NATURAL-THEOLOGICAL UNDERSTANDING FROM CHILDHOOD TO ADULTHOOD

It is commonly assumed that young children only begin to think about God as a result of some educational or cultural influence, perhaps provided by their parents. *Natural-Theological Understanding from Childhood to Adulthood* asks if there is anything about God that children can know independently of any specific cultural input; does their knowledge of God simply come from their everyday encounters with the surrounding world?

Whilst children's theoretical reasoning in biology, physics and psychology has received considerable attention in recent developmental research, the same could not be said about their religious or theological understanding. Olivera Petrovich explores children's religious concepts from a *natural-theological* perspective. Using supporting evidence from a series of studies with children and adults living in as diverse cultures as the UK and Japan, Petrovich explains how young children begin to construct their everyday scientific and metaphysical theories by relying on their own already advanced causal understanding. The unique contribution that this volume makes to the developmental psychology of religion is its contention that religion or theology constitutes one of *the core domains* of human cognition rather than being a by-product of other core domains and specific cultural inputs.

Natural-Theological Understanding from Childhood to Adulthood is essential reading for students and researchers in cognitive-developmental psychology, religious studies, education and cognitive anthropology.

Olivera Petrovich is Research Fellow at the University of Oxford in the Department of Experimental Psychology. Her research deals with the origin and development of natural religious understanding across different cultures.

ESSAYS IN DEVELOPMENTAL PSYCHOLOGY

North American Editors:
Henry Wellman
University of Michigan at Ann Arbor

UK Editors:
Claire Hughes
University of Cambridge
Michelle Ellefson
University of Cambridge

Essays in Developmental Psychology is designed to meet the need for rapid publication of brief volumes in developmental psychology. The series defines developmental psychology in its broadest terms and covers such topics as social development, cognitive development, developmental neuropsychology and neuroscience, language development, learning difficulties, developmental psychopathology and applied issues. Each volume in the series will make a conceptual contribution to the topic by reviewing and synthesizing the existing research literature, by advancing theory in the area, or by some combination of these missions. The principal aim is that authors will provide an overview of their own highly successful research program in an area. It is also expected that volumes will, to some extent, include an assessment of current knowledge and identification of possible future trends in research. Each book will be a self-contained unit supplying the advanced reader with a well-structured review of the work described and evaluated.

PUBLISHED

White & Hughes: *Why Siblings Matter: The Role of Brother and Sister Relationships in Development and Well-Being*

Crone: *The Adolescent Brain*

Needham: *Learning About Objects in Infancy*

Hughes: *Social Understanding and Social Lives*

Sprenger-Charolles et al: *Reading Acquisition and Developmental Dyslexia*

Barrett: *Children's Knowledge, Beliefs and Feelings about Nations and National Groups*

Hatano & Inagaki: *Young Children's Naïve Thinking about the Biological World*

Goldwin-Meadow: *The Resilience of Language*

Perez-Pereira & Conti-Ramsden: *Language Development and Social Interactions in Blind Children*

Bryne: *The Foundation of Literacy*

Meins: *Security of Attachment and Cognitive Development*

Siegal: *Knowing Children (2nd Ed.)*

Meadows: *Parenting Behavior and Children's Cognitive Development*

Langford: *The Development of Moral Reasoning*

Forrester: *The Development of Young Children's Social-Cognitive Skills*

Hobson: *Autism and the Development of Mind*

White: *The Understanding of Causation and the Production of Action*

Goswami: *Analogical Reasoning in Children*

Cox: *Children's Drawings of the Human Figure*

Harris: *Language Experience and Early Language Development*

Garton: *Social Interaction and the Development of Language and Cognition*

Bryant & Goswami: *Phonological Skills and Learning to Read*

Collins & Goodnow: *Development According to Parents*

For updated information about published and forthcoming titles in the *Essays in Developmental Psychology* series, please visit: **www.routledge.com/series/SE0532**

NATURAL-THEOLOGICAL UNDERSTANDING FROM CHILDHOOD TO ADULTHOOD

Olivera Petrovich

LONDON AND NEW YORK

First published 2019
by Routledge
2 Park Square, Milton Park, Abingdon, Oxon OX14 4RN

and by Routledge
711 Third Avenue, New York, NY 10017

Routledge is an imprint of the Taylor & Francis Group, an informa business

© 2019 Olivera Petrovich

The right of Olivera Petrovich to be identified as author of this work has
been asserted by her in accordance with sections 77 and 78 of the Copyright,
Designs and Patents Act 1988.

All rights reserved. No part of this book may be reprinted or reproduced or
utilised in any form or by any electronic, mechanical, or other means, now
known or hereafter invented, including photocopying and recording, or in any
information storage or retrieval system, without permission in writing from
the publishers.

Trademark notice: Product or corporate names may be trademarks or registered
trademarks, and are used only for identification and explanation without intent
to infringe.

British Library Cataloguing-in-Publication Data
A catalogue record for this book is available from the British Library

Library of Congress Cataloguing-in-Publication Data
Names: Petrovich, Olivera, author.
Title: Natural-theological understanding from childhood to adulthood/Olivera
Petrovich, Department of Experimental Psychology, University of Oxford.
Description: 1 Edition. | New York: Routledge, 2019. |
Series: Essays in developmental psychology | Includes bibliographical references
and index.
Identifiers: LCCN 2018021005 (print) | LCCN 2018025024 (ebook) |
ISBN 9781317380740 (ePub) | ISBN 9781317380757 (Adobe) |
ISBN 9781317380733 (Mobipocket) | ISBN 9781138939448 (hardback) |
ISBN 9781138939479 (pbk.) | ISBN 9781315674964 (ebook)
Subjects: LCSH: Children–Religious life. | Adults–Religious life.
Classification: LCC BV4571.3 (ebook) | LCC BV4571.3 .P48 2018 (print) |
DDC 200.83–dc23
LC record available at https://lccn.loc.gov/2018021005

ISBN: 978-1-138-93944-8 (hbk)
ISBN: 978-1-138-93947-9 (pbk)
ISBN: 978-1-315-67496-4 (ebk)

Typeset in Bembo
by Deanta Global Publishing Services, Chennai, India

To the memory of my mother and father and the friends whose interest in this work I always found encouraging and stimulating yet who did not live to see its completion.

CONTENTS

List of figures	*viii*
List of tables	*x*
Preface	*xii*
Acknowledgements	*xiii*

1	Introduction	1
2	Causal understanding: Physical and metaphysical	13
3	Children's theories: Scientific and non-scientific	23
4	Early ontological knowledge: The world and its contents	32
5	In the beginning: Cosmological reasoning in children and adults	68
6	The natural-theological concept of God: A unique causal agent	85
7	Theology as a core cognitive domain	106
8	Innateness of religion within the limits of science alone	121
9	Conclusions, exclusions and some implications	130

References	*137*
Appendix	*153*
Author Index	*154*
Subject Index	*158*

FIGURES

4.1.1   Mean numbers of correct responses (out of eight) for British children and adults across the three conditions in Study 1   42

4.2.1   British children's mean numbers of correct responses (out of six) according to stimulus group, task and condition in Study 2   45

4.3.1   British and Japanese children's mean numbers of correct responses (out of six) across the four conditions of the Origin Task in Study 3   52

4.3.2   British and Japanese children's mean numbers of correct responses (out of six) in the Origin and Animacy Tasks in Study 3   55

4.4.1   British and Japanese children's mean numbers of correct responses (out of six) across the four conditions of the Origin Task in Study 4   57

4.4.2   British and Japanese children's mean numbers of correct responses (out of six) in the Origin and Animacy Tasks in Study 4   60

4.4.3   British and Japanese adults' mean numbers of correct responses (out of six) across the four conditions of the Origin Task in Study 4   61

4.4.4   British and Japanese adults' mean numbers of correct responses (out of six) in the Origin and Animacy Tasks in Study 4   63

Figures **ix**

5.4.1	Origin of matter: Percentages of British and Japanese children selecting "Never began (eternal)" and "Began (created)" options in response to the first cosmological question	76
5.4.2	God's role in the origin of matter: Percentages of British and Japanese children selecting "Matter first" and "God first" options in response to the follow-up cosmological question	77
5.4.3	Origin of matter: Percentages of British and Japanese adults selecting "Never began", "Began" and "Neither" options in response to the first cosmological question	80
5.4.4	God's role in the origin of matter: Percentages of British and Japanese adults selecting "Designer", "Creator" and "No role" options in response to the follow-up cosmological question	82
6.3.1	British and Japanese children's mean scores (out of six) on abstractness of the God-concept	99
6.3.2	British and Japanese children's mean scores (out of six) on abstractness of justifications	99
6.4.1	British and Japanese children's and adults' mean scores (out of six) on abstractness of the God-concept	101
6.4.2	British and Japanese children's and adults' mean scores (out of six) on abstractness of justifications	101

TABLES

4.3.1	Children's mean numbers of correct responses (out of six) and standard deviations (in parentheses) in the Origin Task	51
4.3.2	Children's mean numbers of correct responses (out of six) and standard deviations (in parentheses) in the Animacy Task for *natural* objects	53
4.4.1	Children's mean numbers of correct responses (out of six) and standard deviations (in parentheses) in the Animacy Task according to object category	59
4.4.2	Adults' mean numbers of correct responses (out of six) and standard deviations (in parentheses) in the Animacy Task according to object category	62
5.4.1	Origin of matter: Frequencies and percentages of children's responses according to age and nationality	76
5.4.2	Origin of matter: Frequencies and percentages of adults' responses according to age group and nationality	79
5.4.3	God's role in the origin of matter: Frequencies and percentages of adults' responses according to age group and nationality	82
6.3.1	Children's mean scores (standard deviations in parentheses) on abstractness of the overall God-concept (out of six)	98
6.3.2	Children's mean scores (standard deviations in parentheses) on abstractness of justifications (out of six)	98

6.4.1	Mean scores (standard deviations in parentheses) on abstractness of the overall God-concept and abstractness of justifications (out of six)	100
6.4.2	Children's mean scores (standard deviations in parentheses) on abstractness of the three God-concepts and the corresponding justifications (out of two)	102
6.4.3	Adults' mean scores (standard deviations in parentheses) on abstractness of the three God-concepts and the corresponding justifications (out of two)	102

PREFACE

This book has taken much longer to complete than I could have anticipated when first embarking on research of natural-theological understanding and its development. Unusually for psychology, most of the material in the book has not been previously published, except for two articles (Petrovich, 1997, 1999). I nevertheless benefited greatly from the comments of several anonymous peer reviewers following the attempts to have some of the material published in psychology journals. As the reviewers' feedback seemed to convey, the project involved a number of assumptions and definitions not shared by developmental psychologists working on some closely related issues. It thus became clear that only a monograph would provide sufficient space to justify its rationale and develop those key assumptions *ab initio*. In a nutshell, the studies reported here were not designed either from the theory-of-mind or the anthropological (cultural or evolutionary) perspective but from the science-religion perspective, historically known as "natural theology".

Although much of the material in the book has not been previously reviewed by psychology journals, the design of the studies, the methods used and the hypotheses tested were reviewed by several funding bodies on more than one occasion, when the projects either received the funding sought or I was directed elsewhere as the projects, chiefly on account of the combination of the disciplines involved, were judged to be outside the remit of a particular funding organisation. Working in an interdisciplinary niche can doubtless be greatly rewarding but also a lonely enterprise. The most keenly felt drawback throughout the years has been the lack of regular peer feedback. Such disadvantages notwithstanding, a major and welcome bonus from the delay in publishing the findings has undoubtedly been the opportunity to draw on the achievements made in many areas of developmental research which, although not directly related to the questions pursued in this volume, helped me see more clearly how the key issues addressed here fitted within the broader developmental research and theory.

ACKNOWLEDGEMENTS

The research reported in the volume was funded by grants from The Royal Society, The British Academy and The Great Britain Sasakawa Foundation. Following the research in both Britain and Japan, I received a grant from The John Templeton Foundation to enable me to prepare the material for publication in a book. I am most grateful to each of these organisations. I am also grateful to the Department of Experimental Psychology at Oxford, the Faculty of Integrated Studies at Kyoto during my two research visits there in 1998 and 2000, and to Wolfson College, Oxford, for their support and assistance while researching and writing this book. Over the years I have been welcomed by many primary schools and kindergartens in Oxfordshire, Buckinghamshire, Kyoto, Ibaraki City and Osaka, and spent many enjoyable sessions with the children from those schools. I also thank the students of the University of Oxford and Kyoto University who took part in the research described here and all the other adult participants from both countries who generously gave their time and shared their thoughts. The number of people who have provided assistance and encouragement over the years is too great to list them all on this page. I should like to mention, however, those without whose help I would not have been able to obtain data in Japan: Professor Toshio Sugiman of Kyoto University, Professor Masayuki Ochiai of Otemon Gakuin University and Akiko Rakugi and Tomoko Higashimura, my two invaluable research assistants and translators. I also extend thanks to the colleagues who rated the samples of participants' responses: Kalliopi Chliounaki, Claire Davis, Ann Dowker, Miguel Farias and Fiona Spence. For statistical help I thank Stephen Barlow and Paul Griffiths but accept responsibility for any departure from their expert advice. I thank Anita Butterworth for help with photography and Daniel Walters for assistance with graph editing. Finally, I am indebted to Elizabeth Ashton, Ann Dowker and Tom McLeish for their insightful and generally helpful comments on the manuscript.

1

INTRODUCTION

The current book is about a little-appreciated aspect of young children's theory-building capacity: their ideas about the origin and structure of the world as a whole (i.e., the universe or cosmos) and conjectures about the nature of its ultimate cause. As such, the book complements a growing body of evidence regarding young children's ability to construct theories about different aspects of the world, notably those that correspond with scientific domains such as biology, physics and psychology (e.g., S. Gelman & Noles, 2011). It also suggests that children begin their understanding of the world in many ways like the 17th century "natural theologians" or "physico-theologians" did and, indeed, their forerunners many centuries earlier. The history of modern science demonstrates that the search for answers to scientific questions often terminates in metaphysics as exemplified by natural theology (e.g., White, 1967). In this volume I propose that children start with many of the same questions about the natural world and arrive at broadly similar answers about its structure and origin as those reached by their illustrious predecessors. In other words, children's questions about the physical world lead them, too, to postulate causal agents which transcend the empirical domain altogether.

I will begin by providing a rationale for the main terms in the title of this volume, that is, why "theology" rather than "religion" is a more suitable term for the purposes of describing children's thought studied here. Most dictionaries define *religion* as a term that encompasses not only belief in a supernatural power (i.e., God) but also the ways in which the belief is expressed in different cultures and traditions (i.e., dogma, ritual). In much of the anthropological and psychological literature "religion" indeed signifies a cultural variable on account of its multifaceted nature and "culturally transmitted counterintuitive information" (e.g., Lane & Harris, 2014, p. 146; see also Boyer, 2003; Boyer & Walker, 2000). By contrast, *theology* denotes a theoretical discipline concerned

2 Introduction

with rational analysis of religious belief (*Concise Oxford English Dictionary*, 1995), "the attempt to talk rationally about the divine" (*Fontana Dictionary of Modern Thought*, 1979, p. 632) or "reasoned discourse about God" (Wiles, 1976, p. 1). Given the emphasis in this volume on the theoretical nature of children's thought about the world as a whole, and the concept of God as a causal inference in the context of the world, I will adhere to the distinction between "religion" as a cultural variable, on the one hand, and "theology" as a conceptual domain, on the other. Such a distinction is consistent with Kant's view of "physico-theology" as separate from doctrinal religion (1983, p. 523). More to the point, it is consistent with the natural-theological perspective as a framework for studying children's concept of God as a causal agent, which they construct in the course of processing everyday information about the physical world rather than acquiring it from their culture or religious tradition. Finally, the hyphenated term *natural-theology* has a dual purpose in the current book: first, to convey its many similarities with the historical "natural theology", a period in the development of modern science whose luminaries engaged in the study of nature with the aim of comprehending God's mind as revealed in natural laws (e.g., Brooke, 1991; Hunter, 2009; Lennox, 2009); second, and more pertinently, to highlight its "naturalness", i.e., prevalence in everyday thought about the world from childhood through adulthood and hence its direct psychological relevance.

Concepts of God in natural-theology

The natural-theological concept of God as a causal agent (i.e., First Cause, Creator, Designer), which does not specifically include God's moral attributes (i.e., Judge, Redeemer, Saviour), has led some Christian theologians to reject natural-theology as suspect and argue that only revealed theology, rather than one's own thought, can be the basis for correct reasoning about God (e.g., Moore, 2010). A further criticism of natural-theology is that the very word "nature" is not a neutral term but carries the cultural baggage that we impose upon it, which only reinforces the need for reliance on revelation as a basis for theology (McGrath, 2001). Whilst the emphasis on revelation is undoubtedly of major interest to professional theologians, it is not to the field of psychology, especially developmental. The key psychological issue in the domain of theology is the origin of the concept of God in early cognitive development, something that theologians do not address. Put simply, theologians are not asking the prior, psychological question of how humans come to understand the meaning, and hence accept the possibility, of divine revelation in the first place. To suggest, therefore, that the natural-theological concept of God as a causal agent developmentally precedes the concept of divine revelation does not contradict the mainstream theological view about the importance of revelation but simply draws attention to the core psychological component implicit in all theological reasoning; namely, the concept of God. Finally, although God's moral agency was not a distinct component of the historical natural-theology, this should not be seen as a reflection of the natural-theologians' view that God's moral attributes are irrelevant to human beings but rather that there were no scientific methods available to them for studying those attributes as an aspect of the natural world.

Natural-theology and science: Past and present

As stipulated in The Royal Society Charter (17th century), its Founding Fellows were expected to direct their studies of nature to the glory of God and the benefit of the human race (Brooke, 1991). According to Boyle (1627–1691), for example, science is a religious task in which to "discover the true Nature of the Works of God" (Tambiah, 1991, p. 13). The structure of God's creation is thus inherently worthy of investigation because it can "teach us about the nature of God", "while it incidentally also helped us better to understand the phenomena under study" (Hunter, 2009, p. 202).

Contemporary scientists *cum* natural-theologians have continued to pursue some of its perennial questions in a range of modern scientific fields: biology (Denis Alexander), genetics (Sam Berry), medicine (Francis Collins), materials science (Colin Humphreys), molecular biology (Ken Miller) and physics (Freeman Dyson, John Polkinghorne) as well as mathematics (John Lennox), to mention but a few. Neither in the past nor the present has there been a shortage of scientists seeking to address the questions asked by the original natural-theologians. Claims about scientists as believers or non-believers that are based on public surveys are not always reliable as they offer somewhat superficial and crude categories that lead to contradictory conclusions (e.g., Gross & Simmons, 2009; Larson & Witham, 1999). Whilst some psychologists have recently advanced claims that the majority of scientists are atheists who prefer logic and rational reasoning over an interest in "a reality beyond this world" (Caldwell-Harris, 2012, p. 4), that analytic reasoning promotes religious disbelief (Gervais & Norenzayan, 2012) and that intelligence and religiosity are negatively correlated (Zuckerman, Silberman & Hall, 2013), such claims need to be evaluated in light of the meanings attached to "supernatural agents" and "religiosity" in those studies. As we will see later in the volume, the category "supernatural" has been used to encompass a host of disparate and incongruous notions, including ancestors, ghosts, gods, rituals and sacrifices, spirits and witches as well as God. Clearly, such definitions of "religion" are in stark contrast to the natural-theologians' understanding of religion, which does not put any emphasis on rituals and sacrifices but, instead, on the study of the natural world and its laws, interpreting them as an expression of God's mind. It would be absurd to claim that natural-theologians' *intelligence* did not correlate with "religiosity" just because their belief in the Creator was not motivated by any of the "functions of religiosity" on which contemporary scholars of religion have focused.

The continuing importance of the questions addressed by natural-theology is evident from the contemporary religion–science debate where even non-believing

4 Introduction

scientists play an active role either by challenging, or being challenged by, the opposing views. Hawking (1988), for example, does not rule out the existence of God but rather thinks that God may not be necessary to explain the origin of the universe, which he considers to be, in principle, fully explicable in terms of the laws of physics. But, Lennox (2009), a mathematician and a Christian, is critical of the claim that the laws of physics, and not God's intention, explain how life on Earth began, pointing out that laws are merely descriptions of what happens under certain conditions rather than the laws themselves being endowed with a creative capacity. In agreement with the natural-theologians of the past, Lennox proclaims that it is the beauty of scientific laws which reinforces his own faith in an intelligent, divine creative force at work rather than making the idea of such a force superfluous. I convey the points above mainly to highlight their psychological relevance (i.e., as instances of causal reasoning) and thus as a prelude to describing in this volume evidence from young children asking and answering the very same questions. That these are indeed psychological issues is implicitly acknowledged by Lennox when he appeals to the religious experiences of millions of believers as a given that should not be lightly dismissed.

Science and religion: Psychological issues

The fact that both science and religion make ontological assumptions about the nature of reality and share concerns about the nature of causality is of direct interest to psychology. This is because psychological science is interested in explaining the *assumptions* themselves; that is, how early in development, and under what conditions, do specific assumptions about the world begin to emerge. Put differently, psychology's distinct role among the sciences is to identify the developmental trajectories of concepts from different domains, physical as well as metaphysical, in order to elucidate their respective roles in our theories about the world. Although much more scholarly effort has gone into studying children's scientific concepts than their metaphysical or religious concepts, there is sufficient evidence to suggest that the two conceptual domains interact already in childhood.

Yet a number of scholars have argued that scientific and religious thought are fundamentally opposed. According to the views espoused by this group of scholars, there is no way of resolving the conflict between the two because religion purports to offer scientific explanations even though it conveys none of the truthful statements that science does (e.g., Arieti & Wilson, 2003; Blakemore, 2009; Dawkins, 2006). It is especially interesting that such claims often appeal to some psychological factors (e.g., inferior reasoning capacity among believers, emotional vulnerability) yet without citing any purposely obtained psychological evidence to corroborate them. Paradoxically, the same scholars acknowledge that spiritual beliefs of one form or another are universal, almost as defining of humanity as language is, yet reject any parallels between the capacity for language and that for religion by arguing that the universality of language is grounded in the specialised areas of the human brain, whereas "religion" occurs as a result of a misconception of human intentionality, thus making it akin to visual illusion (Blakemore, 2009). It is pertinent to convey that Blakemore is equally "dubious about those 'why' questions" that humans ask universally and considers them to be either senseless or translatable into the "how" questions "that science answers so well". In other words, he considers both the "why" questions and "religion" to be curious universals in that they lack a specific link to the brain. Instead, Blakemore's conviction is that, once we find out how our brains generate religious ideas and what the Darwinian adaptive value of such brain processes is, nothing will be left for religion. Yet, a number of leading neuroscientists (e.g., Coltheart, 2006; Miller, 2010; Passingham & Rowe, 2015) have dampened such optimism, without even mentioning religion specifically, by pointing out that we first need to develop testable hypotheses about how exactly the brain generates ideas of any kind.

Another example of the "conflict" view to mention briefly is that based on the assertion that science, unlike religion, deals with unambiguous data obtained by independent methods, all of which ensures widespread consensus among scientists and facilitates determining the core concepts that constrain reasoning in each scientific domain so that its progress can be measured (Chinn & Brewer, 2000). Chinn and Brewer's point is only valid if we accept their definition of religion as consisting of "beliefs, dogmas and rituals" rather than the natural-theological one adopted in the current book. As for the claim that only science has core concepts, the simple fact is that *no* psychological research has so far attempted to establish whether there are any core religious or theological concepts, although several psychologists have expressed the view that there could be no such concepts in relation to religion (see below). Suffice it to say at this point that when Chinn and Brewer are contrasting religion (as a cultural domain) and science (as a cognitive domain) they are comparing apples with oranges, which, of course, do have different cores. Last, but not least, their overly positive evaluation of clarity and consensus among scientists is amply contradicted by the history of science, which provides numerous examples of considerable ambiguities in science, too, and hence plenty of scope for interpretation and disagreement about scientific data and theories (e.g., Haldane, 1924; McLeish, 2014).

Although the "conflict" view of the science–religion relationship has been prominent in the literature, some distinguished scientists have argued that science and religion should be seen as completely independent yet complementary (e.g., Einstein, 1940; Gould, 1997). What the independence and conflict perspectives share, however, is the view of religion as a form of culture rather than a conceptual domain. In contrast, two other patterns of the science–religion relationship discernible in the history of modern science, namely, *dialogue* and *integration* (Barbour, 1998), perceive the two domains as sufficiently conceptual to engage with and maintain a relationship. The best known historical representative of integration is "natural theology" ("physico-theology"), discussed above, whilst

6 Introduction

its contemporary perspective is the "theology of science" view (McLeish, 2014, p. 170). According to McLeish, a physicist, the long history of human impulse to understand the world is recorded in the Bible, not least in the form of the questions that appear to foretell science (e.g., Job 39–42). Such a long-standing interaction between the two kinds of quest – religious and scientific – has furnished a basis of a fruitful relationship in the history of science, which has led McLeish to reject both the conflict and complementarity positions but endorse the view that science and theology are simply "*of* each other" (2014, p. 209).

The point of my brief review of the science–religion relationship is not only to draw attention to some of the weaknesses of the "conflict" perspective on the science–religion interaction but, more importantly, to claim that many of the questions commonly perceived as either scientific (i.e., pertaining to physical sciences) or theological are actually psychological, yet not recognised as such by the proponents of either side of the debate. Their passionate arguments, from Hume to contemporary critics of religion, never mention psychological research as at all relevant to the question of whether religious thought, as such, is indeed "non-rational". Thus Grayling, a prominent philosopher, in an interview to *The Oxford Student* proclaimed: "It is very hard to imagine people of real intelligence signing up for the 'man on the cloud' type of view of religion, which of course *many people* do sign up for" (2012, pp. 20–21; italics added). What such misconceptions about "religion" in human cognition clearly demonstrate is the need for separating its two components: (1) cultural and (2) psychological (i.e., conceptual).

Bearing in mind some of the controversies mentioned above, one might conceivably come to the view that scientific study of religious concepts is not at all possible, not least because such concepts involve mental representations of non-material entities. This, of course, depends on the judgement of whether we can have objective evidence about mental states of any content given that mental states, as such, are unobservable aspects of human behaviour. In psychological research, however, verbal and other behavioural responses are the recognised tools for expressing mental states and, as such, can be used for rendering mental states observable as well as measurable, provided that the relevant methodological requirements are met. As a leading experimental psychologist argued forcefully, "It is perfectly legitimate to include [as data] the statements made by human beings, as long as the differences between such responses correspond to differences between other stimuli or other responses" (Broadbent, 1972, p. 41). In the case of "religion", stimuli may consist of any objects or symbols (e.g., words) capable of eliciting the target concept(s) whilst ensuring that they are not confounded with any other, apparently similar, concepts, which can be expressed verbally. Indeed, scholars from cognate disciplines, notably neuroscience, have endorsed Broadbent's point that behavioural evidence is essential in scientific psychology and therefore any progress in the study of mental states depends on the availability of methods for observing and measuring such states and controlling the stimuli that can elicit and influence them (e.g., Miller, 2010).

Scientific reasoning: Common points with theology

The commonalities between scientific and natural-theological reasoning from antiquity to modern times can be highlighted by identifying several components that they share. For example, being able to (1) recognise indeterminacy, (2) evaluate evidence, (3) make judgements about plausibility and (4) coordinate theory and evidence, which Kuhn (2002) singles out as fundamental to scientific reasoning, are equally characteristic of natural-theological reasoning. To further the example, recognising indeterminacy implies the need to establish not only whether the relevant evidence is available or possible to obtain but, also, what may count as evidence in specific situations. This last point is especially important because many scientists are aware of there being impenetrable limits to our understanding that will continue to pose a challenge to science and metaphysics alike (Rees, 2011).

In an attempt to account both for the fluidity and developmental deficits in scientific reasoning, owing to its multiple components, Amsel and colleagues (2008) proposed a dual-processing model of reasoning that encompasses (1) analytic and (2) experiential forms. According to the authors, experiential skills (developmentally early, spontaneous) are never fully replaced by analytic skills (formally acquired, systematic) but continue even among adults despite their fully developed analytic skills. Amsel and colleagues showed, for instance, that even those adults who *could* reason highly analytically sometimes chose not to, and suggested that strategic failures of this kind can be overcome by encouraging a good metacognitive understanding of the conceptual demands in a specific task. Such a general skill would clearly be relevant to theology too, seeing that several psychological studies have reported a coexistence of scientific and supernatural beliefs among children and adults alike (e.g., Legare & S. Gelman, 2008; Shtulman, 2012).

An important contribution of developmental research to the study of concepts in a number of cognitive domains is a well-documented distinction between *everyday* and *specialist* concepts (e.g., Wellman & S. Gelman, 1998). Everyday concepts are *foundational* in that they provide a basis for the acquisition of specialist concepts. For example, although scientific theories of astronomy differ radically from children's everyday conceptions of astronomy, science education in this domain is more effective if it takes into account children's everyday conceptions of astronomy (Kikas, 1998). If, however, such a connection is not made in the educational process, formal learning of scientific concepts is remembered only in the short term (two months after learning) but not several years later. In other words, poorly assimilated concepts suffer from insufficient conceptual rehearsal needed for their retention in memory, which leads to their subsequent disappearance from memory. In Chapter 7 I take up this point and suggest that lack of conceptual rehearsal may be an even greater problem in the case of the early developing theological concepts and one that may account for a belief common among many adults that they had never thought about God as

8 Introduction

young children until this concept was introduced to them by others. What such comments from adults clearly imply is that direct research with children is essential because only such research can validate the distinction between everyday (intuitive) and specialist (formal) concepts and thereby identify the constraints on early memory development that preclude later access to the concepts acquired in early development.

To sum up: In *natural-theology* the concept of God is that of a *causal agent* and consists in an inference based on the stimuli provided by the physical world. Such a process involves many of the steps present in scientific reasoning too, including taking evidence into account, evaluating it, recognising its indeterminacy, as well as assessing the plausibility of particular judgements and inferences based on evidence.

What follows is a brief synopsis of the forthcoming chapters, which jointly provide the background to the research, its main findings, and my conclusions about the development of natural-theological understanding.

Chapter 2 includes a review of selected major studies on causal development from infancy to late preschool years, guided primarily by their relevance to children's metaphysical proclivities as integral to natural-theological understanding. Seeing that the main causal question in this volume concerns children's explanations of the origins of natural things, and whether such enquiry gives rise to the concept of God as a causal agent, I introduce two sets of conceptual distinctions that guide, at least implicitly, children's explanations: (1) *intrinsic* vs. *extrinsic* causal agents and mechanisms and (2) *derived* vs. *primary* conceptions of origin. Causes that are *intrinsic* to entities (i.e., their internal properties and mechanisms) are physical or scientific; in contrast, causes that are thought of as being *extrinsic* to existing entities (i.e., abstracted or inferred relations) are often metaphysical. The intrinsic–extrinsic distinction is critical to young children's ability to differentiate between natural and artificial objects in terms of derived and primary origins and to provide justifications for their origin judgements. Accordingly, *derived* origin explains how an item emerges from its antecedents and through the action of causal mechanism(s) inherent in its structure. By contrast, *primary* origin refers to an object's first coming into being, with no known antecedents of the same kind and thus no intrinsic causal mechanisms from which its origin could be derived, but, instead, requires postulating some extrinsic cause as its ultimate source. Whilst these two notions of origin are clearly differentiated in philosophy (e.g., Harré, 1983; Hospers, 1984; Kant, 1983), no psychological research has so far considered the possibility that the same distinction might be present in children's everyday thought about the world. Instead, developmental researchers have upheld Piaget's claim that the notion of primary or ultimate origin is beyond younger children's grasp and curiosity (e.g., Evans, 2000; S. Gelman & Kremer, 1991; Kelemen & DiYanni, 2005).

It is widely agreed in developmental psychology that causal reasoning plays a key role in the construction of theories and that causal concepts and explanations are the main constituents of children's theories. In Chapter 3 I suggest that children construct not only scientific but also metaphysical theories as part of the same explanatory drive. In contrast to scientific or domain-specific theories (i.e., physics, biology, psychology), metaphysical theories are trans-domain (e.g., theories of the world as a whole), not only because they are stated in terms of some very general categories that do not derive from experience, but also because their explanations may altogether transcend the usual empirical constraints within which science operates. Children's theories constructed in the process of natural-theological understanding, i.e., ontological, cosmological and theological, are of this kind. First, it is pertinent to address the criteria used by developmental psychologists for determining what constitutes a theory in children's knowledge as well as some of the objections to imputing theories to young children. In brief, a common feature of all children's theories, scientific and non-scientific, is their starting point in everyday experience of the physical world and a drive to understand it in causal terms. The coherence of children's theories in general, and of their theological constructs especially, thus critically depends on the validity of their empirical knowledge because only correct and reliable empirical knowledge can give credence to children's conjectures, hypotheses and tentative explanations in general.

Children's *ontological* theory discussed in the current volume holds that the world of objects can be seen as consisting of just two broad categories – natural and artificial – when the criterion for categorising objects is their primary or ultimate origin. What makes this ontological dichotomy a theory is the abstractness of its defining criterion and its fully inclusive and comprehensive scope (i.e., explanatory power). Children's causal stance also leads them to construct a rudimentary *cosmological* theory that concerns the origin of matter as such and not just of its different forms. We will see that, even when inaccurate, children's cosmological theory is manifestly a considered response to the question of whether the matter of which the world is made has a beginning in time or, rather, is a given that elicits no further questions. Finally, children's *theological* theory, which is likewise constructed in the context of their understanding of the physical world, implies that they engage in speculating about the nature of its ultimate cause and infer the uniqueness of its causal agency, i.e., God. In short, the three theories above – ontological, cosmological and theological – are of psychological interest because they emerge from children's earliest efforts to understand the physical world as a unified whole by relying on their everyday experience rather than on formal education or any specific cultural input. Furthermore, trans-domain or metaphysical theories of the world are conceptually simpler and thus easier for children to construct than their everyday scientific theories, because metaphysical theories do not presuppose detailed knowledge of the objects' intrinsic properties (mechanisms) that are typically needed for scientific explanations. Consequently, children's metaphysical theories can be more accurate than their scientific theories when the correctness criterion is their consistency with similar ideas among lay adults and, in some instances, even specialists. This should not come as a surprise given that the skills needed for the construction of such broad

10 Introduction

theories are the same as those that underpin all knowledge acquisition and for which children have considerable relevant experience. In fact, when it comes to direct experience and knowledge that underpins everyday cosmological and theological reasoning, children and adults are equally novices.

Chapters 4, 5 and 6 contain empirical findings regarding each of the three components of natural-theological understanding. Some readers may find that these chapters, especially Chapter 4, contain a more detailed methodological account than necessary for following the main argument. They may thus find it sufficient to peruse the summary and discussion of the main findings at the end of each study within a chapter. In Chapter 4 I describe data obtained from British and Japanese children and adults which show that even children of pre-school age hold a view of the world as consisting of just two ontological kinds, natural and artificial, grouped according to a causal criterion that is extrinsic to an item's structure (i.e., primary origin). I then suggest that children's failure in other studies to evince a reliable natural–artificial dichotomy is owed to the use of inappropriate criteria, which are disparate for each ontological category (i.e., intrinsic for natural items, extrinsic for artefacts). When, however, children are given the opportunity to use the same causal criterion in all instances (i.e., extrinsic to any item), they are able to identify consistently different natural items as belonging in a single ontological group on account of their non-human origin, just as they are able to identify any of the artefacts as members of a single ontological group on account of their origin in human action.

Children's reliable use of an extrinsic causal criterion to arrive at the single, all-inclusive natural category, constituent of the natural–artificial dichotomy, implies that they are likely to have considered in some structured way the notion of absolute or primary origin, not only of the inclusive natural category, but also of the world as a whole (cosmos) and of matter as such. Chapter 5 reports cross-cultural evidence from the same children and adults whose ontological understanding was described in Chapter 4. It shows that children's ideas about the origin of primary matter (cosmology) are distinct from their ideas about the origin of its different forms (i.e., objects and organisms). It also shows that children and adults from two cultures with very different cosmological traditions come up with highly similar assumptions about the beginning of matter and of the world itself. Cosmological reasoning is of interest to psychological research of causal development because it tells us whether children can conceptualise absolute beginning and, also, what they intuitively accept as the best "stopping point" when seeking a complete explanation for the world as a whole: (1) its given structure or (2) a postulated causal agent that brings it about (e.g., Swinburne, 1991).

In Chapter 6 I report data regarding the same participants' understanding of the key attributes of God as a causal agent, which were elicited in the context of their categorising stimulus objects as natural or artificial and answering the cosmological questions. This evidence indicates that children's concept of God as a unique causal agent has two defining characteristics: immateriality and intentionality, which jointly specify God's ontological otherness, i.e., being neither spatial nor temporal but transcendent. I discuss the current findings in relation to other recent studies that have offered different hypotheses regarding children's understanding of God, notably (1) anthropomorphism and (2) preparedness, both of which assume that a theologically correct concept of God (i.e., transcendent) can only be acquired through cultural learning as there is nothing in children's own experience that corresponds with God's transcendence. In contrast, the natural-theological hypothesis advanced here proposes that children's concept of God as a unique causal agent is theologically correct from the outset, and, moreover, that such a concept could not be acquired through cultural learning.

In Chapter 7 I develop further the point that the natural-theological concept of God is an intuitive concept and propose that theology is one of the core cognitive domains on the grounds that it meets the key criteria stipulated by developmental psychologists for identifying core domains (e.g., Chi, 1992; R. Gelman, 2000; Wellman & S. Gelman, 1998). That is, (1) ontological entities in the theological domain are specific or unique to this domain and (2) theological causal principles are uniquely and exclusively associated with the entities belonging in this domain. In addition, theological entities are (3) inherently unobservable and come to be represented through concepts that are coherent and meaningfully integrated (Wellman & S. Gelman, 1998). The concept of God as an ontologically unique causal agent is highly salient in human cognition and hence one of the simplest concepts that humans can acquire spontaneously and invoke subsequently in both scientific and metaphysical theories. In the same chapter I also consider whether any aspects of early cognitive development might constitute the precursors of an explicit core theological concept (i.e., God) and what role, if any, language might play in its onset.

Given its universal occurrence and early onset in cognitive development, in Chapter 8 I allow myself to speculate about the ways in which the concept of God might be innate by considering several psychological accounts of innateness, including connectionism and constructivism. I propose that innateness in the domain of "religion" or theology is a meaningful notion in the same way that it is in physics, biology and psychology, where the core concepts are understood to be innately specified in the sense that even core concepts require experience to become concepts. My account of innateness of the core theological concept is, however, incompatible with those non-developmental approaches that are based on data obtained by fMRI technology and genetic profiling in their search for "hard" evidence that religion has biological bases (i.e., "neurotheology" and the God-gene accounts).

Following a brief summary of the main conclusions arising from the research described in this book, in Chapter 9 I provide a rationale for leaving out some of the prominent literature on the subject of religious cognition, notably that from anthropology, evolutionary psychology and neurotheology. The main reason is that none of those approaches address the concept of God as a causal agent, but all focus on religion as a cultural variable. I then briefly reflect on some of the benefits of our better understanding of the natural-theological reasoning as a psychological topic, including any educational implications. Extant research literature on children's scientific education provides some useful pointers regarding the options that might be conducive to religious education too. I conclude by suggesting that a basic concept of God as a unique causal agent may be an appropriate starting point when seeking to help children learn to articulate the ineffable aspects of this intuitive concept and thereby acquire a more sympathetic understanding of the different teachings about such an agent that their respective cultures seek to provide them with.

2

CAUSAL UNDERSTANDING

Physical and metaphysical

Causal understanding is a fundamental aspect of human cognition that is involved in most domains of conceptual development (e.g., Sperber, Premack & Premack, 1995; Wellman & S. Gelman, 1998). In this chapter I consider its role in the development of natural-theological understanding, notably in children's explanations of the origins of natural things. An almost exclusive research focus on the development of scientific concepts and the causal mechanisms that figure in scientific ("physical") domains (e.g., Gopnik, Sobel, Schulz & Glymour, 2001; Koslowski & Masnick, 2002; Kuhn, 2002, 2012) has meant that much less is known about children's understanding of non-scientific ("metaphysical") causal concepts.[1] Yet, as we saw in Chapter 1, treating the two domains – physical and metaphysical – as conceptually fully separable is at odds with the history of modern science, replete with examples of causal explanation in terms of agents and forces postulated to operate beyond the level of physical mechanisms. One area of developmental research that comes closer to the agency perspective is children's understanding of intentions as causal mechanisms, discussed later in this chapter. First, however, I will look at the main characteristics of scientific, on the one hand, and non-scientific or metaphysical causal thought, on the other.

Empirical phenomena studied by science are typically explained in terms of their antecedent conditions and intrinsic causal mechanisms, which answer the *how* question. It is widely recognised, however, that there are aspects of the world that science cannot explain (e.g., *why* there are any conditions at all) and that such questions, which go beyond the information available in physical reality, require qualitatively different explanations (e.g., Hospers, 1984; Kant, 1983; Swinburne, 1991). Although the majority of developmental accounts have discussed children's understanding and causal explanation of empirical entities and events, some have mentioned the possibility of there being "non-causal explanations" (Lombrozo, 2006, p. 464), including children's ability to "track causal

14 Causal understanding

information in nonmechanistic ways", i.e., in ways "that are 'above' the level of mechanism" (Keil, 2012, p. 330). Of note, Lombrozo suggests that "non-causal explanations" are more likely to occur spontaneously and in "real-world reasoning" than in laboratory experiments (2006, p. 468). In this volume I suggest that a good example of just such explanations occurs in natural-theological reasoning. To provide an account of its origin and development, in the previous chapter I briefly introduced two kinds of causal explanation as relevant to natural-theological understanding: (1) one that deals with *intrinsic* causal mechanisms by which different entities emerge from their antecedents (i.e., *derived* origin) and (2) the other, where no appropriate antecedents or intrinsic causal mechanisms can be stipulated but, instead, a cause *extrinsic* to an entity is postulated to explain its *primary* or ultimate origin, thereby establishing a causal *relation* between an object and the agent that brings it into being.[2] Whilst all causal reasoning is "relational" in the sense that even mechanistic causes are typically inferred rather than directly observed, I use the term to highlight its object-extrinsic, as opposed to object-intrinsic, location.[3,4]

The distinction between *derived* origin (from existing antecedents) and *primary* origin (no antecedents of the same kind exist), on the one hand, and that between *intrinsic* causal mechanisms and *extrinsic* causal agents, on the other, is central to children's ability to correctly identify natural and artificial objects according to their origins and arrive at the natural–artificial ontological dichotomy. Whilst origin derived from antecedent intrinsic mechanisms is at the centre of scientific causal reasoning, primary origin (i.e., in terms of causal relations inferred to exist between objects and their ultimate causes) is characteristic of metaphysical causal reasoning.

The contrast between intrinsic causal mechanism, on the one hand, and extrinsic causal agents, on the other, corresponds with Kant's distinction between mechanistic and purposive or teleological causality. Kant's important point was that both these forms of causal explanation are needed in order to account for "change" in the world (Aristotelian sense) and reduce the manifold of causal laws to a system (Lindsay, 1934; Wallace, 1974). He particularly emphasised that, although the mechanistic principle (i.e., empirical, material) is important in science, and should be pressed as far as possible, humans feel compelled to imagine a different principle in order to explain fully the mechanistic principle itself. In Kant's causal theory, the qualitatively different principle is one that transcends not only any particular object's boundaries but the empirical domain itself. Although Kant held that the transcendent, or God, is unknowable and thus, strictly speaking, not a cause but the "ground of all possibility", he acknowledged that transcendent God is a necessary postulate of causal reasoning whilst maintaining that such a postulate does not constitute a proof of God's existence (Wood, 1992, p. 398; Kant, 1983). In his critique of Kant, however, Hegel (1959) made a useful point that although humans have no knowledge of transcendence itself, they are conscious of the boundary that demarcates the empirical and the transcendent and, by implication, may be able to articulate this awareness. The connotation of *transcendence* in the current volume is in keeping with the accounts above, i.e., reference to a realm of thought that is completely outside of and beyond the world of our sensory and perceptual experience and hence unknowable, except as an intuition of its being distinguishable from the empirical domain.

Another way of conveying the distinction between the two causal principles – mechanistic and purposive (teleological) – is by following Harré (1983) and considering whether change occurs in an existing item or object (mechanistic) or, rather, pertains to an item being created anew (teleological). It is pertinent to point out that the methods commonly used to study children's explanations of natural objects' origins do not differentiate between the two concepts of origin outlined above, even though both can involve postulating non-verifiable causal agents as a way of completing an empirical "causal story" that could not be completed by reference to causal agents from the same explanatory domain (e.g., Harré, 1986). For example, Harré's "Realm 3" and its entities are postulated to belong in the empirical domain yet are described as profoundly unknowable, or "beyond all possible experience" (1986, p. 192). This clearly makes Realm 3 entities conceptually indistinguishable from the entities postulated to belong in the non-empirical or transcendent realm. In brief, the relevance of the distinctions involving the two causal principles above is in their implicit correspondence with the empirical-transcendent distinction which underpins natural-theological understanding. In spite of the many studies investigating children's "non-natural", "supernatural", "religious" and other "counterintuitive" tendencies described as persisting into adulthood, none have addressed the empirical-transcendent distinction as relevant to those tendencies and potentially available to children.

Causes in "physics" (science) and in "metaphysics" (theology): Knowledge and speculation

Although causal explanations in some sciences involve considerably more speculation (e.g., cosmology) than in other scientific domains (e.g., physics, biology), even in physics and biology scientists engage in speculative causal reasoning in order to arrive at the best and most coherent explanations of observed and inferred phenomena. The role of speculation in causal reasoning is not sufficiently understood in psychology and natural-theological reasoning provides a suitable framework in which to examine the interplay between "physics" and "metaphysics" more systematically. There is indeed a long, informal record of young children asking the apparently metaphysical questions. Piaget described such children's questions as "pre-causal" while some of his critics declared them to be "anomalies" of causal reasoning (e.g., Huang, 1930, 1943; Isaacs, 1929). According to Isaacs, for example, children's questions of this kind are not actually causal, that is, not a product of "ordinary" intellectual tools but represent "conversational problems" that elicit people's "fantasies" and hence belong to matters of agreed opinion among adults (Isaacs, 1929, p. 512). Huang similarly suggested

16 Causal understanding

that any questions about the "clouds, heavenly bodies, rivers, and other things in nature" should be topics for mythology and fairy-tales (1930, p. 178) because they give rise to "anthropomorphic, magical, and other non-physical causal concepts" (1943, p. 117). In short, the early developmental psychologists were of the view that children could only give correct explanations of those natural objects that were nearby or "familiar" rather than remote. Yet, children's questions and explanations of natural objects that Isaacs and Huang interpret as "anomalies" and "fantasies" often seem to be instances of children's implicit grasp of the distinctions between derived and primary origins, on the one hand, and intrinsic and extrinsic causal principles, on the other. Huang indeed acknowledged that, when speculating about distant natural events, children's speculations were not radically removed from real life or from those of adults. "Where the correct but difficult concept was not available, the adult explained the event by whatever simpler concepts they had, naively, just like the child" (1930, p. 179).

The proposal that children are better at explaining the origin of familiar natural objects was upheld in subsequent research even when the data obtained from children did not seem consistent with such a proposal. For instance, S. Gelman and Kremer (1991, p. 401) predicted that it should be more difficult for 4- to 7-year-olds to explain the origin of "remote" (e.g., sun, moon) than "familiar" natural objects (e.g., dogs, flowers) on the grounds that the knowledge of "precise creation processes" develops with age (p. 398). Contrary to the researchers' prediction, children in the study performed significantly better on remote (82%) than on familiar natural kinds (66%). It should be said that this finding is only surprising on the assumption that the same causal mechanisms explain the origin of both remote and familiar natural objects, which, it seems, young children do not share. Instead, 4- to 7-year-olds seem to understand that there are no "precise creation processes" to appeal to in order to explain the origin of remote natural objects, many of which are unique occurrences (e.g., the sun) and hence could not be derived from any antecedents in the way that dogs and flowers can. Whilst the researchers accepted children's references to God as correct responses for the origin of natural objects, it is important to recognise that responses in terms of God do not even approximate "precise creation processes" of natural objects' origins but are qualitatively different, i.e., explain the objects' primary origin by postulating an extrinsic causal agent rather than some intrinsic physical mechanism(s). S. Gelman and Kremer's findings are thus consistent with my prediction that primary origin should be inherently easier than mechanistic origin at any age, precisely because primary origin does not presuppose detailed knowledge of the objects' intrinsic properties but can be fully explained by establishing a plausible relation between an object and its postulated or inferred causal agent that is extrinsic to its structure. The same hypothesis is also consistent with the researchers' finding that children performed significantly better in the Direct Question Task, which only demands that children should deny human intervention as the cause of natural items, than in the Open Ended Task, where they had to specify a cause, including that of the remote natural kinds, leading the authors to conclude simply – and rightly – that children "may not need knowledge about specific creation processes to distinguish natural kinds from artifacts" (S. Gelman & Kremer 1991, p. 401).

Because of the importance attached in developmental literature to children's direct experience with objects as a way of learning about the objects' origins, one other point relevant to natural-theological understanding may be made. It is arguable that all natural objects, regardless of their size and proximity, are equally remote (or equally familiar) when considered from the viewpoint of their primary origin. While our direct, often hands-on, experience with animals and plants undoubtedly increases familiarity with those objects' species-specific mechanisms of origin, it does not help us better understand how any such object may have first started. On the other hand, familiarity with remote natural objects can be enhanced through mental engagement, such as reflecting upon, speculating about and imagining the different possible sources of those objects' origins. It follows, therefore, that derived (mechanistic) origin of natural objects is only easier for children when they can have first-hand experience of the causal mechanisms involved (e.g., witnessing the birth of animals, plant growth from seeds) but not when they have to learn about natural causal mechanisms from others. By contrast, children almost always have sufficient background knowledge to come up with a hypothesis of how *any* object, familiar or remote, may have started from scratch, most easily so when judging whether or not human action may have caused it.

Completeness of explanation in science and theology

As mentioned earlier, it is an inherent characteristic of causal reasoning to seek a complete explanation of the observed. There is some evidence from research with children that they, too, seek complete explanations. Frazier, S. Gelman and Wellman (2009) looked at the relationship between children's causal questions (*how*, *why*), the responses that children receive from others and children's reactions to those responses. Frazier and colleagues reasoned that, if the purpose of children's causal questions is to seek theory-building knowledge, there should be variation in the pattern of their reactions based on whether they have received a causal or non-causal explanation. Their findings with 48 children aged 2- to 5-years showed that children indeed reacted differently to adults' explanatory vs. non-explanatory answers by either asking follow-up questions or merely restating the question, respectively. Such a pattern seems to imply that, before asking others, children had already constructed tentative explanations of their own (i.e., hypotheses) and used them to judge whether a received explanation was sufficient. What is not clear from Frazier and colleagues' study is whether the children had asked any metaphysical and religious questions. Whilst the earlier developmental literature cites numerous instances of children mentioning non-empirical, i. e., metaphysical and religious, issues in the tasks involving natural phenomena, it is interesting that no such trends have been reported in the more recent developmental literature even when the studies investigated children's understanding of natural phenomena

18 Causal understanding

(e.g., Callanan & Oakes, 1992; Greif, Kemler Nelson, Keil & Gutierrez, 2006; Kelemen, Callanan, Casler & Pérez-Granados, 2005). Lack of such evidence is partly due to the researchers' stated aims to focus on children's grasp of causal mechanisms; for example, Callanan and Oakes instructed the parents to report children's questions about "how things work" or "why things happen" (p. 224). Consistent with such a focus, any potentially religious questions (e.g., "Does Santa Claus make Christmas?") the researchers categorised as "Cultural and Social Conventions" (p. 219), without exploring further their meaning.

Children's willingness to speculate about the nature of the cause responsible for a witnessed event by mentioning some specific and plausible, albeit naively phrased, possibilities such as "invisible batteries" and "invisible person" (e.g., S. Gelman, Coley & Gottfried, 1994, p. 349) is of direct interest to our main topic. The cogency of hypothetical causal reasoning about empirical events depends at any age on having the relevant background information, which, understandably, younger children cannot possess to the same degree as older children and adults can. But children are fast learners and, between 2 and 4 years of age, they can successfully infer causal relations on the basis of variation and covariation of different components of fairly complex mechanical sequences (Gopnik et al., 2001). As Gopnik and colleagues point out, it is remarkable that very young children learned a novel fact of no direct ecological significance by just observing three empirical events and imputing "an underlying nonobvious, causal power" to the blocks included in the task (2001, p. 627). In a related study, 4- to 5-year-olds were able to use limited perceptual data to infer abstract physical laws and consistently uphold them by postulating, when appropriate, an unobservable object rather than abandon the law(s) when faced with apparently anomalous evidence (Schulz, Goodman, Tenenbaum & Jenkins, 2008). Such findings imply that when the events to be explained are ecologically significant (e.g., pertaining to the actual world), children may be expected to show an even greater proficiency in hypothetical causal reasoning than when reasoning about events of little or no ecological interest.

Children's search for complete explanations suggests that they implicitly adhere to the rationale that it is preferable to postulate entities in order to account for events fully than leave them unexplained. In other words, not only do scientists infer the existence of unobserved variables so as to explain anomalous data (Schulz, 2012) but children do, too. The nature of postulated entities – material or immaterial – is what accounts for the differences between causal reasoning in science and in theology, respectively. Although no psychological research has compared directly and systematically causal reasoning in the two domains, some scholars have argued that the differences outweigh any apparent similarities between scientific and religious causal reasoning (e.g., Chinn & Brewer, 2000; McCauley, 2000). Without addressing those arguments in detail, it should be sufficient to point out that they are not based on any systematic and direct evidence from either children or lay adults about how each group's reasoning in the two domains actually proceeds. Moreover, they define religion as a cultural rather than cognitive variable and then contend that only science involves causal concepts, which makes it "reflective", whereas religion (i.e., religious culture or tradition) is non-reflective by virtue of lacking causal concepts (McCauley, 2000).

Plausible and implausible causes and causal agents

Seeing that the outcome of causal reasoning in any domain is always, ultimately, a guess about plausibility (Koslowski & Masnick, 2002), some criteria for evaluating the appropriateness of a particular guess are needed. The criteria for judging the adequacy of postulated causal mechanisms can be either *pragmatic,* such as in science where manipulative success of our experimental operations strengthens our belief in the existence of postulated entities (Harré, 1986), or *formal* (e.g., consistency with established facts and laws, plausibility, simplicity and parsimony). The often tentative and hypothetical nature of reasoning about causality, and the recognition that a plausible mechanism can be "any kind of connection through which causes are effective" (Harré, 1983, p. 118), has been corroborated by developmental research. For example, several studies have found that children can think of a variety of mechanisms as providing such a connection: biological processes (e.g., Ahn et al., 2001), intentions (e.g., Shultz, 1982) and supernatural forces, including God (e.g., Bullock, R. Gelman & Baillargeon, 1982; S. Gelman & Kremer, 1991).[5]

Taking intention as an example of a plausible causal inference, Shultz established that children of preschool age judged intention to be a correct or plausible cause of the leg's movement only when there was no sufficient external cause in the experiment to explain the movement of the leg (e.g., a tap on the leg). When a sufficient external cause was present, however, children tended to say that no intention was involved. In other words, children of preschool age do not seem to invoke intention by default but only when they cannot identify a sufficient physical cause for the observed effect. Later research found that competence at construing intentions as causes seems to be evident by 18 months of age, and possibly at 15 months, when infants appear to differentiate between people's observable behaviour, on the one hand, and their intentions, on the other (e.g., Meltzoff, 2002). In Meltzoff's experiment, for instance, when infants were shown directly contrasted movements of machine and man, but which were closely matched spatially and temporally, they differentiated the two kinds of movement by appearing to attribute a goal or intention only to human agency but not to the machine. In other words, infants in their second year of life seem capable of selecting a single cause as the most plausible in a given situation, a tendency also observed in adults under more complex task conditions (e.g., Goedert, Ellefson & Rehder, 2014; Lombrozo, 2007).

Causal mechanisms and causal relations: Evidence from infants and young children

The emergence of causal reasoning in early cognitive development strengthens the argument that causal reasoning is one of the primary ways of making sense of

20 Causal understanding

the world. Because of its early onset as well as little variability according to age, education or culture, human capacity for causal reasoning has been described as a "developmental primitive" (Corrigan & Denton, 1996). Furthermore, its early development and vital role in adaptive behaviour has prompted suggestions that causal thinking may have a genetic basis (e.g., Baillargeon, 1994; R. Gelman, 1990). The main function of causal reasoning in any domain is to motivate the search for a complete explanation by adhering to the principles of determinism (every event must have a cause), mechanism (causes bring about their effects by transfer of causal impetus) and priority (causes always precede their effects). For example, even young children seem to assume that no event can be caused "by itself" but must have a cause outside itself (Bullock, 1984; Shultz, 1982). Evidence that pre-verbal infants behave in accordance with the principle of determinism comes from a study with 10-month-olds who inferred the correct cause of a moving target when the choice was either an inanimate object or a person (Kosugi, Ishida & Fujita, 2003). Similarly, 10- and 12-month-olds made correct inferences about a hidden agent (i.e., human hand rather than an inanimate object) as the actual cause of a moving inanimate target (Saxe, Tenenbaum & Carey, 2005). Such behaviour seems to imply that infants have a prior expectation of what kind of a cause is appropriate to the movement observed, i.e., have an intuition about the correct mechanism and select one that is plausible from among several possibilities on the basis that it best explains a certain effect (Shultz, 1982). Selection of plausible, even if incorrect, mechanisms is consistent with having some knowledge of the objects' intrinsic natures or "powerful particulars" (Harré & Madden, 1975). In short, children's readiness to assume that there must be "a primary cause" of an event (Saxe et al., 2005) and then consider its possible nature implies that their judgements are guided by causal principles rather than the perceived stimuli (Shultz & Kestenbaum, 1985). In fact, when perceptual appearances or prior experience of particular cause–effect sequences appear to contradict children's expectations, they show a preference for relying on causal principles (e.g., Bullock, 1984; Schulz et al., 2008). It is important to recognise that such general causal principles, whose role is to guide interpretation of temporal and spatial cues in cause–effect relations rather than specify the exact causes of events, do not arise out of experience but are inherent in human cognition (e.g., Lindsay, 1934).

Further evidence for children's adherence to causal principles comes from the studies revealing their understanding that, with the passage of time, existing physical systems move towards greater randomness and disorder (Shultz & Kestenbaum, 1985), that random phenomena are characterised by uncertainty and unpredictability (Kuzmak & R. Gelman, 1986) and that random forces cannot create order in a disordered set of objects (Friedman, 2001). Conditions of uncertainty and unpredictability are especially conducive to engendering speculative attempts when trying to identify the likely mechanisms in that they elicit children's postulates of invisible causes, including supernatural ones, as mentioned earlier. None of this should be surprising in light of Holyoak and Cheng's

(2011) cogent argument that, given that causality is unobservable, it is rational to assume that the occurrence of certain causes is impossible to rule out. Although Holyoak and Cheng's examples are all empirical (i.e., physical), the same assumption is even more pertinent in the context of causal reasoning that occurs in the domains of cosmology and theology.

Causal understanding and ontological categories

There is a broad consensus in developmental research that causal reasoning plays a key role in the construction of ontological knowledge as it dictates the "most fundamental conceptual cuts one can make in the world" (Keil, 1989, p. 196). Data from categorisation studies provide evidence that infants form conceptual or abstract categories by the age of 7 months (Mandler & McDonough, 1993) and possibly earlier (Quinn, 2002a). Certainly by 12 months of age infants engage in different types of categorisation and learn about a large number of categories, including animals, food, vehicles, quantities and furniture (e.g., Mandler, 1999; Ross, 1980; Strauss, 1979). Sugarman interprets young children's habituation to similar stimuli as an indication that "some kind of categorizing function is present virtually from birth" (1982, p. 436). In short, cumulative evidence from developmental research shows that children in their first year of life start to respond to stimuli as members of *conceptual categories* rather than as individual objects and do so on the basis of non-observable properties such as causal powers and liabilities, whether biological, physical or psychological (e.g., S. Gelman, Coley & Gottfried, 1994). Put differently, even very young children seem to understand that non-obvious (i.e., hypothetical) entities and causal mechanisms might account for and predict manifest occurrences (Wellman & S. Gelman, 1998).

According to some research, the ability to form "hypothetical representations" appears by 18 months of age as a uniquely human function, when infants begin to conceptualise what they had not previously experienced (Meltzoff, 1990). By age 5-years, children are able to postulate intentions as causes of bodily action even though they themselves have not experienced those intentions (Shultz & Shamash, 1981). The sophistication of children's postulated empirical causal mechanisms is even more impressive when we consider the complexity of variables that they must take into account before coming up with a plausible mechanism. By comparison, postulating entities which transcend the spatial domain altogether and for which no specific information needs to be processed and memorised must be easier for both children and adults. This is not to say that children's postulated entities will be indistinguishable from those of adults, not least because younger children's vocabulary is less developed to allow them to communicate their ideas clearly. My point is that hypothetical causal reasoning associated with physical or empirical entities is more complex at any age as it depends on experience and education.

Seeing that causal understanding plays a key role in the construction of theories in any domain of knowledge, and that hypotheses are fundamental to theoretical

22 Causal understanding

reasoning in that they provide tentative explanations of empirical phenomena in general, in the next chapter I take a closer look at the main characteristics of children's theories, especially those that are integral to natural-theological understanding: ontological, cosmological and theological.

Notes

1 Throughout this book I refer to metaphysics in the sense given by Aristotle to the study of things "beyond physics", or nature (*meta-ta-physica*), and not in the broader sense found in developmental publications (e.g., Harris, 1997, 2000; Johnson, 1997; Subbotsky, 1996). The latter is used as a reference to any departure from physical or empirical concepts and may encompass magic, superstition and other "culturally and historically biased" beliefs (Subbotsky, 1996, p. 2).
2 Primary or ultimate origin discussed in the current volume differs from the apparently similar terms of "prior" (Callanan & Oakes, 1992) and "ultimate" causes (Mayr, 1961). The latter two terms always refer to physical or empirical causes, which account for different objects' antecedent-derived origin, whilst the term "primary" in the current volume is a counterpart of "derived" origin and accounts for objects' origins when no antecedents of the same kind can be specified.
3 In their account of relational concepts, Doumas, Hummel and Sandhofer (2008) proposed a model which stipulates that causal relations can be acquired from perceptual experience, i.e., can be detected from the objects' "featural invariants", rather than being imposed on perceptual experience. Whilst Doumas and colleagues stress that little is known "about how people acquire relational concepts" (2008, p. 29), and are open to the possibility that causality might be innate (2008, p. 1), their model addresses causal relations that obtain among existing objects and their features rather than the causal relations that are inferred or postulated to exist between an object and the cause bringing it about.
4 Gentner, Angorro and Klibanoff likewise use the term "relational" as a reference to "extrinsic relations with other entities" (2011, p. 1173), i.e., already existing objects, rather than as a reference to a causal relation between an entity and its source of origin.
5 Harré (1993) cites Leibniz's philosophy of science as an example where God provides or represents the causal connection.

3
CHILDREN'S THEORIES
Scientific and non-scientific

One of the main functions of theories in general is to provide a coherent account of the phenomena considered or observed by identifying their causes and thereby enabling predictions based on the nature of those causes. In the preceding chapter we saw that children, too, organise their experience and interpret the surrounding world in causal terms as well as make predictions on the basis of those interpretations. First, however, we need to address a preliminary issue of what constitutes a theory, especially in childhood. Although many adults may see it as somewhat extravagant to attribute theories to young children, the criteria used in developmental psychology allow us to see that children's theories are not always radically different from those of lay adults.

According to some definitions, theory is "any cognitive representation of the way things are, no matter how simple, implicit, or fragmentary" (Kuhn, 2002, p. 372). Theories are also "imaginative posits" invented for explaining nature, not only by scientists but also by ordinary people and even children (Kuhn, 1989). At a higher remove, theory represents an organised system of knowledge, or a coherent belief system that provides a unified account of observed phenomena (Goldstone, 1994; Murphy & Medin, 1985; Wellman & S. Gelman, 1992). There is evidence that children's theories meet most of the criteria mentioned above, i.e., provide coherent and unified accounts of their everyday experience of the world, even when factually incorrect (e.g., Brown, Metz & Campione, 1996; Gopnik & Wellman, 1994; Wellman & S. Gelman, 1998). Some of the examples of children's reliance on their rudimentary theories include different ways of categorising objects, learning words or estimating the probabilities of what they observe (S. Gelman & Koenig, 2003; Rhodes, S. Gelman & Karuza, 2014; Waxman & S. Gelman, 2009). In spite of the substantial cumulative evidence that children are theory-builders, the capacity for theoretical thought in younger children has sometimes been questioned (e.g., Piaget, 1977; Sloutsky, 2009).

24 Children's theories

Whilst it is generally agreed in developmental psychology that children spontaneously construct theories in a number of scientific domains, much less is known about their acquisition of non-scientific or metaphysical theories. The preponderance of studies dealing with children's scientific understanding compared to non-scientific is usually explained in terms of the greater relevance of scientific concepts and theories to children's education and cognitive development, chiefly because of their greater complexity, informativeness and potential to allow further discoveries about specific phenomena (Keil & Silberstein, 1996). The view that scientific concepts have a privileged position in cognitive development has inevitably skewed developmental research towards investigating children's concepts of scientific mechanisms of origin (i.e., antecedent-derived) whilst disregarding any alternative ideas about natural origins, i.e., metaphysical, even when such ideas are appropriate and occur in conjunction with scientific explanations.

A consequence of focusing solely on scientific theories is that we have little insight into the variety and scope of children's non-scientific theories. The question of whether children are indeed biased to develop scientific theories in preference to, and earlier than, metaphysical theories is, of course, an empirical question that should be answered by examining their theoretical reasoning in a broad range of domains while taking account of any prior knowledge that children may have acquired in a particular domain. In other words, to gain a more complete view of their understanding of the world in its manifold aspects, we need to know what role, if any, children's non-scientific theories play in their cognitive development. As noted in Chapter 1, explanations of the world as a whole, as opposed to its particular aspects, are not solely in terms of the scientific principles but go beyond them and are thus more abstract. What the history of Western science reveals is that the two kinds of explanation – physical and metaphysical – have often been coexistent in the thought of many early scientists (e.g., Boyle, Copernicus, Kepler & Newton; see Barbour, 1998; Brooke, 1991; Lloyd, 1995; McLeish, 2014; Tambiah, 1991), including their philosophical predecessors, and continue to be so for many contemporary scientists (e.g., Collins, 2007; Humphreys, 2003; Polkinghorne, 1987). To the extent that the history of modern science can be a guide to finding out how children might go about explaining the world around them, it would be reasonable to expect a greater prominence of metaphysical explanations in children's theories, too.

Assessing the cogency of children's metaphysical theories, especially those that postulate non-empirical entities as causal agents, raises the question of the criteria to be used for judging the validity of such theories. Given that postulating the existence of non-empirical or transcendent entities as causal agents does not require one to have direct knowledge of them but only be able to relate meaningfully such entities to empirical phenomena (e.g., by not contradicting what science has established about empirical phenomena), the validity of such postulates and theories should be easier to verify than that of scientific theories. In other words, whilst children cannot be expected to have acquired sufficient factual knowledge specific to different scientific domains, their metaphysical theories can be evaluated in terms of whether they meet the formal criteria used to judge the validity of hypotheses in general, such as plausibility, coherence, consistency, comprehensiveness, simplicity and integrating power (Mitchell, 1973; Ward, 1985).

Empirical criteria for identifying core domains and theories

The current view in developmental psychology is that children's earliest or "core" theories emerge in those domains of knowledge that correspond with the particular sciences, notably physics, biology and psychology (e.g., Carey & Spelke, 1994; Keil, 1991, 1995; Wellman & S. Gelman, 1992). Although the notion of what constitutes a core domain of knowledge is not always clear, most researchers agree that a domain of knowledge is defined by its distinct ontology and the causal principles specific to the domain's ontology (Chi, 1992; R. Gelman, 1990, 2000; Wellman & S. Gelman, 1992). Accordingly, a domain's ontology consists of the basic ideas about the entities included within a domain (e.g., objects, organisms, mental states) while its domain-specific causal principles identify the types of action that are appropriate for the entities of a domain (e.g., mechanical force, metabolic processes, intention). For example, 5-year-olds' intuitive understanding that biological and psychological processes operate according to fundamentally different causal mechanisms (Erickson, Keil & Lockhart, 2010), albeit without detailed and accurate knowledge of the causal mechanisms specific to each domain, suggests that children of this age differentiate conceptually biology and psychology as domains of knowledge. There is a broad agreement among developmental psychologists that core domains represent those aspects of children's knowledge that are (a) acquired early and spontaneously, i.e., without explicit teaching, (b) remain similar across age, i.e., little or no development with age and are (c) cross-culturally universal. These criteria jointly imply that core domains are, to some extent at least, innately specified (e.g., Carey, 1995; R. Gelman, 2000; Keil, 1989; Wellman & S. Gelman, 1998). Identifying domains of knowledge that are "core" is important in developmental psychology because such domains are seen as providing a conceptual foundation for all subsequent knowledge acquisition within a domain.

The recognition by developmental researchers that determining core domains in human cognition is an empirical question which ought to be answered in accordance with the criteria mentioned above is central to my consideration later in this volume of theology as a possible core cognitive domain even though theology (or religion) has hitherto been explicitly ruled out as a potential candidate (e.g., Boyer & Ramble, 2001; Keil & Silberstein, 1996; Wellman & S. Gelman, 1998). Whilst I cannot embark at this junction on a more detailed discussion of the reasons for discounting theology as a core cognitive domain, it is pertinent to mention the following two. First, religious concepts are commonly seen to be products of culture and social learning rather than spontaneous cognitive

26 Children's theories

development; as such, they cannot be "core". Second, because early cognitive development is typically studied via perception, and theological entities cannot be accessed by any perceptual mechanisms, investigation of theological concepts in pre-verbal children has been practically impossible. In Chapter 7 I revisit both these constraints when pondering the existence of any conceivable psychological precursors in the development of theological concepts.

Domain-specific and trans-domain theories[1]

As I noted earlier, the currently prevailing view in developmental research that theories, as such, are domain-specific and correspond with individual sciences (e.g., S. Gelman & Noles, 2011) cannot encompass those explanatory attempts that address the world as a whole and which therefore cross several knowledge domains. Because such "trans-domain" explanations and theories go beyond a domain's empirical boundaries in their search for causal explanations, they are metaphysical (e.g., cosmology, theology). Two questions regarding the scope and intension of such theories arise for developmental research. The first is whether children, too, construct similarly broad or trans-domain (i.e., metaphysical) theories, and, second, whether such theories could be said to have a distinct ontology and any correspondingly distinct causal principles. Taking cosmological theory as an example, which is essentially and ultimately concerned with the origin and nature of primary matter, it is clear that matter or substance can be said to constitute its ontology; however, the nature of cause specific to the cosmological domain is more ambiguous and even controversial. Whilst the question of causality in scientific cosmology remains open and is expected to be settled through empirical research (e.g., Coles, 2005; Hawking, 1988), in philosophical cosmology the cause of primary matter is usually conceived of as transcending the material universe and extending into theology. Needless to say, even greater uncertainties about the nature of domain-specific ontological entities and causes arise when we consider the theological domain: Whilst its ontology is conceptually distinct (i.e., an immaterial, intentional agency), any causal principles specific to ontological entities in the theological domain are beyond human reach and verification. Notwithstanding the uncertainties just aired, conceptual domains such as cosmology and theology should be studied as psychological topics, that is, in accordance with the developmental criteria for identifying core knowledge domains. In short, their status in human cognition as core or non-core ought to be settled through empirical research.

Natural-theological theory: Some predictions

To restate the point made in Chapter 2, children's readiness to appeal to unobservable entities and causes when explaining events in the physical, biological and psychological domains implies that conceiving of unobservable entities in the non-empirical or transcendent (i.e., theological) domain need not be any more difficult for them but, in fact, may be easier, and for two reasons. The first is that there is no specific factual information about the non-empirical domain that children could be said to lack compared to adults. Second, because any postulated non-empirical entities are absolutely unobservable, there are no multiple ways of processing them cognitively as there are when processing the unobservable entities from the empirical domain, where there is a great deal of relating and differentiating to do, even when categorising objects (Spelke & Hespos, 2002). Put differently, the concepts of invisible entities belonging in the physical world (e.g., causal mechanisms) are probably harder to conceptualise than the invisible entities that are never encountered in the empirical domain as there is nothing for the child to learn to differentiate within such a domain but merely recognise its ontological difference from any of the empirical domains.

When studying children's metaphysical concepts and theories we are therefore faced with a limited range of possibilities: Either the two kinds of concept – physical and metaphysical – rely on the information obtained from very different sources and thus cannot be treated as commensurable (i.e., the physical world vs. culture) or, as implied by the natural-theological theory, both kinds of concept ensue from the same wealth of information contained within the physical world but come to be processed in accordance with distinct ontological and causal principles that are already in place in infancy and can be deployed in response to questions inherent in each. Although study of conceptual development in infancy is not easy, and the ambiguity of its findings can be frustrating, I concur with the argument that it is the best available way in which "to approach many difficult questions concerning the structure and content of human knowledge at later ages", not least because "many of our foundational concepts are clearest during the infancy period" (Spelke & Hespos, 2002, p. 244).

Construing an early development of transcendent concepts along these lines is congruent with the Kantian epistemological position, implicitly endorsed by a number of developmental researchers when affirming that "the main organizational features of the adult mind appear to be present in infancy" (Leslie, 1988, p. 207). It is nonetheless important to reiterate Kant's point that these structures inherent in human cognition do not amount to fully fledged concepts but are best thought of as epistemological tools or Aristotelian "categories", whose function is "instrumental", namely, sorting the sensory raw material that reaches infants' sensory organs into meaningful percepts and concepts.

In the next sections of this chapter I look briefly at three well-studied domains of children's scientific theories – physics, biology and psychology – with a view to their potential relevance in the development of children's natural-theological theory.

The most basic aspect of intuitive or everyday *physics* concerns the existence and behaviour of inanimate objects and forces. Research with human infants suggests that they acquire a great deal of knowledge about physical objects by being able to extract increasingly complex information about the physical world soon after birth. For example, 3- and 4-month-old babies seem to "expect" solid

28 Children's theories

objects to continue to exist when they are no longer in view. They show this by looking longer at anomalous displays where events seem to violate the principles of solidity and continuity of objects (Baillargeon, 1994; Needham, 2016; Spelke, 1994). In contrast, babies of this age need to see which objects fall to the ground when dropped and which remain suspended in the air in order to acquire the principles of gravity and inertia. Such behavioural patterns among infants imply that solidity (i.e., there can only be one object in one location) and continuity (i.e., objects exist continuously in space and time) are more fundamental in every-day physics than gravity (i.e., objects move downward in the absence of support) and inertia (i.e., objects continue in motion in the absence of obstacles). Put differently, the principles of solidity and continuity represent core or foundational knowledge on which later learning about physics depends. Yet whilst an early onset and foundational role in the development of object knowledge suggests that such elementary concepts of physics may be innately specified (Baillargeon, 2002; Bertenthal, 1996; Carey, 2002; R. Gelman, 1990; Mandler, 1988; Spelke, 2000), it is also possible that they result from infants' own experience of themselves as continuous and solid objects (available from birth). By the same token, their learning about gravity and inertia can come either through experiencing themselves falling off a surface or observing other objects fall. Whether innate or acquired early under well-defined conditions, evidence of physical knowledge in infancy is compatible with the assumption that children approach the world of experience with certain "expectations" about its structure and behaviour.

How might children's early physical concepts be relevant to their metaphysical theories? Young children's concepts of matter as having a permanent existence even when it consists of invisible particles (Au, 1994) or of matter as distinct from any objects derived from it, both of which understandings seem to be in place by the age of 4 years (e.g., Kalish & S. Gelman, 1992), suggest that young children begin to reflect on matter as such and arrive at intuitions about its nature as well as origin.[2] Of further interest to the question above is well-established evidence regarding infants' ability to form representations of permanently exist-ing yet "hidden" material entities (i.e., object permanence concept). Such evidence is consistent, in principle, with being able to form representations of other "hidden" entities, some of which may be imagined to belong outside of the empirical domain. Scarcity of information about children's ability to form concepts of non-existence leaves room for speculation that the ability to conceptu-alise hidden or unobservable empirical entities is continuous with the ability to conceptualise non-empirical entities, such as God. Any attempt to address such questions directly would require research with infants in their first year of life rather than children a few years old which, admittedly, poses methodological obstacles that have yet to be overcome.

A similar construal of children's earliest experiences of themselves and other humans as being both objects and agents may account for an early or intuitive *biology*. Put simply, infants have numerous opportunities to acquire knowledge about living organisms as distinct from inanimate objects and do so according to a variety of criteria. For instance, 12-month-olds reliably discriminate biological from mechanical motions (Bertenthal, 1996) and 2-year-olds know that animate objects move by themselves (Golinkoff, Harding, Carlson & Sexton, 1984) as well as differently from mechanical objects (Massey & R. Gelman, 1988). Researchers have also established that by age of 3 years, children acquire biological principles such as heredity which enable them to predict what parental features would be inherited by their offspring (Springer & Keil, 1989) and begin to understand that innate potential is something that predisposes both animals and plants towards certain characteristics (Wellman & S. Gelman, 1998). Furthermore, young children start to treat animals and plants as a single category (i.e., animate) that is distinct from inanimate natural kinds and do so on the basis of inferred rather than perceived characteristics (Backscheider, Shatz, & S. Gelman, 1993; S. Gelman & Koenig, 2003; Hatano & Inagaki, 1994; Hickling & S. Gelman, 1995). Taken together, findings obtained with children of preschool age strongly imply that they understand biological causal processes to be distinct from other causal processes, notably intentional and mechanical, and differentiate biology as a domain from other scientific domains.

The relevance of children's biological knowledge to their theological understanding is most direct when it comes to their representations of God. For instance, children's knowledge that organisms are embodied (i.e., bounded by their skin, feathers or fur), which makes them subject to a host of changes in their lifetime and ultimately death, has a direct bearing on the question of whether they conceptualise God as physically anthropomorphic, that is, constrained by the same biological laws that govern the existence of empirical agents. Hence the relationship between children's biological understanding, on the one hand, and the concepts such as immortality and immutability, on the other, neither of which could be said to derive from their actual experience of other living beings, has direct implications for their theological understanding.

Encounters with other humans provide neonates with much relevant information to begin constructing an early *psychology*, by allowing them to develop different expectations about the behaviour of persons as distinct from physical objects. As mentioned earlier, babies attribute goals and intentions to persons but not to mechanical objects (Meltzoff, 2002) and 3-year-olds know that while physical force is necessary to manipulate mechanical objects, mental states are influenced by "just thinking" (Estes, Wellman & Woolley, 1989). Also by the age of 3 years children represent other minds as having independent existence ("theory-of-mind") which, according to a currently leading hypothesis, is the main source of children's concepts of God. There is also evidence that preschool children are aware that perception informs belief and that distinctive mental states are caused by different sources of information (Pratt & Bryant, 1990). In short, children's psychological understanding suggests that they are able to infer appropriate relationships between mental and perceptual events as characteristic of empirical intentional agents (humans). Their relatively advanced understanding of human mental states raises the question of whether young children can

30 Children's theories

also arrive at appropriate inferences about non-empirical agents, notably God, as having mental states but not sensory experience. Such tests are critical for verifying the hypothesis that children's quite sophisticated understanding of human action enables them to understand human action as ontologically different from divine action and to contrast the two explicitly and consistently.

My brief review of how children go about organising and systematising their early knowledge of the surrounding world indicates that much of their understanding about the unobservable characteristics of the physical world is coherent and theoretical, allowing them to make appropriate predictions about its different aspects. Above all, it provides them with a basis for inferring or postulating causal agents that are qualitatively different from humans in not being subject to the laws that govern entities in the domains of physics, biology and psychology. In short, children's knowledge of "physics" is the context for their emerging metaphysics.

Adequacy and limitations of children's theories

Given that even scientific theories make assumptions that are not always verifiable, determining the adequacy of non-scientific theories, especially those constructed by children, presents additional challenges. One path open to psychologists is to perform direct comparisons between children and adults as well as cross-culturally (Coley, 2000). Another approach is to examine the specific concepts in each age group, "in the context of related concepts and the intuitive theories in which they are embedded" (Carey, 1991, p. 269). Such comparisons can have distinct advantages when studying the development of theoretical, i.e., abstract, forms of understanding, whether scientific or theological. As Harré put it, when non-observability is a permanent characteristic of a theory, i.e., when we have "no idea what it would be like to perceive a subatomic particle, a quantum state or a field of potential" (1993, p. 97), we can still have a very good idea of the dispositions and powers of these mysterious entities through scientific research by adhering to the criteria mentioned earlier – plausibility, simplicity and overall coherence with experience. In the case of non-scientific theories, plausibility is of particular importance when it comes to judging the appropriateness of any unobservable and untestable components of explanation because *theory*, by definition, entails such components.

In agreement with the considerations above, each of the metaphysical theories considered in this volume – ontological, cosmological and theological – strongly implies, and indeed requires, reliable, even if rudimentary, understanding of the empirical conditions relevant to those domains. Put simply, without a correct intuitive understanding of the many empirical laws and specific causal mechanisms characteristic of the different natural kinds, it would be impossible to hold a plausible ontological theory of the world and its contents (i.e., to know what kinds of things can and cannot exist). Similarly, without a reasonably valid implicit understanding of the basic physical properties of matter and its causal powers and liabilities, it would be impossible to make plausible conjectures about its origin. The coherence of theological propositions (e.g., the nature of postulated transcendent entities) should likewise be judged in terms of whether or not the postulated entities contradict what is known about empirically occurring entities and their causal powers, notably human. In short, my account of children's theological conjectures in this book leans upon the coherence of their ontological knowledge and the basic compatibility of their cosmological inferences with those of lay adults.

Evidence presented in the current volume was obtained with those concerns in mind; that is, by directly comparing children and adults from two markedly different cultures and religious traditions in their understanding of the world as a whole – its basic structure and likely origin. The rationale for such comparisons was driven by one further concern specific to the nature of the questions investigated in the volume: Whenever we can reasonably assume that different age groups have the *same* access to the relevant information, such as when it comes to explaining the basic structure and ultimate origin of the world as a whole, children and ordinary adults are in a similar, if not identical, position. This is even more strongly the case when it comes to the information about God that can be abstracted from the world. Whilst adults undoubtedly have the advantage of being able to couch their conjectures in a more sophisticated language, as well as benefit from their greater general knowledge and better communication skills, none of those advantages should make a qualitative difference to how humans of any age construct everyday theories of the world of such a broad scope as those addressed in this volume, i.e., ontological, cosmological and theological.

Notes

1 "Domain-general" might also be a suitable term, however, this term is commonly associated with Piaget's developmental theory and refers to cognitive operations as distinct from concepts and conceptual content.
2 Although Carey (1991) concluded that children's concepts of matter are incommensurable with those of adults, we should note that her data derive from the tasks involving those properties of matter that children are unlikely to acquire spontaneously (e.g., having mass, density), but depend on specific experience and educational input for their acquisition, neither of which they need when mastering a simple material–immaterial distinction.

4

EARLY ONTOLOGICAL KNOWLEDGE

The world and its contents

In the preceding chapters, discussion centred on the relevance of children's "physics" to their metaphysics, that is, taking children's empirical knowledge as the starting point for their emerging metaphysical concepts and theories. In the current chapter, we look at those aspects of children's knowledge about the world that provide a springboard for their ontological theories.

Whilst developmental research has corroborated young children's knowledge of biology, physics and psychology as some of the most basic modes of understanding of the world, the world is much broader than the phenomena covered by those domains. To see the world in its breadth and as a whole, adult thinkers typically invoke non-scientific, i.e., metaphysical, concepts. Such concepts do not derive from experience but are inherent in human reasoning and enable us to organise sensory and perceptual data provided by everyday experience. A branch of metaphysics that deals with such general concepts is ontology, also defined as the study of real, as opposed to apparent, existence. The nature of "reality", however, is what differentiates between ontology as a philosophical topic, on the one hand, and as a topic in science, including psychology, on the other. For example, some metaphysicians consider abstract entities and Kant's noumena to have real existence even though not being accessible to empirical verification, whereas they consider many things studied by science and having material form as being only the appearances or manifestations of that which does have real existence.

Following Keil's (1979) publication *Semantic and conceptual development: An ontological perspective,* psychological research of ontological knowledge has addressed children's concepts of what exists within the world (e.g., animal, artefact, living thing, plant). Such real-world categories are determined by the nature of their entities and entity-specific causal mechanisms, which jointly ensure that a category has a stable existence and identity, i.e., cannot be transformed physically from one category to another (Carey, 1985; Chi, 1992; R. Gelman, 2000; Wellman & S. Gelman, 1998). Ontological categories studied by psychologists are of interest to developmental research because they tell us how young children begin to carve the world into conceptually distinct domains and whether those domains might constitute core knowledge in human cognition. In this volume, I will refer to "ontology" in the sense that it has acquired in psychology; namely, children's knowledge of what exists within the world. In the greater part of the current chapter, I dwell on one particular aspect of children's ontological knowledge: the natural–artificial dichotomy, i.e., mutually exclusive grouping of extant objects into just two categories and based on a single causal criterion. The relevance of this dichotomy, and hence of the current chapter, is in showing that such a rudimentary theory of the world is a key component of natural-theological understanding in children and adults alike. For theological conjectures at any age are only credible to the extent that they proceed from an essentially correct and coherent understanding of the empirical world.

Ontological dichotomies: The special case of natural–artificial

One of the most fundamental ways of conceptualising the world as a whole is in terms of a small number of highly general and inclusive categories that are often of dichotomous nature (Keil, 1981b, 1983), for example, animate–inanimate, mental–physical, natural–artificial and the like. Given that dichotomies are ubiquitous in human thought and represent some of the most elementary forms of categorisation (Emmet, 1966), it is perplexing that such systems of classification have not been studied more directly and systematically in children.[1] In other words, whilst children's understanding of the animate–inanimate and mental–physical dichotomies has been studied quite extensively, the same is not true of the natural–artificial dichotomy. Lack of research on the natural–artificial dichotomy is especially surprising given the volume of research on children's acquisition of knowledge about diverse natural kinds as distinct from artefacts with regard to their origins. According to a number of scholars, the natural–artificial dichotomy is inherently ill-defined or fuzzy because of the impossibility of establishing an all-inclusive *natural* (comparable to *artificial*) category. Put differently, whilst researchers agree that it is easy to see what makes all artefacts to be the same kind of ontological entity, there is no similarly obvious criterion that could allow one to see all the natural objects as also being the same kind of entity. Instead, it has been suggested that "natural" is a philosophical concept rather than one corresponding to anything existing in the world (Carey, 1985, 1988) and that "natural kind" does not occur universally as a concept but is peculiar to Western culture and philosophy (Atran, 1995; Ogawa, 1986, 1998). Furthermore, a single, all-inclusive natural category may be impossible to form seeing that natural and artificial entities can be differentiated according to several criteria, thus representing a continuum rather than a clear-cut division (Keil, 1989, 1995).

34 Early ontological knowledge

When it comes to children's reported failure to sort natural and artificial items into two mutually exclusive categories, the most common explanation has been that children's knowledge of the natural objects' intrinsic characteristics is insufficient to allow them to identify the mechanisms of natural objects' unique paths of origins (e.g., S. Gelman, 1988a; Keil, 1986, 1991). As Keil put it, we rely on the distinct causal chains intrinsic to a natural item in order to determine its category of origin, whereas even children can establish that the essences of artefacts are "in the intended function of the creator" (1986, p. 139). It is worth noting that whilst Keil recognises the crucial role of causal criteria for explaining both natural and artificial entities, he argues that the causal criteria used for the two ontological categories are fundamentally different, i.e., intrinsic in the case of natural objects and extrinsic in the case of artefacts. I argue for a different view; namely, the use of different causal criteria for natural objects and for artefacts inevitably leads to overlapping or "fuzzy" categories, thus precluding the formation of a well-defined natural–artificial dichotomy. For a dichotomy of any kind to be possible, a single criterion is needed in terms of which an object can be categorised as either X or Y.[2] In the case of the natural–artificial dichotomy, this requirement means that its defining criterion ought to permit *all* natural entities to be seen as belonging in the same group, just as the criterion used for artefacts permits all such objects to belong in one and the same ontological group, i.e., artificial.

The defining criterion of the natural–artificial dichotomy: Extrinsic cause and primary origin

Whilst there is a consensus in developmental literature that children have a clear concept of artefacts as being members of the same ontological category because of their common origin in human causal activity, it is commonly overlooked that this causal criterion (i.e., human action) is not intrinsic to an object but extrinsic to it. More specifically, it is a relational criterion in that it merely connects an object's existence to its source of origin rather than specify a causal mechanism by which the object is created. Furthermore, the extrinsic causal criterion that defines artefacts (i.e., human action) explains such objects' *primary* or ultimate rather than *derived* origin (i.e., from antecedent causal mechanisms intrinsic to each kind). The most relevant consequence of the disparity in locating the causes of natural (*intrinsically)* and artificial (*extrinsically)* objects is the imposition of a causal asymmetry between the two ontological categories, which necessarily precludes the emergence of a well-defined natural–artificial dichotomy.[3] My proposal is that by using the same criterion for both categories of the dichotomy, the category *artificial* becomes fully explained as consisting of objects that are caused by human intentional action, whilst the category *natural* is equally fully explained as one that consists of objects which *cannot* be brought into existence by human intentional action.[4] That such a simple yet abstract criterion (i.e., an object-extrinsic causal relation) should be available even to young children is a premise consistent with much extant research on causal development, infant categorisation and early theoretical reasoning reviewed in the earlier chapters. What is new in my proposal is that the natural–artificial dichotomy is a rudimentary ontological theory of the world, integral to children's natural-theological understanding, and one that they construct by considering the world as a whole rather than its separate components that they master as part of their scientific knowledge.

It is also important to stress that the more abstract or inclusive a dichotomy, the greater is the need to make its defining criterion explicitly available to children and adults alike. This requirement, however, was not met in most studies bearing on the issues discussed here. For example, the most widely used procedure for studying categorisation in all age groups has been "free sorting" or object-manipulation task (i.e., sequential touching). Researchers typically provide participants with an array of stimuli, such as pictures or small objects, and instruct them to group the objects that "go together", i.e., in any way they may see them as similar (e.g., Rosch, Mervis, Gray, Johnson & Boyes-Braem, 1976). In the case of infants, researchers simply observe and record how long and in what order infants manipulate or touch a set of objects in front of them (e.g., Mandler, 2000). The rationale for using the free categorisation procedure is to see whether, and at what age, children spontaneously detect any abstract, rather than just perceptual, similarities among the stimuli. One of the uncertainties associated with this approach is that it is unclear whether the spontaneity in laboratory conditions can ever match that in the everyday conditions of the actual world (Goswami, 1992).[5]

To begin with, in laboratory settings participants see a much smaller number of stimuli that are also representative of a narrower range of ontological categories than what they encounter in the real world. In addition, stimuli used in the laboratory are often unrealistic, consisting of schematic drawings of real and novel objects rather than faithful copies or 3-D representations of real objects (e.g., Cimpian & Petro, 2014; Keil, 1989; Needham, 2016; Simons & Keil, 1995). Furthermore, some studies include only artefacts but no natural objects (e.g., Matan & Carey, 2001) or use an independent groups design where each group of participants receives either natural or artificial objects but not both (e.g., S. Gelman, 1988b). Such methods clearly do not provide as rich and realistic arrays of stimuli from which children could abstract the relevant criteria and establish the relations that their everyday environments typically afford. Yet there is substantial research evidence that multiple comparisons and contrasts are highly beneficial for relations to become salient and available as criteria. This is because only such rich matrices of diverse dimensions and stimuli can enable children (and adults) to recognise the more abstract commonalities even when stimuli consist of geometric shapes and other schematic and novel stimuli (e.g., Kotovsky & Gentner, 1996; Kurtz, Boukrina & Gentner, 2013; Roberts & Cuff, 1989; Ross, 1980). The ability to abstract and use relations in a variety of stimulus displays is well documented in both children

36 Early ontological knowledge

(Bryant, 1974) and animals.[6] In brief, what developmental evidence suggests is that the more the test stimuli approximate the everyday world in its variety, the easier it becomes for children to detect diverse causal relations and ontological categories that occur in the real world. This is because judgements about membership in relational categories are "determined not by common intrinsic properties of the members, but by common relational structure" (Goldwater & Gentner, 2015, p. 151).

Ontological dichotomies in babies and young children

Although no research has directly studied pre-verbal children's understanding of ontological dichotomies as mutually exclusive categories, there is some evidence that very young children perceive the surrounding world in terms of dichotomies. For instance, when presented with a set of toy models, 3- to 4-month-olds formed categories of mammals vs. furniture (Behl-Chadha, 1996; Quinn, 2002a, b), 2- to 11-month-olds formed separate groups of animals and vehicles (Arterberry & Bornstein, 2001; Mandler & McDonough, 1998), while 11-month-olds differentiated between animals and furniture (Pauen, 2002). Such behaviour in the first year of life is consistent with evidence that neonates are able to detect regularities in the physical world and form abstract representations of objects (Baillargeon, 2002; Bertenthal, 1996; Leslie, 1988; Spelke, 1994; Spelke & Kinzler, 2007). Crucially, many such regularities that babies detect are based on causal relations rather than perceptual characteristics of the objects (e.g., Booth, 2008; Golinkoff et al., 1984) and thus resemble superordinate categories, which can only be formed on the basis of some abstract characteristics shared by a group of objects (e.g., function). Researchers working with infants and toddlers have thus proposed that pre-verbal children evince the ability to abstract such characteristics when they pay attention to the objects, compare them and reflect upon the comparisons (e.g., Mandler, 2000; Ross, 1980; Sugarman, 1982). According to some evidence, even 2-year-olds "attempt to make inferences from comparisons of comparisons" by reflecting on the relations that they infer among objects (Sugarman, 1983, p. 202). Such behaviour suggests that pre-verbal children seek to establish meaning in what they perceive (Nelson & Ware, 2002) and do not seem to depend on receiving explicit linguistic input when abstracting ontological types (Cimpian & Erickson, 2012). In short, evidence from research with pre-verbal children indicates that their early categories are embedded in abstract conceptual knowledge and not in perceptual features (Booth, Waxman & Huang, 2005; Rhodes et al., 2014).

Studies with older children and adults bring out more clearly the critical role of the criterion needed for arriving at a dichotomy and make it possible to study such groupings directly. Evidence from those studies also suggests that the inherent ambiguity of the free classification method affects the performance of children and adults alike in that it rarely yields strict dichotomies (e.g., Annett, 1959;

Currie-Jedermann, 1984; Denney & Acito, 1974). For instance, in Annett's study only one child out of 303 (age range 5 to 11 years) and one adult out of 42 (age range 18 to 73 years) made a complete dichotomy (animate vs. inanimate) under the "free" conditions. By contrast, in "directed" classification, where the experimenter stipulates the dimension of similarity to attend to when judging an object's ontological category, even three-year-olds produced taxonomic categories (Currie-Jedermann, 1984). In another study, preschool children correctly formed a dichotomy between real vs. pretend objects when instructed to do so, but not in a free sorting task (Morrison & Gardner, 1978). There is also evidence that even an implicitly available criterion can assist children to sort a set of objects taxonomically (Markman, Cox & Machida, 1981). Thus, when children aged 3 to 4:7 years were presented with an array of toy furniture, vehicles, people and trees and were asked to "put things that are alike together" either (1) on the table or (2) into plastic bags, their performance evinced significantly more taxonomic sorting in the plastic bag condition. The researchers attributed children's better performance when sorting into bags to the effect of bags on reduced saliency of spatial configuration. Yet it is equally possible that the provision of bags supplanted the missing instruction by reminding the children what bags are for (to hold things of the same kind), informed, perhaps, by their own experience of visiting supermarkets. In summary, the two methods of categorisation – free (no criterion given) and directed (criterion given) – consistently lead to different outcomes in that the more explicit the criterion, the more taxonomic children's categories become.[7]

Animate–inanimate dichotomy

Sustained interest among researchers in the development of biological knowledge has instigated many studies looking at children's understanding of those ontological distinctions that involve biological kinds. For instance, animates vs. artefacts or animals vs. artefacts (e.g., Erickson et al., 2010; R. Gelman, 1990, 2002; R. Gelman, Spelke & Meck, 1983; S. Gelman & Opfer, 2002; Leddon, Waxman & Medin, 2008; Mandler, 2004; Margett & Witherington, 2011; Richards & Siegler, 1986; Simons & Keil, 1995). As I noted earlier, no similar research effort exists in connection with the natural–artificial dichotomy, largely because of the scholarly doubts about its feasibility. Yet there are grounds for considering the natural–artificial dichotomy as either preceding or emerging simultaneously with the other ontological dichotomies that involve natural kinds, notably the animate–inanimate dichotomy. In other words, although researchers have generally interpreted children's groupings such as mammals vs. furniture or animals vs. vehicles as instances of the animate–inanimate dichotomy, the same groupings can equally represent instances of the natural–artificial dichotomy.[8] Put simply, because it is not clear what criteria pre-verbal infants are using when forming such groups of items, the

38 Early ontological knowledge

possibility that they are using an extrinsic causal criterion (i.e., relational) cannot be ruled out, not least because such a criterion is simpler than the criteria which define animate and inanimate objects.

The animate–inanimate distinction is likely to be harder for young children to master because it can, indeed must, be made on the basis of several criteria (e.g., growth, death, movement) rather than just one, as is the case with the natural–artificial dichotomy (i.e., whether human action is needed for an object's existence). Further, many of the biological criteria children cannot acquire spontaneously through everyday observation but require educational input. As well as this, because most of the animacy criteria leave out the inanimate natural objects, whilst the criterion of autonomous movement leaves out both inanimate natural objects and plants, the animate–inanimate is a less inclusive dichotomy than the natural–artificial.[9] For the category *natural* encompasses all the natural kinds (animate, inanimate, mobile or static) and the category *artificial* encompasses all and any artefacts. The greater simplicity of the defining criterion of the natural–artificial dichotomy (an object-extrinsic causal relation) implies that children may acquire it early and spontaneously, as well as rely on it when learning about different objects' intrinsic properties (Petrovich, 1999). Notwithstanding the criterial differences mentioned above, the two dichotomies clearly interact in children's thinking, as shown by their frequent justifications of a natural item as natural rather than man-made on the grounds that it is alive and, conversely, of a living item as living on the grounds that people cannot make it (see below; also R. Gelman et al., 1983).[10]

Development of the natural–artificial dichotomy: A hypothesis

In view of the simplicity of its defining criterion, which is causal and thus a conceptual "primitive" that underpins cognitive development in several knowledge domains, I envisage that children begin to differentiate natural and artificial objects in causal terms from early on and in proportion to their contact with different kinds of object. For example, neonates have opportunities within their environment to differentiate between natural things and artefacts according to texture, temperature, motion, sound and any other characteristics afforded by the different objects, while also simultaneously establishing multiple causal relationships among the objects and their characteristics. More pertinently, babies may begin to discern events in terms of whether or not other human agents have arranged or provided them, thereby accumulating a great store of experience about what adults generally could or could not do. For instance, it is within one's early experience to discover that adults cannot bring on daylight when it is dark, stop the rain and wind or reliably alter the infant's physical sensations and meet their needs even when trying. Once they become able to perceive more of the world (e.g., owing to increased mobility), and generalise the perceived relationships to novel objects and contexts, pre-verbal children can establish an even greater number of causal relations between different objects and human agents. Based on those experiences, infants can begin to infer either that many things around them are the effects of agents like themselves (i.e., people) or that those agents cannot produce the same effects. My point is that there are plenty of situations in infants' daily lives that they can relate to themselves directly and to their insight of themselves as causal agents. Thus, when encountering diverse natural and artificial objects, a correct heuristic for determining the identity of the objects might be one that enables young children to judge an item as artificial if it looks like something that others "like me" can do, along the lines suggested by Meltzoff (2002). Meltzoff's hypothesis about how babies might use their own body to build concepts provides a more plausible framework for explaining how children rely on their own body as a reference point for constructing knowledge about the world than Piaget's notion of egocentrism. Accordingly, when categorising natural and artificial objects as causally different, children may begin by abstracting the relation between an object and human causal action (initially the child's own) as its possible source. By extending the "like me" analogy, children may be able to deduce from their first-hand knowledge of human causal powers which objects could and could not be made by people and build "expectations" that allow them to generalise further what people, as such, can and cannot do. Whilst they are bound to make mistakes in the process, young children must be very fast learners seeing that, by the time that they can speak, no evidence of gross conceptual errors in differentiating natural and artificial entities has emerged. My hypothesis is also consistent with Kuhn's (2012) proposal that children's "own action is the earliest locus of causal inference", which enables them to create and elaborate "mental models of a myriad of causes" as well as construct causal inferences bottom-up and top-down (p. 328). What may be added here is that such inferences imply a capacity for reflection upon the relations that children infer to hold among the observed objects and events and do so in causal terms. Evidence from pre-verbal children suggests that this appears to be well within infants' cognitive potential (e.g., Sugarman, 1982) and can, in principle, account for their ability to transcend any particular objects' boundaries, while also abstracting the relevant causal relations and imagining new ones. Developmental research indeed suggests that young children can use a variety of criteria when categorising by similarity (S. Gelman & Koenig, 2003; Morrison & Gardner, 1978) and when constructing basic ontological categories (Arterberry & Bornstein, 2001).

In the remainder of this chapter, I describe the findings from four studies investigating the natural–artificial dichotomy in children and adults from Britain and Japan. Before describing the main findings as consistent with my hypothesis that natural vs. artificial is an early yet well-defined system of ontological knowledge, which is stable across age and cultural experience, I provide the

40 Early ontological knowledge

background and rationale for the studies and describe the method used. Evidence in the current chapter serves to underpin the central argument in this book; namely, that natural-theological reasoning emerges in conjunction with children's developing knowledge of the world, and that such knowledge provides a starting point for constructing hypotheses and theories about its origin and the nature of its ultimate cause.

Background and rationale for the studies

My interest in children's natural-theological understanding began with investigating their ability to use an object's primary origin as a criterion for differentiating between natural and artificial objects in general.[11] I expected that such a basic categorisation should be available to children of preschool age and regardless of any prior familiarity with particular objects; in other words, even if children had not seen an object before, they should be able to tell whether it is something that people can or cannot make. In all the studies that I have undertaken, my key assumption has been that children are most likely to evince such knowledge if tested by a method that mimics real-life conditions, that is, includes realistic representations of natural and artificial objects that children encounter in the everyday world and where they construct concepts and theories unaided by specialist teachings.

As a first step in devising such a method, I created a collection of photographs of diverse natural and artificial objects taken at close range to highlight any cues potentially relevant to identifying the objects' origins. In addition to different kinds of natural objects and common artefacts, I created a novel stimulus category consisting of imitations or replicas of the matching natural items. Photographed objects were mounted on 3.5" × 5.2" laminated cards with a neutral background. A trial consisted of seeing two objects either from the same ("dummy pairs") or different ontological categories ("conditions pairs"), which were placed in individual unmarked envelopes. The stack of envelopes was shuffled and participants were asked to open each envelope and "find out if any of the two things inside the 'letter' is something that can be made by people or something that people can't make". The objects were presented in pairs rather than singly for two reasons. First, to highlight and maximise the relevant contrasting features of the items and thereby capitalise on children's inherent tendency to notice contrasts (Koslowski & Masnick, 2002); second, to reduce any ambiguity associated with presenting the items singly, which is a particularly important concern when dealing with imitations of natural objects instead of genuine natural objects. In the first two studies described below, stimuli were presented in three conditions (i.e., different combinations of natural and artificial objects): Clear Contrast, Matched Contrast and Unmatched Contrast.[12] The number of each type of pair varied across the studies, which I shall specify in due course. To illustrate the contrasts involved in the conditions and dummy pairs used in Studies 1 and 2, see the Plate section at the end of the book.

In each study reported in the volume, participants were tested individually in a quiet room within their school (children) or in the university's psychology department (adults). Rather than introducing children to a "game", I began each session by stressing that I was interested in finding out what *they* really thought even if they had not learnt about the matter at school or talked about it before. Adults received the same instruction with the additional information that the study looked at cross-age comparisons involving young children. Following each trial of identifying the items in an envelope according to their possible origin in human causal activity, participants provided justifications for their judgements (on approximately 70% of randomly selected items) and then answered a few speculative questions about the objects. This basic format was adapted to the aims of each study. For instance, in Study 2, also with British participants, children and adults performed two tasks on each item: Origin and Animacy, followed by their justifications and the same speculative questions as in Study 1. In Study 3, participants were British and Japanese children whereas in Study 4 both children and adults from the two countries participated. After the origin and animacy questions, participants in all four studies provided data about their representations of God (Chapter 6) while those in Study 4 also answered two cosmological questions (Chapter 5). The point to stress here is that children received the questions about God in the context of their knowledge of the physical world rather than as a concept acquired through religious instruction and other cultural input. This inevitably meant that for some children, particularly the youngest, a testing session lasted longer than what they had previously experienced in a formal setting. I will first briefly describe Studies 1 and 2, whose findings were published previously (Petrovich, 1999), while providing more detail about the findings obtained in the two cross-cultural studies (Studies 3 and 4).

Study 1. Primary origins of natural and artificial objects: Evidence from British children and adults

An earlier, unpublished study with 60 children of preschool age (Petrovich, 1988) revealed that imitations of natural objects were quite ambiguous when it comes to identifying them as either natural or artificial, for instance, when children had to decide whether a toy dog in the photo merely represents a natural dog or is a 3-D model in its own right. This ambiguity became apparent in children's justifications when some of them construed imitations of natural items to be representations of the real things (i.e., citing characteristics of real dogs) and others were clearly referring to pictures or models of real objects when describing how people painted and shaped them. Children's performance on imitations of natural objects is highly relevant in this area of research because of the substantial literature reporting children's greater competence with artefacts than with natural objects, when, in most cases, natural objects in those studies consisted of imitations or replicas of natural objects. It was therefore important to ascertain whether children's apparently inferior performance on "natural" items, and a

42 Early ontological knowledge

failure to demonstrate the natural–artificial ontological dichotomy, could have occurred because of the ambiguity of the imitations rather than any difficulties with natural objects as such.

Thirty preschool children aged 3:9 to 5:0 years and 30 adults aged between 18 and 27 years were tested by the same procedure. Each participant saw 48 objects (24 natural, 24 artificial) including animals, humans, plants, inanimate natural items and common artefacts as well as the imitations of animals, humans and plants. Half of the items were included in the three conditions described above and another half were control or "dummy" combinations, with both items in a pair from the same category of origin (e.g., two different natural dogs, two different toy rabbits or two different common artefacts).

As expected, adults' scores exceeded those of children in all three conditions but the effect of conditions was significant ($p < .001$) for both children and adults (Figure 4.1.1). Because the two conditions comprising imitations of natural objects achieved lower scores among all participants, it was clear that imitations of natural objects, rather than natural objects, as such, were more difficult to identify correctly, especially for children.

Indeed, children's performance in Clear Contrast condition (without any imitations), approximated that of adults ($M = 7.40$, $SD = 0.90$, $p < .001$), who scored the maximum (eight). Furthermore, in the two conditions comprising imitations of natural objects, children performed significantly better ($p < .001$) on natural

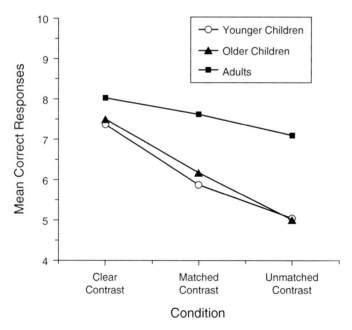

FIGURE 4.1.1 Mean numbers of correct responses (out of eight) for British children and adults across the three conditions in Study 1. Reprinted with permission from Petrovich (1999).

items (maximum correct four), whether animate ($M = 3.83$, $SD = 0.38$) or inanimate ($M = 3.77$, $SD = 0.50$), than on imitations, whether of the matched natural items ($M = 2.16$, $SD = 0.95$) or of unmatched items ($M = 1.10$, $SD = 0.82$). Children were also more accurate on those dummy pairs that included natural items and common artefacts but made significantly more errors on the imitations of natural items (81.6%) than on genuine natural items (17.8%). Presenting imitations of natural items with their matching originals (Matched Contrast) clearly helped children disambiguate the ontological status of such objects compared to presenting imitations without any matching natural items (Unmatched Contrast). Adults' errors on imitations (36%) additionally support the hypothesis that imitations of natural objects are an inherently ambiguous category of item when it comes to identifying their origin.

Children's scores in the Clear Contrast condition are most consistent with the hypothesis that their understanding of the natural–artificial ontological dichotomy is reliable when the stimuli are unambiguous, when the instruction stipulates the defining criterion and when the criterion is a familiar causal concept (i.e., human action). It is important to point out that the natural–artificial dichotomy logically implies a concept of "natural" as a single all-inclusive category that is counterpart of the category "artificial". Children's mean scores on the four categories of natural objects (when maximum correct is two) were indeed quite similar (animal, $M = 1.85$, $SD = 0.60$; human, $M = 2.00$, $SD = 0.00$; plant, $M = 1.90$, $SD = 0.30$; inanimate natural, $M = 1.88$, $SD = 0.50$), suggesting that they see the four natural categories as equivalent in terms of the objects' extrinsic or primary origin.

Participants' justification responses were analysed to determine, primarily, whether they were congruent with the origin judgement made about an object. For example, identifying a toy dog in the picture as natural and then consistently attributing to it the properties of a living dog implies that the error is a perceptual rather than category mistake. The majority of children's justifications (89%) met this criterion, i.e., were congruent with the judgement about an item's ontological category. Although children produced a variety of justifications, the highest percentage cited the objects' Biological-Intrinsic (36%) characteristics (e.g., "It's got blood inside", "It grows from seeds"), followed by Category Label (29%), such as "It's a toy" or "She is a people", and External Features (20%). External Features included justifications that often stipulated cues to the items' intrinsic and essential characteristics which imply intrinsic causal mechanisms (e.g., "He's got real skin", "His ears are pink", while pointing to the visible blood vessels of a natural rabbit shown together with its lookalike fluffy copy) rather than some superficial features. I should also stress that children frequently appealed to their own experience (or lack thereof) when judging an item's identity as either natural or artificial (e.g., "I know mountains"; "I've never seen a crab"). Among the incorrect justifications were mainly those less informative and vague responses, such as "Because it is" or "I know", as well as a small number of factually incorrect or irrelevant justifications (e.g., following a correct identification of a male

44 Early ontological knowledge

mannequin as artificial, the justification stated "Because real men don't wear red trousers").

The high frequency of justifications in terms of biological properties (or lack thereof) suggests that the two ontological dichotomies, (1) natural–artificial and (2) animate–inanimate, interact in children's reasoning about different objects. For instance, they frequently cited biological characteristics of animals and plants when identifying such objects' origin as natural rather than manufactured (e.g., when shown a porcupine, "It's got to be born somehow, a person couldn't make him. He's got to be growned like flowers and people") but did not do the same when justifying the origin of inanimate natural objects (e.g., stone, water), except negatively or indirectly by pointing to an absence of such attributes (e.g., "It just sits there"). Study 2 was designed to determine more directly the role of biological criteria in the natural–artificial dichotomy and ascertain that children's use of biological criteria is properly restricted to animate kinds only, whilst they continue to group animate and inanimate natural items together on account of their common extrinsic origin (i.e., as objects that people cannot make).

Study 2. The role of biological criteria in the natural–artificial dichotomy: British children and adults

In this study, each participant performed in two tasks: Origin and Animacy, but in only one of two stimulus groups: Animals or Plants. The rationale for separating animals and plants was that a number of studies had reported children's failure to treat plants as biological kinds and their inconsistent use of biological criteria when dealing with plants. To test a possible discrepancy in children's understanding of animals and plants, it was important to include the same number of animals and plants in the test. Accordingly, each stimulus group (Animals or Plants) consisted of either 15 animals or 15 plants in addition to five inanimate natural objects, five imitations of natural objects and five common artefacts, so that individual participants in each of the two stimulus groups saw 30 objects in total. This time, imitations of natural objects were included in the Matched Contrast condition only while dummy combinations of items (i.e., both items from the same category) were the same as in Study 1. Participants in the study were 45 children (30 in the Animals Group and 15 in the Plants Group) aged 3:6 to 5:1 years and 24 adults aged between 21 and 40 years (12 in each stimulus group). In the Origin Task, participants followed the same procedure as in Study 1, i.e., identifying objects according to whether or not people make them. In the Animacy Task, participants provided two measures of biological understanding: first, they identified each item according to whether or not it is "alive" and second, they answered four questions about each item's life attributes, i.e., whether it (a) was born/grown, (b) can die, (c) lives and (d) needs food/water. Several other studies investigating children's animate–inanimate dichotomy had used a similar procedure (Bullock, 1985; Carey, 1985; Dolgin & Behrend, 1984; R. Gelman et al., 1983; Massey & R. Gelman, 1988; Ochiai, 1989). Because of the greater complexity of the current study's design, and thus potential relevance of different developmental factors influencing children's understanding of the two ontological dichotomies, all participants completed a vocabulary test (children the English Picture Vocabulary Test (EPVT), adults the Mill Hill Vocabulary Scale). This was useful because many of the words associated with "alive" can convey a range of meanings, including non-biological, and because young children's limited vocabulary may not encompass certain connotations available to adults. In brief, the main aim of the current study was to directly compare children's understanding of the two ontological dichotomies on the same objects and verify the previous reports that children find it harder to identify items as "alive" than answer the questions about life attributes and perform less well on plants than on animals.

As anticipated, adults performed significantly better than did children ($p < .001$) but both age groups were affected by the conditions ($p < .001$). Both made more errors on the imitations of natural objects than on genuine natural objects. Only children, however, were influenced by the combined effects of task, condition and stimulus group as well as vocabulary scores by performing significantly better in the Origin than Animacy Task, in the Clear Contrast condition of both tasks and on animals than plants (Figure 4.2.1).

As in Study 1, imitations of natural items were the hardest stimulus category to identify correctly according to origin, which accounts for children's significantly inferior performance in the only condition comprising imitations, i.e., Matched Contrast.

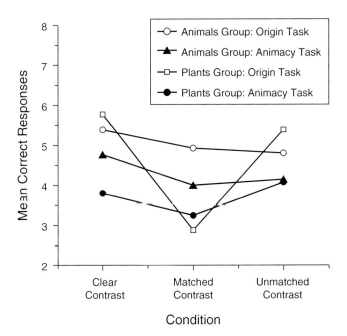

FIGURE 4.2.1 British children's mean numbers of correct responses (out of six) according to stimulus group, task and condition in Study 2. Reprinted with permission from Petrovich (1999).

46 Early ontological knowledge

A comparison of children's scores on the three categories of natural objects (when maximum correct is five) indicated that they scored significantly higher on each natural category (animals $M = 4.11$, $SD = 0.85$; inanimate natural objects $M = 4.51$, $SD = 0.72$; plants $M = 4.26$, $SD = 0.62$) than on imitations. Such a pattern is consistent with that observed in Study 1 and suggests that, from the viewpoint of primary or extrinsic origin, preschoolers seem to construe different kinds of natural object as equivalent. By contrast, in the studies investigating children's ability to use intrinsic causal criteria for categorising objects according to origin (e.g., reproduction), no evidence emerged that children had a concept of an all-inclusive natural category but rather seemed to conceive of animals and plants as "totally different types of things" (Carey, 1985, p. 180; Richards & Siegler, 1986).

Whilst children's understanding of plants in the current study is consistent with several other studies reporting children's difficulties when identifying plants as "alive" (e.g., Hatano et al., 1993; Ochiai, 1989; Richards, 1989; Stavy & Wax, 1989), the current data show that children had no difficulties identifying plants as natural according to their primary origin. For example, whilst failing to recognise that plants are "alive" or that they "live" (43% in Animacy Task), children often mentioned plant growth as a reason for stating that people cannot make plants (Origin Task). It is also noteworthy that children were significantly more accurate on the second measure of their understanding of animacy (i.e., responding on the four attributes of life) than on "alive". Furthermore, seeing that children's vocabulary scores were significantly related to their performance in the Animacy Task but not in the Origin Task, their difficulties with *alive* and *lives* appeared to be of a linguistic rather than conceptual nature. Differential effects of language on the two dichotomies imply that their developmental trajectories may be different; that is, young children need to learn the meanings of *alive* and *lives* that these words have in adult vocabulary, whereas they do not need to learn through language that people cannot make certain objects. Until such learning has taken place, children's use of *alive* and *lives* is often idiosyncratic. For instance, when answering questions about a natural horse, a child explained that "Horses don't live; they stay outside" while another said "the road is alive for ever". Indeed, it frequently seemed that preschool children's most common references to *live* and *alive* were associated with location or habitat, function and even sheer existence. Yet judging by their correct use of the four attributes of life and the justifications given for natural objects' origins, children's biological knowledge seems to be coherent and reliable, implying a correct basic understanding of the different objects' intrinsic characteristics and causal mechanisms. The current findings are thus in agreement with a study which concluded that children's understanding of the category *animate* depends on whether they are asked about the living attributes of the items or whether something is "alive" (Leddon, Waxman & Medin, 2008).

As in Study 1, children in this study also frequently identified natural objects as those that God makes. Such responses appear to suggest that children of preschool age implicitly conceive of the origin of natural objects in a "dual" sense, that is, antecedent-derived as well as primary and, when not instructed which one to use, their strategy appears to vary according to the object. Hence their tendency to explain some natural objects' origins in terms of their antecedent-derived causal mechanisms (e.g., "Born from its mother", "Grown from seeds") but other objects, notably inanimate natural, they more readily explain in terms of primary origin, i.e., an object-extrinsic cause (e.g., "Made by God"). To address the availability of this dual-origin assumption in preschool children's understanding of the natural objects' origins, and to find out whether the same conceptual trends are present cross-culturally, in the next study I compared British and Japanese children in the same tasks.

Study 3. Primary and derived origins of natural and artificial objects: British and Japanese children

Diverse literature on Japanese culture is replete with claims alleging marked differences between Western and Japanese people's views of nature (e.g., Cyranoski, 2010; Watanabe, 1974; White, 1967). Nakamura (1964), for example, titles one of his chapters, "Non-rationalistic tendencies in Japan", and a section therein "The lack of knowledge concerning the objective order" (Chapter 36). Especially relevant to the current volume are the claims that Japanese people are not inclined to engage in causal reasoning spontaneously but have acquired this ability under Western influences (e.g., Kawasaki, 1990; Ogawa, 1986, 1998; Watanabe, 1976). Japanese youngsters are thus said to view all objects as having the same origin (i.e., natural) and only later come to learn that many objects are produced by human industry (Kobayashi, 1993). As well as this, scholars from different disciplines have argued that native Japanese perceive the world holistically, as a harmonious and organic whole that is also alive (i.e., animism), rather than in terms of different categories of existence (e.g., animate, inanimate, natural, artificial). Some writers have also argued that Japanese people prefer to think about particular natural things rather than in general terms because "natural" as an abstract concept does not figure in their culture (Nakamura, 1964, p. 535, 537–8; Ogawa, 1998; Watanabe, 1976). What makes such claims particularly striking is that they are at odds with a vast body of developmental research, some of which I reviewed earlier in this volume, showing that very young children, before being influenced by their culture's linguistic idiosyncrasies, engage in causal reasoning, postulate unobservable causes and categorise objects according to their inherent characteristics.

In fairness to the scholars above, some have acknowledged that their description is that of "the typical view of nature in traditional Japan" rather than arising from psychological research (Watanabe, 1976, p. 282). "Typical" views are those espoused by the "representative thinkers" in the history of Japanese thought and recorded in religious scriptures, mythology and literature, as well as based on "personal observations" (Nakamura, 1964, p. 392). Indeed, Nakamura expressed hope that "perhaps social scientists will finally furnish us with statistical verification" of those impressions (p. 392). Nevertheless, many of the claims about "typical" Japanese cognitive traits have penetrated the psychological literature and gained acceptance even among psychologists. I was

48 Early ontological knowledge

thus not too surprised when several Japanese colleagues aired their scepticism regarding Japanese children's ability to understand my questions in the same way that Western children do, particularly those questions that ask them to think about the origins of natural entities. Their concern emanated from the widely held assumption that Japanese people lack a concept of God as creator of the universe but instead believe that the cosmos and matter as such have always existed (e.g., Nakamura, 1964; Ono, 1962; Watanabe, 1974).

Because of the implications of any such profound cultural differences in the conceptions of the world for my theory that natural-theological understanding is a universal aspect of cognitive development, a comparison with Japanese children seemed uniquely appropriate. Taking account of extant developmental research and theory, my main prediction was that Japanese children should be able to differentiate between natural and artificial objects in terms of the objects' origins when tested by the same method as British children. Furthermore, I expected that Japanese children, too, might show a more sophisticated understanding of different objects' origins than just in terms of whether or not people can make an object. In addition, and in the context of pervasive claims about animism in Japanese thought and culture, I included the same test of animacy for children from both countries. Finally, seeing that Japanese culture does not encourage speculation about the ultimate origin of natural objects, or postulating God as a causal agent when thinking about the origin of natural objects, I was interested to see whether Japanese children would mention God spontaneously when identifying the origin of natural items or select this option when included among the response choices.

Whilst I continued to use the same basic procedure as that with the British participants described above, the test format in the current study altered somewhat in order to ensure that data from the two cultural groups were comparable. Because it seemed impractical to attempt to replicate the Matched Contrast condition in Japan, whilst at the same time meeting the criterion of equal familiarity of the objects for both national groups, I focused on achieving the latter. An approximately equal familiarity of the selected stimuli for children from both countries was determined by pre-testing several Japanese adults with a larger set of objects and then asking children to name each item included in the test.[13] The downside of achieving such a balance is that the number of objects finally included in the test was smaller (12) than in the previous two studies with British participants. From the viewpoint of the overall design and the duration of each testing session, however, this turned out to be an optimal number of stimuli. Most important, the objects included in the test were representative of the variety existing in the world, i.e., animals, plants, inanimate natural objects and common artefacts.

The key modification of the Origin Task in the current study was the inclusion of two concepts of origin – derived and primary – in connection with each item. Hence, in the new Origin Task, children were asked to identify, first (1) antecedent-derived origin of the item in the photograph (e.g., *this dog*) and then (2) primary origin of the same kind of item but not shown in a photograph (e.g., *the first ever dog*), stressing that this would be the time when no other dogs were around.

The order in which children were asked about natural and artificial items varied across children but all children were asked about antecedent-derived origin first. Further, children answered both origin questions by selecting one of three options, one of which was correct, one incorrect and the third was open-ended, allowing them to respond in their own words. For example, the derived origin question (i.e., about "this dog") was followed by the options "Born/Grown", "Made by People" and "In Some Other Way", whereas the primary origin question (i.e., about "the first ever dog") was followed by "Always Existed", "Made by God" and "In Some Other Way". The option "Always Existed" was included to accommodate the Japanese cultural preference, according to which matter (and some of its forms) has eternal existence. In the case of artefacts, the options for both origins were "By People", "By God" and "In Some Other Way". Following the origin questions, children received a simpler version of the Animacy Task than that used in Study 2, which asked them only to say if any of the two items shown in the photographs was "alive". As in Study 1, children gave justifications for a selected number of items on each of the two concepts of origin and for a certain number of their animacy responses, regardless of whether they were correct or incorrect. Finally, children's concepts of God were elicited in the context of their reasoning about natural objects (data described in Chapter 6).

In a separate session, which took place a few days later, each child completed a picture vocabulary test (EPVT in Britain, PVT in Japan) in order to monitor any effects of language on the different components of the study. Children from both countries were tested individually in a secluded space within their school or kindergarten. In order to test a sufficient number of children in Japan, comparable to the size of the British sample, several psychology students from Kyoto and neighbouring universities assisted me in collecting data. Because in some of the schools children were tested in several locations simultaneously, I was able to be present in about 50% of the sessions in Japan.

50 Early ontological knowledge

In total, 90 British and 102 Japanese children aged 4, 5, and 6 years of both sexes and of a similar average age took part. Children in both countries came from state schools/kindergartens. Not all 102 Japanese children provided data in all the parts of the test, partly because of the duration of the test but, also, the shyness of many younger Japanese children. We thus decided to focus on obtaining their responses about natural objects mainly and ask them a reduced number of questions about artefacts. Consequently, whilst all 102 Japanese children answered both origin questions about natural objects, the natural objects' animacy status and about the derived origin of artefacts (i.e., about "this X"), only 23 children (13 at age 6, six at age 5 and four at age 4) were asked about the primary origin of artefacts.

When analysing children's data (ANOVA), I first looked at whether object familiarity was a significant factor by comparing children's mean scores on familiar and unfamiliar objects from each ontological category (natural, artificial) and according to both origins (derived, primary). These tests indicated that prior familiarity with the objects did not have a significant effect on the children's ability to correctly identify objects' origins, so that data for familiar and unfamiliar items were treated as a single category in the remaining analyses.[14] Put simply, children from both countries seemed able to make a plausible guess about an item's identity as either natural or artificial, often prefixing their response by saying, "I don't know what it is but [it] can (or can't) be made".

Origin Task

Because neither children's age or sex were significant factors in their overall performance in the Origin Task, whereas nationality and verbal age (VA) were consistently and highly significant, comparisons according to nationality were of the greatest interest. As predicted, children from both countries discriminated reliably between natural and artificial objects according to the objects' origins, scoring higher on artificial than on natural items and higher according to the objects' derived than primary origin (Table 4.3.1).[15] In three of the four conditions of the Origin Task, British children scored significantly higher than did Japanese children: Natural Derived, t (190) = 6.97, $p <$ .001, Natural Primary, t (189) = 4.02, $p <$ .001 and Artificial Derived, t (190) = 2.53, $p =$ .012, but the two groups did not differ statistically in Artificial Primary.

Although natural primary was the hardest condition for both groups, a number of children from each country scored a maximum (i.e., six) in this condition (18 British, eight Japanese). Overall, the trends observed within each national group in the Origin Task suggest that what is easy or hard for British children is also easy or hard for Japanese children (see also Figure 4.3.1).

It is pertinent to note that, whilst Japanese children's mean scores in Natural Primary did not exceed the 50% cut off point, their performance in this condition (well above zero) casts doubt on the claim that Japanese have no concept of natural objects' primary origin and thus may not understand the origin questions. Moreover, children's justifications seemed consistent with the assumption that natural objects began at some point. Rather than respond randomly, my impression was that, when uncertain, Japanese children refrained from responding instead of venturing a guess, even when encouraged to do so.

Whilst children's better performance on artefacts than on natural objects is consistent with other studies, data from the current study suggest a different

TABLE 4.3.1 Children's mean numbers of correct responses (out of six) and standard deviations (in parentheses) in the Origin Task

Condition	British N = 90	Japanese N = 23
Natural Derived	4.89 (1.12)	3.13 (1.36)
Natural Primary	3.38 (2.06)	2.43 (2.11)
Artificial Derived	5.39 (1.21)	4.78 (1.81)
Artificial Primary	4.09 (2.00)	3.57 (1.93)

52 Early ontological knowledge

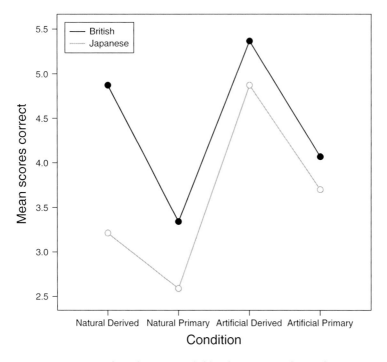

FIGURE 4.3.1 British and Japanese children's mean numbers of correct responses (out of six) across the four conditions of the Origin Task in Study 3.

explanation for such a discrepancy, in agreement with the dual origin hypothesis mentioned earlier. In other words, seeing that the origin of artefacts cannot be derived from any intrinsic causal mechanisms, their origin is straightforward to conceptualise in terms of a single cause (i.e., human action). By contrast, many natural objects' origin can be thought of in two senses (antecedent-derived and primary), thus making it harder for children to answer the origin question in a principled manner without knowing which concept of origin to use as a criterion. Moreover, children's better performance on derived than primary origin clearly implies that they understand enough about intrinsic causal mechanisms from which natural objects derive yet do not use this knowledge to answer the questions about primary origin. To verify this interpretation, I looked at the two object categories (natural, artificial) in Derived Origin condition first, where both nationalities provided complete data, and then in Primary Origin, where only 23 Japanese children's data were used in the analysis (Artificial Primary condition). There was no statistically significant difference between the two object categories in either origin condition whilst the effect of origin concept was highly significant ($p < .001$). Such a finding strengthens the hypothesis that what makes the natural category harder for children is not lack of knowledge about natural objects'

Early ontological knowledge **53**

intrinsic causal mechanisms but, rather, their implicit assumption that such objects can have two origin explanations and the uncertainty regarding which of the two is the correct one to use. Put simply, a dual origin concept relevant to many natural objects is an intuition available to young children but they apparently find one of the two origins easier to handle (derived) than the other (primary). I discuss later some of the possible reasons for children's inferior performance on primary origin of natural objects in the current study compared to the two previous studies where children performed better when using primary origin as the criterion.

Animacy Task

The overall trend for British children to score higher than Japanese children in the Origin Task was reversed in the Animacy Task, where 4- and 5-year-old Japanese children performed somewhat better than their British counterparts did (Table 4.3.2); by age 6, however, British children's marked improvement rendered the overall difference between the two nationalities nonsignificant.

The similarities and differences between British and Japanese children in the two tasks (Origin, Animacy) may be accounted for in terms of both their vocabulary scores (VA) and nationality, both of which were consistently highly significant factors ($p < .001$) and, in fact, overlap. For example, whilst the two groups' average calendar age (CA) in months is quite similar (British, $M = 66.43$, $SD = 9.18$; Japanese, $M = 65.23$, $SD = 10.55$), Japanese children's average VA score ($M = 62.73$, $SD = 15.90$) is significantly lower than British children's average VA score ($M = 73.22$, $SD = 19.44$), $t (190) = 4.113$, $p < .001$. In view of such discrepancies, Japanese children's frequently superior performance in the Animacy Task is even more remarkable and best explained by the specific effects of the Japanese language. The precision of the Japanese terms for "alive" (*ikiteiru*) and "not alive" (*ikiteinai*), which are used exclusively for referring to the presence and absence of biological attributes (the same kanji character signifies "alive", "perishable" and "fresh"), undoubtedly facilitated Japanese children's good performance in the Animacy Task.[16] Conversely, the multiple meanings of *live* and *alive* in the English language (e.g., live music, dead battery, shelf life, dead end) seem to hinder British children's capacity to adhere to consistent criteria when judging different objects' animacy status. By age 6, however, most British children in the study seemed to

TABLE 4.3.2 Children's mean numbers of correct responses (out of six) and standard deviations (in parentheses) in the Animacy Task for *natural* objects

Age	British N = 90	Japanese N = 97
4	3.76 (0.72)	4.06 (1.09)
5	4.06 (0.61)	4.21 (1.17)
6	4.56 (0.88)	4.25 (0.99)
Total	4.16 (0.81)	4.18 (1.07)

54 Early ontological knowledge

have learned the biological meanings of these terms and at times exceeded Japanese children's scores.

The difference between the two nationalities in their readiness to provide justifications, with British children being generally more forthcoming than Japanese children, can also be attributed to the influences of their vocabulary and nationality. Notwithstanding such differences, some Japanese children offered equally informative, or similarly mistaken, justifications as did British children. For example, children from both countries seemed ready to confer animate status to artefacts when such objects are directly handled by people (e.g., "*Shoe is alive when you are walking*", British; "*If people have money, it is alive*", Japanese) and they offered similar justifications for attributing the primary origin of natural objects to God (e.g., "*God only makes alive stuff, not furniture*", British; "*Absolutely Kamisama, people can't make animals*", Japanese). Although only two (out of 23) Japanese children attributed the first artefacts to God rather than to "*the first people*", they justified such attributions in the same way that many British children did: "*Because no people were alive then*", "*People wouldn't know how to make the first X*" or "*People didn't have metal then*". Albeit erroneous, children's attributions of the first artefacts to God often seemed to be of some philosophical interest (Platonist Ideas or Pre-existing Forms) rather than implying a failure to integrate immediate and final causes as previously suggested (e.g., Evans, 2008).

In brief, evidence obtained in the two tasks suggests that children from both countries find it easier to answer the questions about different objects' derived origins and their animacy status than about the same objects' primary origin. When British and Japanese children's judgements about derived origin, primary origin and animacy status were compared directly as separate tasks, a significant difference emerged ($p = .002$). Pairwise comparisons further indicated that whilst derived origin and animacy judgements were not statistically different, they each differed significantly from primary origin judgements (Figure 4.3.2). One obvious similarity between derived origin and animacy questions is that they both pertain to actually existing objects whilst primary origin questions require children to switch attention to a level of explanation that they rarely deal with in everyday communication. The finding that British children too performed significantly less well on primary origin judgements contradicts the claims that Japanese, but not people from Western cultures, find it difficult to think in terms of primary origin.

The similarity between the two nationalities regarding primary origin may seem to contradict my prediction that primary origin should be easier for children of preschool age than derived origin because it does not presuppose any knowledge of specific intrinsic causal mechanisms. One possible explanation for children's inferior performance on primary origin questions in the current study is that the question format used in Study 3 is more complex than that used in the previous two studies, where children had to identify natural objects' primary origins merely by indicating whether people make such objects. In the current study, by contrast, children had three possibilities from which to select one;

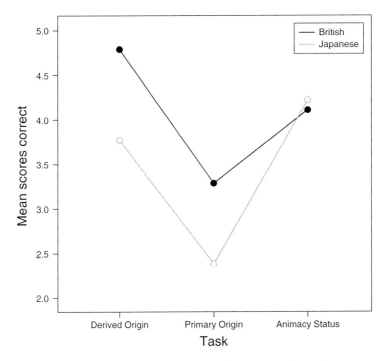

FIGURE 4.3.2 British and Japanese children's mean numbers of correct responses (out of six) in the Origin and Animacy Tasks in Study 3.

moreover, none of the three possibilities involved human agency. Furthermore, two of the options ("Always Existed", "By God") children did not seem to differentiate well; frequently, they seemed to construe "Always Existed" as meaning "Ever since God had made it". Most pertinently, however, children of this age and in both countries are unlikely to have had sufficient experience (or none at all) of discussing primary origins and thereby acquiring the relevant vocabulary and building the confidence that comes with using it. In contrast to children, adults were able to identify such obstacles explicitly by pointing to a general lack of opportunities for discussing ideas about primary origins.

In summary, the main findings of this cross-cultural study are consistent with my prediction that children from both countries should be able to differentiate consistently natural and artificial as distinct ontological categories on the strength of their everyday knowledge of causal mechanisms and causal relations that obtain in the physical world. Crucially, however, evincing such knowledge under formal testing conditions depends, first, on having the criterion and, second, on the criterion being extrinsic to the object. Earlier in the volume, I argued that the easiest extrinsic origin criterion for children to acquire and use is in terms of human action, whose presence or absence permits categorisation of diverse objects as either artificial or natural.

56 Early ontological knowledge

The ambiguity associated with children's implicit understanding of natural objects' dual origin concepts suggests that a different approach may be more useful in research that seeks to establish whether children of preschool age can conceive of primary origin as an absolute or ultimate beginning. I addressed this concern in the next study by using a test of cosmological understanding in conjunction with the Origin and Animacy Tasks, which findings are described in Chapter 5. In the final study of the current chapter (Study 4), British and Japanese children's understanding of the natural–artificial ontological dichotomy was investigated further by using the same tasks as above, albeit with additional modifications, as well as by comparing their performance with that of adults from both nationalities.

Study 4: Origin by evolution: Conceptions among children and adults from Britain and Japan

In the current Origin Task, the main modification consisted in replacing the open-ended option in the question about primary origin of natural items with an evolutionary response option. (For artefacts, the open-ended option, i.e., "Some Other Way", remained the same.) Children's version of the evolutionary option was put in terms that they could understand, such as, "X (animal) started from being something like a fish millions of years ago and then slowly developed to become X". For the two inanimate natural objects the equivalent wording was "X started from some stuff that millions of years later became water/rock". As in Study 3, all participants also made animacy judgements about each item in the test and provided justifications for a number of selected items in each task. Following the two tasks, participants answered the questions designed to elicit their God-concepts. To reiterate my earlier point, the rationale for asking participants to answer the speculative questions immediately after asking them about physical objects (Origin and Animacy Tasks) was to address their concepts of God in the context of their knowledge of the world rather than as an aspect of their cultural learning.

Eighty-three British children aged 4, 5 and 6 years, 48 Japanese children aged 4 and 5 years (including three children aged 6), as well as 62 British and 60 Japanese adults participated in the study. British children came from several state schools whereas the majority of Japanese children came from two private kindergartens. One British and two Japanese children did not provide VA scores so some statistical analyses are based on 82 British and 46 Japanese children's data. Adults from each country were divided into a younger (18 to 25 years) and an older (40 to 67 years) group. Whilst older adults from both countries came from diverse educational and social backgrounds, the younger adults were almost entirely students of the University of Oxford and Kyoto University, studying mainly psychology but also other science and humanities subjects. An approximately even number of participants from each country and within each age group were male and female. All participants also completed a vocabulary test: British and Japanese children completed EPVT and PVT, respectively, younger British adults completed the vocabulary subtest of

Wechsler Adult Intelligence Scale (WAIS), older British adults completed the Mill Hill Vocabulary Scale and all Japanese adults completed WAIS (vocabulary subtest), which scores were included as a covariate in all the analyses.

Children and adults were tested in an identical manner and by the same procedure as in Study 3, either by me (in Britain) or by two native Japanese researchers working with me as translators, who also assisted me with participant recruitment. This time I was present during each testing session in Japan and was able to intervene when needed (e.g., when a child departed from the response options on the test sheet). Several Japanese adults spoke fluent English so that I was able to test them in English in the presence of the translator. I will first report the main findings with children before drawing comparisons with adults within and across the two countries.

Children: Origin Task

As in Study 3, familiarity with the objects was not a significant factor in children's performance so that the scores on familiar and unfamiliar items were combined in the subsequent analyses. Whilst British children as a group scored higher than did Japanese children in all the conditions of the Origin Task (Figure 4.4.1), children

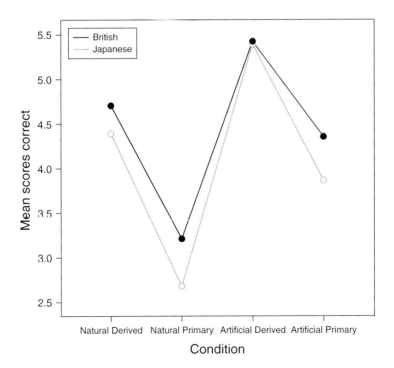

FIGURE 4.4.1 British and Japanese children's mean numbers of correct responses (out of six) across the four conditions of the Origin Task in Study 4.

58 Early ontological knowledge

from both countries scored higher on derived than primary origin and on artefacts than natural objects (paired t-tests, $p < .001$).

The similarity of findings in the current Origin Task (Figure 4.4.1) to those in Study 3 (Figure 4.3.1) is evident from the pattern of variation across the conditions of the Origin Task in the two studies. It is worth noting that, although British children scored higher in each condition, the gap between them and Japanese children is smaller in the current study than in Study 3. I am inclined to attribute Japanese children's somewhat better performance in the current study primarily to the fact that more of them answered the questions rather than just stating "I don't know", as they frequently did in Study 3. Thus, when children in the current study responded "I don't know", we encouraged them to say what *they* thought, even if it was something that they had not yet learned about. Such interventions rarely occurred in Study 3, where student researchers perceived them as alien to Japanese children's ways of interacting with adults and to Japanese culture in general. Another possible reason for Japanese children's better performance in the current study than in Study 3 are their higher VA scores than those in Study 3 (details below). This, in turn, may have resulted from the fact that the majority of children in the current study attended private preschools, with smaller class sizes and the educational benefits ensuing from this.

Whilst natural primary was again the hardest origin condition for both national groups ($p = .015$), children's mean scores in this condition (well above zero) together with the appropriateness of their justifications imply that they understood the origin question. It is perhaps intriguing that among both British and Japanese children the mean scores in this condition are lowest at age 6 (i.e., British 4-, 5- and 6-year-olds scored 3.72, 4.02 and 3.60 respectively and Japanese children of the same ages scored 3.21, 3.41 and 2.88 respectively). Such a developmental trend suggests that by age six either children engage less in speculating about natural objects' primary origins or, more likely, become less confident about expressing their conjectures, possibly because formal education increasingly conveys to them the importance of factual knowledge.

Although the current version of the Origin Task included an evolutionary option as a possible explanation of natural objects' primary origin, only a handful of children gave a response that resembled evolutionary change. The majority of children from each country (75%) selected the creation option (i.e., 62 British, 36 Japanese), stating that God made the first natural objects and that God's ideas were the source of the first artefacts' existence. For example, "God made people and then people made the same thing that God did" regarding a wooden dish (British), "God made the materials and people put them together" regarding a shoe (Japanese). Even those children who selected the evolutionary response (21 British, 12 Japanese) also mentioned God's involvement, usually stating that God was the initial cause but that the original item later changed. Only two British children responded in a way that suggested some learning about evolution: one of those mentioned the origin of humans from apes and the other said

Early ontological knowledge **59**

that "The first dog would be a wolf and then God made it to a different dog, like a pet". Among Japanese children, those who responded by selecting the evolution option frequently said that the dog and badger "developed" from other animals and then offered a variety of transformations, such as a dog developing from a pig, zebra or cat and a badger emerging from a panda, rabbit or elephant. The naivety of children's evolutionary ideas is less surprising in light of evidence that even biologically educated adults, including medical students, do not consistently adhere to Darwinian evolutionary explanations but instead evince a number of misconceptions that are incompatible with the main tenets of Darwin's evolutionary theory (e.g., Alters & Nelson, 2002; Bishop & Anderson, 1990; Nadelson & Sinatra, 2009; Southcott & Downie, 2012). As a Japanese academic helpfully pointed out to me, there may be a major ambiguity regarding the apparently evolutionary explanations among both children and adults in Japan in that such explanations are often acceptable to Japanese people because they seem compatible with cultural beliefs in reincarnation (i.e., turning from one species into another in each subsequent incarnation).

Children: Animacy Task

Children's performance in the Animacy Task also replicated the pattern observed in Study 3, whereby Japanese children scored higher than did British children in several instances, albeit not significantly so partly because British children improved by age 6 (Table 4.4.1).

Seeing that the children in the study differed significantly according to both nationality ($p = .020$) and VA score ($p < .001$), which overlap, VA scores can account for some of the observed differences in their performance. For instance, Japanese 4- and 5-year-olds' calendar age in months ($M = 61.54$, $SD = 6.92$) and their verbal age ($M = 64.35$, $SD = 14.92$) were not significantly different, whereas British 4- and 5-year-olds' VA scores ($M = 65.59$, $SD = 14.87$) were significantly higher than their calendar age ($M = 60.79$, $SD = 5.83$, $p = .008$). Japanese children's lower VA scores may also account for their greater reticence when answering primary origin questions and giving justifications. Importantly, however, Japanese children's answers to the primary origin questions were not substantially different from those of British children and in several instances

TABLE 4.4.1 Children's mean numbers of correct responses (out of six) and standard deviations (in parentheses) in the Animacy Task according to object category

Age	Natural Animate		Artificial Animate	
	British	Japanese	British	Japanese
4	3.66 (1.04)	3.61 (1.08)	4.59 (2.23)	3.87 (1.94)
5	3.81 (0.89)	4.35 (0.99)	4.96 (1.95)	5.60 (0.68)
6	4.44 (0.89)	4.33 (0.58)	5.89 (0.42)	6.00 (0.00)
Total	3.96 (1.00)	4.09 (0.88)	5.13 (1.80)	5.16 (0.87)

achieved the same maximum score (i.e., six). Again, it is worth noting that such a pattern runs counter to any suggestions that children of this age, not least those from Japan, lack a concept of primary origin as distinct from antecedent-derived origin.

Comparing children's performance on derived, primary and animacy judgements as three separate tasks, this time including both natural and artificial items, revealed similar overall patterns (Figure 4.4.2) to those observed in Study 3 (Figure 4.3.2); namely, significantly lower scores on primary origin than on derived origin and animacy questions for both nationalities.

Adults: Origin Task

British and Japanese adults performed significantly better than did children in all the conditions and in both tasks; nevertheless, they too made errors occasionally and of a similar kind as those that children made (Figure 4.4.3). As predicted, the concept of origin was highly significant ($p < .001$), eliciting higher accuracy on derived than primary origin questions among all participants. This performance, however, interacted with participants' vocabulary scores ($p < .001$), so that Japanese adults scored higher than British adults did on derived origin of natural objects (British: $M = 5.77$, $SD = 0.61$; Japanese: $M = 5.93$, $SD = 0.25$) whereas

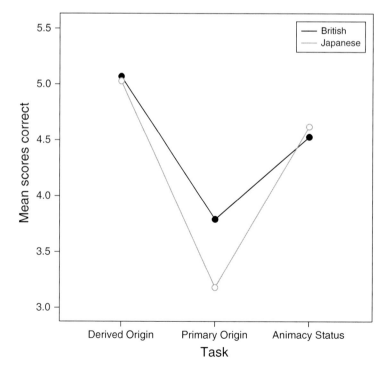

FIGURE 4.4.2 British and Japanese children's mean numbers of correct responses (out of six) in the Origin and Animacy Tasks in Study 4.

Early ontological knowledge 61

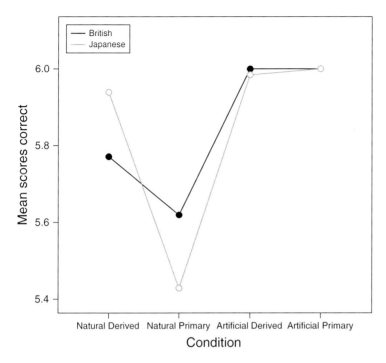

FIGURE 4.4.3 British and Japanese adults' mean numbers of correct responses (out of six) across the four conditions of the Origin Task in Study 4.

British adults scored higher on primary origin of natural objects (British: $M = 5.63$, $SD = 0.75$; Japanese: $M = 5.42$, $SD = 1.01$).

Japanese superiority on natural derived is evidenced by their lowest correct score of five (out of six), whereas in the British sample score of two was the lowest in the same condition. Nevertheless, the overall similarity between children and adults from the two countries in the Origin Task is evident from Figures 4.3.1 and 4.4.1 (children) and Figure 4.4.3 (adults). It is clear that both age groups in both countries achieved the highest scores when identifying the origins of artefacts and lowest when explaining the primary origin of natural objects. In contrast to children, the effect of object category was highly significant among adults ($p < .001$), mainly because their scores had reached a ceiling (i.e., six) in the conditions comprising artificial objects (except for one 5.97 score). Object familiarity was also significant in adult performance although it is difficult to interpret this effect in view of their frequent at-ceiling scores.

As for the frequency of selecting the evolutionary option in response to the question about natural objects' primary origins, adults' data differed substantially from those of children in that the majority of British adults (83% older, 97% younger) selected evolution whilst only five older and one younger adult selected creation by God. Among Japanese adults, too, the majority selected the evolutionary response

62 Early ontological knowledge

option although, surprisingly, twice as many adults (i.e., 11 or 37% older and one younger) selected the creation option. It would be impossible to verify from the current data to what extent adults' understanding of evolution was Darwinian and, in many cases, it was apparent that the reverse was true. For example, British adults selecting this response option often stated that the first animal of its kind "Evolved from slightly different parents" or "From another animal", while Japanese adults' justifications were not very different from those that Japanese children offered. Thus, a badger "Evolved from a cat-like or dog-like animal", grass "Evolved from its pre-existing seed on earth" and the like. A response that aptly illustrates the idiosyncrasies in understanding Darwinian evolution came from a life sciences student in Japan who put it succinctly: "Evolution, but I don't believe in the theory of Darwin. The seed of every kind of animal existed from the beginning", also adding that the whole process occurred by chance.

Adults: Animacy Task

Adults' performance in the Animacy Task yielded somewhat unexpected results in the current study. In contrast to Japanese children, who often scored higher than British children on the animacy questions, in the current study Japanese adults had a tendency to score lower than British adults, albeit not statistically significantly so (Table 4.4.2).

Differences between adults and children on animacy judgements are apparent when comparing Figures 4.3.2 and 4.4.2, on the one hand, and Figure 4.4.4, on the other. Whilst the two children's figures both indicate that preschoolers scored higher on animacy than on primary origin judgements, Figure 4.4.4 indicates that adults scored lower on animacy than on primary origin judgements.

This finding is of interest because it is unlikely to result from Japanese adults' failure to benefit from the precision of the Japanese terms for animacy status, as I suggested could explain Japanese children's superiority in relation to British children earlier in Study 3. Rather than linguistic, Japanese adults' performance in the Animacy Task suggests a cultural explanation. Let me elaborate: A longer exposure to Buddhist teachings about life pervading all matter appears to account for Japanese adults' somewhat less correct animacy judgements. Conversely, Japanese children's good performance in the Animacy Task (i.e., they do not lag behind British children in this task as they do in the Origin Task) reflects not only their

TABLE 4.4.2 Adults' mean numbers of correct responses (out of six) and standard deviations (in parentheses) in the Animacy Task according to object category

Age group	Natural Animate		Artificial Animate	
	British	Japanese	British	Japanese
Younger	5.81 (0.53)	5.73 (0.52)	6.00 (0.00)	6.00 (0.00)
Older	5.40 (0.81)	5.30 (0.70)	5.93 (0.25)	5.80 (0.48)
Total	5.61 (0.71)	5.52 (0.65)	5.97 (0.18)	5.90 (0.35)

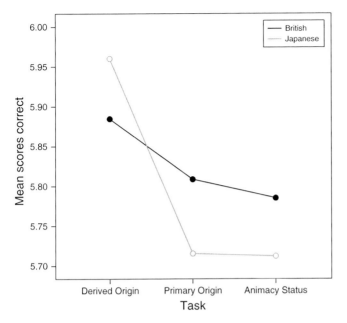

FIGURE 4.4.4 British and Japanese adults' mean numbers of correct responses (out of six) in the Origin and Animacy Tasks in Study 4.

ability to master Japanese terms for animacy and apply them correctly but also young children's insufficient assimilation of their culture's quasi-animistic attitudes to nature. British children, on the other hand, master the relevant vocabulary terms a little later (by age six), but thenceforth use them largely correctly. Yet this cultural advantage for British participants (i.e., low exposure to Buddhist animistic ideas) makes it harder to explain the relatively high frequency of the "typical" Japanese responses among British adults, who often made statements of the following kind: "I can't say that water is dead", "Everything in nature is alive", "It [water] has a mind of its own… It has a way. To me, it's a live thing" and the like. Such notions among British adults are indistinguishable from the Japanese equivalents: "Water flows under gravity but it is alive, I feel it when I look at it" or "It [water] is part of nature and it is not made by people". Examples of this kind manifestly contradict generalisations such as White's (1967) that individuals from Christian cultures do not perceive nature as sacred or endow natural objects with life.

As with children from the two countries, adults differed significantly on their verbal scores ($p < .001$), according to both nationality and age. Thus, younger British adults ($M = 93.51$, $SD = 11.00$) scored significantly higher than older British adults ($M = 58.04$, $SD = 26.25$), $t(60) = -6.86$, $p < .001$, as did younger Japanese adults ($M = 92.33$, $SD = 11.64$) compared to older Japanese ($M = 56.90$, $SD = 30.95$), $t(58) = -5.87$, $p < .001$. Put simply, younger adults from the two

64 Early ontological knowledge

countries were more similar than were younger and older adults from the same country. As we shall see later in the volume, these differences held in the other components of the tests used.

In summary, evidence described in the current chapter suggests that children's understanding of the world as consisting of natural and artificial objects is systematic and theoretical. In other words, children use an abstract causal principle in terms of which it is possible to see any object as belonging in one of the two mutually exclusive ontological categories, natural or artificial. I suggested earlier that children's greater accuracy on artefacts than natural objects may be best explained not in terms of their greater familiarity with artefacts, but in terms of their uncertainty in how to answer the questions about natural objects' origins that do not specify which of the two intuitively available concepts of origin to consider: (1) antecedent-derived or (2) primary. Once children have the correct origin criterion (i.e., an object-extrinsic causal principle) for identifying both natural and artificial objects' primary origin, they can evince a strict, that is, mutually exclusive natural–artificial ontological dichotomy. Not only is the use of a single criterion in all instances of identifying objects' origins computationally simpler than the use of multiple criteria (i.e., intrinsic causal mechanisms specific to different natural kinds), but a well-defined natural–artificial ontological dichotomy is only possible if based on a single criterion.

I also argued earlier in the chapter that children's knowledge of this ontological dichotomy is most reliable when the criterion is stated in terms of human causal action (i.e., whether people make an X) but becomes harder when it is put in a format that requires them to select from among several options (e.g., "Always Existed", "Made by God" and "In Some Other Way"). Refining the primary origin question further by introducing the evolutionary option made it even harder for children to answer such a question correctly. In my view, they are hindered, primarily, not by their limited knowledge about the evolutionary mechanisms but because such a question, even among adults, often seems to confound the concepts of derived origin, i.e., of species, and primary origin, i.e., of living matter (see, for example, Tracy, Hart & Martens, 2011). In other words, the main difficulty with understanding biological evolution may not be in grasping the idea that natural kinds can undergo significant transformations over time but, rather, in misconstruing Darwinian evolutionary mechanism as pertaining to the origin of life itself rather than emergence of its different forms (Beecroft, 2014).

The cross-cultural comparisons described in the chapter have revealed important and hitherto overlooked conceptual similarities between British and Japanese participants. Japanese children's inferior performance in the Origin Task, especially in the primary origin condition, seems to be a consequence of cultural and linguistic influences rather than their causal cognition. Lack of exposure to a language suitable for expressing ideas and concepts investigated in the Origin Task undoubtedly limits Japanese children's ability to convey their implicit understandings of such concepts. Conversely, by virtue of living in a culture that does not discourage thought about natural objects' origins, British children have a somewhat greater exposure to the vocabulary needed for communicating such reasoning. As a result, they were more willing to talk about their understandings and often did so with great enthusiasm. Yet the fact that both groups achieved lowest scores on the questions about primary origin of natural objects suggests that British children's cultural milieu, perceived as being more advantageous to their ability to articulate ideas about origins, may be an overestimate. For although British children live in a culture that is more open to discussing natural objects' origins, the emphasis is usually on derived (physical) rather than primary (metaphysical) origin. A number of British adults put this point rather eloquently by stressing a distinct lack of social opportunities to discuss primary or ultimate origins as the main reason for not having articulated their own views on the subject. Lack of opportunities for verifying one's own judgements through comparisons with the judgements of others, especially those pertaining to metaphysical issues, appears to be a universal obstacle to elucidating the nature of one's own beliefs at any age. This leads me to conclude that both British and Japanese children's inferior performance when identifying primary origin of natural objects occurs predominantly for cultural, including linguistic, reasons rather than cognitive reasons.

In spite of the significant differences between British and Japanese children's scores in many parts of the study, the similarities between the two groups are all-important, not least when considered against the background of the broader literature claiming profound differences between Japanese and Western people's conceptions of nature. Bearing in mind some of the important cultural constraints that Japanese children have to overcome, the overall similarity between British and Japanese children's responses in the two tasks is quite considerable. Thus, in spite of there not being a single word in the Japanese language denoting a concept of *natural*, or natural phenomena in general, but only the names for concrete natural things (Ogawa, 1998, p. 145), Japanese children nevertheless form a working concept of an all-inclusive category consisting of animals, plants and inanimate natural objects.[17] They do so by relying on the same abstract criterion as British children; namely, objects' origins in terms of their relation to human causal action. Seeing that such a criterion is not dependent on either language or formal instruction, the current findings are consistent with the suggestion that even pre-verbal children may be able to construct category representations, i.e., generalisations or abstractions of what they perceive (cf., Quinn, 2002a).

One of the more striking similarities between British and Japanese children to mention briefly in this chapter is in their references to God as a causal agent. Even though Japanese culture discourages references to God in this context, and a number of Japanese scholars expressed scepticism that Japanese children would understand my questions in the same way that British children do, their mentioning God in the context of the current study plainly contradicts such generalisations. It also shows that Japanese children are prepared to say what they think when given an opportunity to do so. This is no mean feat seeing that children in Japan commonly expect to learn from their seniors what to think, especially about the matters addressed in the current study, rather than be asked what *they* think.

66 Early ontological knowledge

Notes

1 I refer to "dichotomy" rather than "distinction" in order to highlight the strictly bipartite, i.e., mutually exclusive, nature of such a system of categorisation.
2 A single criterion in the current context resembles, but does not amount to, the classical view of category representation (Medin, 1989; Murphy & Medin, 1985). Without embarking on a more detailed account of the similarities and differences between the two positions, suffice it to say that the defining criterion of the natural–artificial dichotomy is not any "feature", "attribute" or "property" as the classical model stipulates (Murphy & Medin, 1985, p. 290), but a relation inferred to exist between an item and its ultimate cause.
3 White's (2006) reference to causal "asymmetry" as a bias to overestimate the importance of the causal object and underestimate the significance of "the effect object in bringing about the outcome" (p. 132) is unrelated to my use of the same term for referring to "extrinsic" and "intrinsic" causal criteria as asymmetrical when applied to the natural and artificial categories. White's point is that the two objects involved in an interaction (the causal object and the effect object) equally contribute to the resulting effect.
4 To say that the defining criterion of the natural–artificial dichotomy is extrinsic to objects in no way implies that intrinsic criteria play no role in children's judgements about natural objects' origins. Rather the reverse: intrinsic criteria are uniquely important when explaining the origins of objects from their antecedents (i.e., derived origin) but not when there are no antecedents, such as when new entities come into being (i.e., primary origin). Hence, when explaining an object's primary origin (whether natural or artificial), postulating *extrinsic* causes is necessary (see, for example, Harré or Kant mentioned earlier in this volume).
5 Whilst the limited ecological validity of the laboratory context can be advantageous in some tasks (see Rakison & Yermolayeva, 2010), it is unlikely to be beneficial when studying categorisation based on different causal criteria.
6 Evidence from animals far simpler than humans (e.g., honeybees, pigeons, baboons) additionally implies that the ability to abstract relations and use multiple comparisons when responding to sameness is an early and basic cognitive competence. The capacity to recognise sameness at abstract levels can be facilitated by increasing the number of stimuli (Van den Berg et al., 2012). Even bees can form abstract concepts from pictures and use the abstracted relational concepts to combine them in a rule for subsequent choices (Avargués-Weber et al., 2012). In short, the ability to categorise by relational similarity appears to be a basic adaptive mechanism needed for survival of human as well as many non-human organisms and hence may be present, in some form, prenatally (Cohen, 1988).
7 The "free" method resembles a test of "divergent" (many solutions possible and desirable) vs. "convergent" (only one correct solution possible) abilities that Guilford (1967) proposed as characteristic of two types of intelligence, which predominate in arts and in sciences, respectively.
8 Functional magnetic resonance imaging (fMRI) studies do not elucidate the basis for such groupings either, except report that distinct neural systems sub-serve person vs. object knowledge (Mitchell, Heatherton & Macrae, 2002) and indicate differing activation levels in the brain when participants were responding to human faces vs. robotic faces (Gobbini et al., 2011).
9 I use "animacy" as a term of reference to life status of both animals and plants.
10 Although mental–physical is also a well-supported ontological distinction in young children (e.g., Estes et al., 1989; Watson et al., 1998), I do not discuss it further in the current chapter because it is not directly relevant to children's use of different causal criteria for categorising natural and artificial objects according to their origins. See Chapter 6 for further discussion on mental–physical dichotomy.

11 The natural–artificial categorisation discussed in the current volume pertains to whole objects that occur in everyday space rather than natural substances of which objects are made, complex machines or artificial intelligence (AI) phenomena.

12 I am indebted to an anonymous reviewer of a previously submitted manuscript for publication in a journal for suggesting the current labels for the conditions as I had hitherto been using my original, provisional and somewhat cumbersome labels when starting to test children in 1981.

13 The most unfamiliar artefact in the set, for participants from both countries, proved to be the image of an electric Light (flat, attached to the ceiling), which even many adults misidentified (e.g., as an egg, pancake, pill, stone fruit, toilet seat). Other unfamiliar objects (i.e., those incorrectly identified in the pictures) included: Dish (frequently identified as lid, penny, wheel), Mortar (identified as bell, leg of bed, musical instrument), Badger (identified as bear, jaguar, pig, skunk, squirrel), Pumpkin (identified as coconut, egg, peanut, pebble, rice, seed, shell, turtle's back) and Mineral (identified as ant, crab, hand of shrimp, nest, straw).

14 One significant interaction involving familiarity, object category and nationality, F (2, 185) = 5.413, p = .021, occurred because 4-year-old Japanese children performed slightly better on unfamiliar artefacts than their British counterparts. There is, however, no obvious explanation for this particular interaction.

15 I should point out that Japanese scores in Table 4.3.1 derive from only 23 children because the SPSS statistical programme selects by default the lowest common number when comparing different groups (in this case, only 23 Japanese children provided data in the artificial primary condition). When, however, all 102 Japanese children's data were used in the analysis, their scores were as follows: natural derived (M = 3.59, SD = 1.42), natural primary (M = 2.23, SD = 1.89), and artificial derived (M = 4.88, SD = 1.49).

16 According to the comments of the Japanese researchers testing the children, Japanese preschoolers were more confident and responsive to questions about animacy than about origin. My observations of British children suggested the opposite pattern in that they had shown greater interest in answering the questions about the objects' origins than about animacy.

17 The nearest Japanese term corresponding to "natural" is *shizen*, translated into English as signifying "by itself" or "spontaneously" (Kawasaki, 1990).

5

IN THE BEGINNING

Cosmological reasoning in children and adults

Evidence that children of preschool age engage in speculating about the likely causes of witnessed events (described in Chapter 2) and about causes that bring natural objects into existence (described in the preceding chapter) implies that they may also be able to entertain causal ideas pertaining to the beginning of matter as such. Although children's ideas about unobservable entities and causes are often incorrect, engendering such ideas is consistent with a tendency to seek complete explanations for what they observe. In keeping with the philosophical arguments that seeking causal explanations for natural objects is continuous with seeking explanations for the origin of primary matter, I suggested in Chapter 1 that children's ideas about the beginning of matter and the universe (cosmological reasoning) should be studied as an aspect of their causal understanding.

The interest of cosmological reasoning for psychological research is two-fold. First, it is a form of causal understanding whose starting point is the actual physical world (e.g., Hawking, 1988; Hospers, 1984; Kant, 1983; Rees, 1999; Swinburne, 1991) and which is therefore likely to be a universal component of causal development. Studying its early development may thus yield further insights into children's ability to adhere to the principles of determinism, mechanism and priority that they adhere to in other instances of causal reasoning. Second, the highly speculative nature of cosmological reasoning allows us to compare children and lay adults more directly on the grounds that both age groups are equally novices when it comes to the most fundamental cosmological question; namely, origin of matter as such and the assumptions underpinning it.

Cosmology: Scientific and lay

Whilst it is true that scientific cosmology relies on input from the various branches of science (e.g., astronomy, physics or geology), its subject matter is distinct, namely, origin of the universe and its matter, including any initial conditions that could have led to the world as it is (Carr, 2006). Because no research of "the whole" (i.e., the universe) is possible (e.g., Barbour, 1998), seeing that such a whole "has no exterior, no outside world, no 'rest of the universe' to which one could appeal for boundary or initial conditions" (Halliwell, 1991, p. 83), those engaged in cosmological reasoning necessarily impose a concept or model of the whole upon the world of experience (Harré, 1983). Precisely because all cosmological models rest on certain assumptions about the initial conditions, it is the nature and origin of those assumptions that psychological research can address, thereby making cosmological theorising a psychological topic, too.

What are the main cosmological assumptions and theories that could be of interest to psychological research? According to the prevailing cosmological view, the world began with the formation of primary matter from an explosion within the initial conditions ("the big bang"). Both scientists and philosophers aim to answer the questions regarding when and how this took place. Seeing that their main tool in this process is speculative reasoning, it is interesting that cosmology specialists have often highlighted the similarities between their own "ultimate" questions and those asked by children (e.g., Halliwell, 1991; Medawar, 1984). What differentiates children from professional cosmologists is that the latter are able to couch their quest in more technical terms and say "What happened before inflation?" or "How did the universe actually begin?" (Halliwell, 1991, p. 78), whereas the same questions asked by children are phrased in notoriously "childish" terms. Put differently, cosmologists know that such questions cannot be answered conclusively regardless of the advances that science continues to make (Berry, 1986) and that the scientific goal of understanding "the very beginning" may in fact be unattainable (Rees, 1999, p. 176–7). Children, however, keep on asking the "ultimate" questions, unperturbed by the predicament inherent in all cosmological endeavour. Turner aptly illustrated the nature of this predicament by citing Hawking's multiverse theory as an example of a cosmological theory that still "does not explain why there is something rather than nothing" (2010, p. 658).

The other major cosmological view is one that assumes an eternally existing universe (e.g., "steady state" or continuous creation of matter) and hence makes no assumptions about a big bang or anything that happened before it but simply takes the existence of the universe for granted. Whilst such a theory is conceptually simpler (Brush, 1992), there is little psychological evidence that people of any age find this hypothesis satisfactory. Even Hume accepted that human beings cannot resist making conjectures about the cause of the world as a whole but succumb to "an arbitrary act of the mind" that inevitably comes up with a proposal (in Swinburne, 1991, p. 122). In contrast to Hume, however, the very same tendency to come up with a proposal Kant elevated to the status of a regulative principle of human cognition.

A third cosmological view to mention briefly, which has its adherents among both scientists and philosophers, is that the universe may turn out to have a

70 In the beginning

mechanistic explanation (including chance) which is at present unknown. This cosmological view is represented in philosophical reflection by agnosticism or scepticism, a version of which dismisses the origin question as redundant and even irrational.

I have reviewed briefly these divergent cosmological positions because of their direct bearing on the outcomes of natural-theological understanding in that each implies a different concept of God and God's role in the origin and structure of the world. For instance, the beginning-of-matter cosmological view often corresponds with *theistic* cosmology, which postulates a transcendent God who creates matter from nothing pre-existing (ex nihilo) and is distinct from it. The eternal-matter hypothesis, by contrast, usually corresponds with pagan cosmology (i.e., *pantheism*), which makes room for God's causal role in the structuring (designing) of a pre-existing matter but not in its creation ex nihilo (Tambiah, 1990). Finally, cosmological agnosticism or scepticism considers God to be an unnecessary postulate of a causal agent, unlikely to be involved with the material world, so that any judgement about God's existence and role is either suspended or dismissed.

By way of ending this brief overview of the highly speculative nature of cosmological theories, we may concur with Ellis and Silk's (2014) verdict on all cosmological theories (e.g., string, multiverse or any pre-big bang variety) as consisting of essentially untestable and unprovable hypotheses. Physical science will thus never solve the many mysteries in cosmology, such as provide reasons for the existence of the universe, of any physical laws at all or of the nature of those physical laws that do hold (Gibbs, 1998). As Lennox (2009) put it, all of these issues science takes for granted rather than investigate. Bearing those caveats in mind, it seems both fitting and desirable that we put the same fundamental questions about the world to children and lay adults, unrecognised experts in speculative reasoning, to find out how they represent the beginning of entities that have no known antecedents, namely, the universe and its primary matter.

Development of cosmological reasoning: Pre-causal or metaphysical?

What children think about the origin of the world as a whole, or matter as such, has so far not been studied in developmental research. The best-known attempt to gauge young children's cosmological ideas is still that made by Piaget in the 1920s when he noticed that already at age 2 or 3 years, long before any religious education takes place, children begin to ask about the origins of things, including "Who made the world?" (1977, p. 399). Whilst admitting that such questions are abundant in children by the time they are 4- or 5-years-old, Piaget maintained that children do not ask them in the first-cause or "cosmogonic" sense (1925, p. 207), i.e., "ex nihilo" (1977, p. 379), but in accordance with "theological artificialism" (1977, p. 399), which amounts to a pre-causal intuition that a human or human-like being manufactured it. In Piaget's view, children only begin to raise "the most metaphysical questions, such as that of the primal cause" after the age of 6 or 7 years (1977, p. 410), once they have acquired a concept of physical cause and can thus begin to answer metaphysical questions "rationally", that is, by explaining things either in terms of their antecedent causes or adopt a stance of "tentative agnosticism" by refusing to speculate (1977, p. 313).

It should be said that Piaget's claims about the nature of physical and metaphysical causal reasoning often seem confusing and in need of being evaluated in the context of his own philosophical predilections. According to Piaget, for example, metaphysical causal postulates are by their very nature pre-causal or non-rational; as such, they bias children to view the natural world as created by an anthropomorphic being rather than by "chance or mechanical necessity" (1977, p. 402). It is also important to stress that Piaget did not investigate directly and systematically children's understanding of primary origin of natural objects or of matter as such and thus had no evidence that children's origin questions imply one and the same causal agent as creator of all kinds of object and who is anthropomorphic (Petrovich, 1988). Furthermore, the two senses of origin – primary ("ex nihilo") and derived ("from antecedent causes") – are confounded throughout Piaget's interviews with children so that many of the questions that he put to children would be just as difficult for adults to answer (e.g., "How did the sun begin?", "Where did the fire [of which the sun is made] come from?"). In spite of his limited and mostly anecdotal evidence, Piaget concluded that, instead of a cosmological theory, children hold an artificialist conception of the world ("over-audacious cosmogony"), believing that the universe was made by humans or human-like agents, even if called God (1977, p. 313).

Post-Piagetian research of cosmological understanding

The gap of almost a century in the study of children's cosmological understanding is perplexing, not least because of the extensive research in the last few decades of children's causal understanding, including that of natural objects' origins. What seems to account for this gap is that whilst Piaget considered the two domains of thought, physical (science) and metaphysical (religion), to be conceptually directly related, albeit inappropriately, contemporary developmental research has focused almost entirely on children's concepts in the scientific domains and hence on scientific but not metaphysical aspects of cosmological reasoning (Bryce & Blown, 2013; Siegal, Butterworth & Newcombe, 2004; Siegal, Nobes & Panagiotaki, 2011; Vosniadou, 1994; Vosniadou & Brewer, 1994). For example, researchers have looked at how children conceptualise the shape of the earth, day-night cycles and planetary relationships, but not at their ideas about the origin of the universe or its primary matter. There is, however, some indirect evidence from research on children's understanding of the origins of natural entities that they may well have ideas about origin in the first or ultimate sense and engage in speculating about the nature of its cause. One source of such evidence is the research on children's teleological understanding (Kelemen, 1999a, b) and the other is that involving their ideas about the origin of species (Evans, 2000).

72 In the beginning

In her investigations of preschool children's understanding that only arte-facts and parts of organisms have functions or purposes whereas whole natural objects, whether animate or inanimate, do not, Kelemen found that children ascribed functions and purposes to all kinds of object (i.e., "promiscuously"). She attributed such a tendency to two major biases which lead young children to assume that natural things, like artefacts, have been designed by an intentional, albeit "under-specified", agent (1999a, p. 245): (a) limited knowledge of physi-cal causal mechanisms and (b) familiarity with human intentionality. It should be said, however, that children in the study were not asked to "specify" their ideas about the agent who designs natural objects; consequently, the evidence reported does not demonstrate that children indeed represent the intentional agent who designs natural objects to be the same as the human intentional agents who design artefacts. In a subsequent study, Kelemen and DiYanni addressed the question of whether children's "purpose-based reasoning about nature is actively related to their intelligent design reasoning in any systematic fashion" (2005, p. 3) by questioning 6- to 10-year-olds about (a) origins of natural and artificial objects' ("Why did the first ever X object/event exist/occur)?" and, also, about (b) "intelligent design" ("Did someone or something make the first ever X or did it just happen?"). Although the majority of children (82–84%) associated natural entities with God, that is, linked intentional explanations of natural objects' origins with their intuitions about the "nonhuman intelligent" design in nature, whilst linking artefacts with human causal activity, Kelemen and DiYanni nev-ertheless concluded that children of this age treat natural objects "as though they were artifacts" (2005, p. 15). The researchers reached this conclusion on the grounds that children intuitively think of "purpose" as the primary explanation for the origin of both artefacts and natural objects and do not volunteer responses which demonstrate that they differentiate between the two kinds of "purpose". As I noted above, children's intuition that "purpose" (i.e., intention) explains the origin of both natural and artificial objects does not constitute evidence that they do not differentiate between the purposes or intentions associated with each ontological kind. Yet such evidence is needed in order to sustain the "promis-cuity" argument, not least because data show that children in the study made systematic connections between natural objects and "non-human" intelligence, on the one hand, and between artefacts and human causal activity, on the other. Without corroborating evidence that children systematically confound between the two kinds of purpose, their responses in the study do not imply lack of inter-est in theorising about first origins or that such reasoning represents an "esoteric a topic" for 6- to 10-year-olds (Kelemen & DiYanni, 2005, p. 23).

Although Evans similarly concluded that "the world of the 5- to 7-year-old appears to be one in which organisms always existed" (2000, p. 250), children's frequent responding in creationist terms implies a reference to the first cause. In a subsequent study involving children as well as adults, Evans replicated the find-ing that all age groups and from both fundamentalist and non-fundamentalist backgrounds gave creationist (i.e., intentional) responses, leading her to conclude that the human mind is "susceptible" to creationism and resistant to "naturalistic explanations for the origin of species" (2001, p. 252). Whilst it may be a valid observation that humans have a tendency to appeal to intentional causality in such a context, children's "intentional" explanations of natural entities (in this case biological species) do not necessarily imply that children think of those intentions as being identical with human intentions. Seeing that the terms "first species" or "the very first things on earth" can be ambiguous for participants of any age, in that such terms can be construed as also pertaining to the very substance of which the entities, or life as such, are made, "creationist" references require further probing, especially when made by young children.

In short, children's concepts of "the very first" and their ability to theorise about the "first origins" suggest that a more direct way of addressing them would be to investigate children's cosmological reasoning (origin of primary matter) in the context of their ideas about the first origins of particular objects.

Cosmological conjectures: British and Japanese children and adults

The reasons for comparing British and Japanese children as well as adults in their understanding of natural origins were mentioned earlier in this volume; those of specific relevance to the current chapter include the claims that Japanese people believe in an eternally existing matter, partly because they cannot conceive of unidirectional time ("an absolute 'onceness' of time"; Watanabe, 1974, p. 281) and, also, lack a concept of God as creator (e.g., Ono, 1995). Abstract concepts such as "God" and "nature" are said to be Western cultural products that native Japanese have simply assimilated (e.g., Ogawa, 1998). Comparing British and Japanese participants' cosmological views thus seemed appropriate as a way of attempting to verify the validity of widespread claims in the scholarly literature about vast conceptual differences between Western and Japanese cosmological views.

Data presented in the current chapter were obtained from the same children and adults in Britain and Japan who took part in Study 4 (participants' characteristics described in Chapter 4). Following the questions in the Origin and Animacy Tasks, each participant also answered two cosmological questions. The first cosmological question asked them to state their preferred view regarding the origin of primary matter by selecting from among the three options corresponding with the main cosmological hypotheses mentioned earlier: (1) eternally existing matter, (2) beginning-of-matter and (3) agnosticism about whether the question can be answered. Based on the evidence from research on causal development (Chapter 2) as well as young children's ability to engage in theoretical reasoning (Chapter 3), my prediction was that preschool children from both countries should be able to grasp the meaning of each of the cosmological possibilities if stated in simple terms. In other words, it should be straightforward to determine whether young children prefer the view that (a) the world (i.e., stuff

74 In the beginning

of which it is made) has always been there (without a beginning), or that (b) it began at some point in time or that (c) the question was too difficult to answer and thus should not be asked.

To ensure that participants' responses represent their own judgements and inferences, both children and adults were explicitly encouraged to say what they think rather than look for a "correct" answer that they may have learned from others. Accordingly, the instruction given to participants stipulated that even specialists, such as scientists and philosophers, did not always agree in their views about the matters in question. In the children's version, I used the following wording:

> Scientists – people who have studied a lot – say that the whole world came from a tiny speck of stuff called "atom", which no one can see and which took millions and millions of years to grow and gradually become different things. But no one is sure how the first speck of stuff came to be. Some people say (a) it had been "always there" (*eternal-matter*), others say (b) it began, probably when God made it (*beginning-of-matter*), and others say that (c) no one can know for sure and we shouldn't be asking the question (*agnosticism*). What do you think: (a), (b) or (c)? [Repeating each option in an abbreviated form.] Adults received the same question format with a slightly modified wording.

After stating their preferred response option to the first cosmological question, each participant then received a follow-up question designed to elicit their views on the role of God, if any, in the origin of matter. Adults' version of the follow-up cosmological question asked each participant to say whether they ruled in or out God's involvement in the origin of matter, by selecting one of the three options corresponding with God's role as (a) *designer* who imposes structure on an existing matter, (b) *creator* of matter or (c) *no role* for God in either. Children's version of the follow-up question asked them to say whether matter or God came first, whereby the order of mentioning God and matter varied in a random pre-determined fashion across participants. The rationale for asking children to state whether God or matter came first was to ensure a correct interpretation of the "always there" option, which many children appeared to use for meaning "existed for a long time". From the viewpoint of the aim of the cosmological test, i.e., to find out whether children have an understanding of the "first cause" idea, the current question format seemed both simple and sufficient. In sum, both children and adults provided two pieces of information in this part of the study; first, their preferred cosmological conjecture regarding the origin of primary matter and, second, their judgement regarding God's role in the origin of matter.

The test of cosmological reasoning used here makes it thus possible to establish whether children understand the meaning of *first* as a starting point in a series of subsequent events or, rather, take the series for granted and hence decline to speculate about its origin. Put differently, the current test is another way of finding out whether young children adhere to the principles of determinism and priority when reasoning about the world as a whole. As for the responses to the follow-up cosmological question, one of the research interests was to see whether they were consistent or inconsistent with the same participant's response to the main cosmological question. The inconsistencies occurred more frequently among children than adults, notably when saying that matter was "always there" and then affirming that God came before matter.

Three scorers,[1] including myself, sorted a sample of 82 complete cosmological statements (i.e., 82 participants' responses to both questions), 36 from children and 46 from adults, according to an initially suggested set of 10 response categories that was subsequently reduced to the current three. Following a discussion of the specific examples, and the use of the three response categories, the final inter-rater agreement was 94%.

Children's conjectures about the origin of matter

Because only 10 children (five from each country) responded in a manner that appeared consistent with agnosticism, and all 10 responses could be classified as either "eternally existing matter" or "beginning-of-matter" (i.e., in light of children's responses to the follow-up question), the children's data were analysed by 2×2 Chi-square tests for independence (computed with continuity correction). The aim of the tests was to determine whether children's cosmological judgements were independent of their nationality, age and sex.

Although British and Japanese children differed significantly in their responses to the first cosmological question, X^2 (1, $N = 116$) = 14.71, $p < .001$, $phi = .38$, and the differences were often consistent with their culture's dominant view, important similarities between the two groups also emerged. As Figure 5.4.1 indicates, the majority of British children (77%) selected the beginning-of-matter option whilst the majority of Japanese children (61%) selected the eternal-matter ("always there") option. Importantly, however, within each nationality were the children who diverged from their respective culture's dominant view by selecting the opposite culture's "typical" preference: 23% of British children selecting the eternal-matter option and 39% of Japanese children selecting the beginning-of-matter option.

When children from the two countries were compared according to age, the two nationalities differed significantly at age 4, X^2 (1, $N = 41$) = 3.97, $p = .046$, and at age 5, X^2 (1, $N = 44$) = 7.97, $p = .005$, but not at age 6. Whilst British children at each age preferred the beginning-of-matter hypothesis, Japanese children showed an increasing preference for this hypothesis with age. Thus, 33% of Japanese 4-year-olds responded by selecting the beginning-of-matter option, 39% of them did so at age 5 and 67% at age 6 (Table 5.4.1). Sex differences were not significant in either national group.

Because of the small number of Japanese 6-year-olds (i.e., 3), it was only appropriate to compare 4- and 5-year-old children from the two countries, and

76 In the beginning

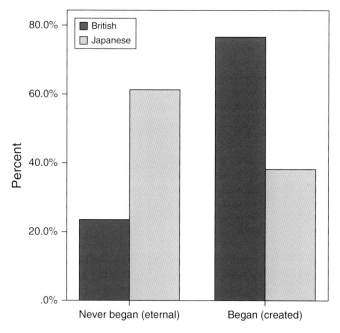

FIGURE 5.4.1 Origin of matter: Percentages of British and Japanese children selecting "Never began (eternal)" and "Began (created)" options in response to the first cosmological question.

TABLE 5.4.1 Origin of matter: Frequencies and percentages of children's responses according to age and nationality

Age	Eternal	Created
4 years (N = 41)		
British	7 (30%)	16 (70%)
Japanese	12 (67%)	6 (33%)
5 years (N = 44)		
British	4 (15%)	22 (85%)
Japanese	11 (61%)	7 (39%)
6 years (N = 31)		
British	7 (25%)	21 (75%)
Japanese	1 (33%)	2 (67%)

these comparisons are consistent with the overall comparison of the two nationalities. The increasing age trend among Japanese children to make a causal conjecture, i.e., that matter "began" rather than being "always there", may suggest a greater confidence among 5- and 6-year-old than among 4-year old Japanese children to speculate and/or articulate their thoughts about a question that is not commonly discussed within their culture.

In brief, the pattern of children's responses to the first cosmological question implies that preschoolers from both nationalities were able to understand its meaning and answer accordingly. Further, both groups of children made judgements about the origin of primary matter that were "atypical" of their respective cultures. Japanese children's responses in particular could not be construed as merely conveying what they had learned from others, but are likely to represent their own judgements and inferences.

Children's judgements about God's role in the origin of matter

When answering the follow-up cosmological question, which asks child participants to judge whether matter or God came first, the majority of both British and Japanese children stated that God came before matter (Figure 5.4.2) but the frequency with which the two nationalities affirmed God's primacy (British 83%, Japanese 60%) was significantly different, X^2 (1, N = 118) = 6.21, p = .013, phi = .25.

What is important to highlight in this overall similarity between the two national groups is that Japanese children's judgements contravene their culture's dominant view but are in accordance with the principles of causal understanding, notably determinism and priority. Seeing that 17% of British children also took the view that is not typical of their culture, such as stating that matter

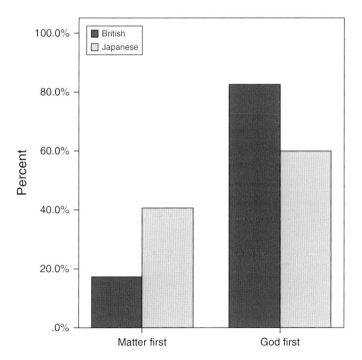

FIGURE 5.4.2 God's role in the origin of matter: Percentages of British and Japanese children selecting "Matter first" and "God first" options in response to the follow-up cosmological question.

preceded God, the assumption that culture is the key determinant of people's cosmological ideas, which is held more strongly in Japan, seems unjustified.

Comparing children from each age group with their counterparts from the other nationality revealed no significant differences in the frequency with which British and Japanese children judged whether God or matter came first. For instance, at age 4 years, 82% of British children stated that God came first whilst Japanese children were evenly divided between those who said that God came first (50%) and those who said that matter came first (50%), X^2 (1, $N = 43$) = 3.34, $p = .067$. At age 5, however, more children from each nationality (85% British, 61% Japanese) stated that God preceded matter, but the difference was not statistically significant, X^2 (1, N = 44) = 2.01, $p = .157$. At age 6, 82% British and 100% (i.e., all three) Japanese children stated that God came before matter, also non-significant, X^2 (1, N = 31) = .018, $p = .754$. The increasing age trend among Japanese children to say that God preceded matter is, again, consistent with the key principles of causal reasoning rather than their culture's view.

Although only a small number of children responded to the follow-up cosmological question in terms that could not be identified as either God or matter having precedence, such responses may be of greater theoretical interest than it at first seems. For example, there were children in both countries who suggested that *both* God and matter have "always existed" or that both had started at the same time, as the following statements from British children illustrate: "God and dust came together from the beginning", "God came when the world was made … God was always there with the dust" and "God just made himself, from the dust". Whether children's responses of this kind represent a genuine intuition akin to *panentheism* in theological and philosophical thought, which some scientists have endorsed (e.g., Peacocke, 1993), is impossible to say on the basis of the current data but might be of interest in future studies.

In short, British and Japanese children have shown both similarities and differences in their responses to the two cosmological questions. Whilst the two nationalities differed significantly on the first cosmological question (origin of matter), they were considerably more similar on the follow-up cosmological question (God's role in the existence of matter).

Adults' conjectures about the origin of matter

In contrast to children, adults responded to both cosmological questions by using all three included options and with sufficient frequency so that their data were analysed by 2 × 3 Chi-squares for independence, rather than 2 × 2 as in the case of the children. Several comparisons involving adult data were relevant although not all of them yielded equally significant results. The first comparison involved (a) the two nationalities regardless of age, followed by (b) the two age groups (younger, older) regardless of nationality, (c) the two age groups across the nationalities (i.e., older British vs. older Japanese; younger British vs. younger

In the beginning **79**

Japanese) and, finally, (d) the two age groups within each nationality. No significant sex differences emerged either within or across the nationalities.

Although British and Japanese adults (regardless of age) differed significantly in their preferred view regarding the origin of matter, X^2 (2, $N = 120$) = 6.32, $p = .043$, Cramer's V = .23, thus matching the cultural stereotype, this overall significant difference conceals a major similarity between the two nationalities in that adults from each country selected the beginning-of-matter hypothesis with an almost identical frequency (52% British, 50% Japanese). The frequencies and percentages for each response category according to nationality and age group are shown in Table 5.4.2.

In other words, although the overall difference between the two nationalities is consistent with the cultural accounts, such accounts are incomplete as they do not reveal how ordinary Japanese adults think about the origin of matter when asked this question in the context of their own experience and everyday understanding of the world. When compared in this context, the two nationalities' views are noticeably more similar. The overall pattern of similarities and differences between the two national groups in response to the first cosmological question is shown in Figure 5.4.3.

Age was a significant factor only when comparing older, X^2 (2, $N = 58$) = 8.19, $p = .017$, Cramer's V = .38, but not younger adults from the two countries, X^2 (2, $N = 62$) = 3.06, $p = .216$. Post-test residual analysis indicated that the greatest discrepancy between older British and older Japanese adults was in relation to each group's preference for the eternal-matter hypothesis (18% vs. 53% respectively). Again, what the significant overall difference between older adults from the two countries obscures is that 40% of older Japanese adults in the study think that matter is *not* eternal. In a similar vein, the 18% of British participants who opted for the idea that matter has existed eternally also contradicted the literary stereotypes of there being stark differences in cosmological reasoning between Japanese and Western people. Whilst younger British and Japanese adults did not differ significantly in their preferred cosmological conjectures, it is interesting that younger Japanese participants exceeded their Western counterparts in terms of the frequency with which they selected the beginning-of-matter hypothesis

TABLE 5.4.2 Origin of matter: Frequencies and percentages of adults' responses according to age group and nationality

	Eternal	Created	Neither
British			
Younger	8 (25%)	13 (41%)	11 (34%)
Older	5 (18%)	18 (64%)	5 (18%)
Total	13 (22%)	31 (52%)	16 (26%)
Japanese			
Younger	7 (23%)	18 (60%)	5 (17%)
Older	16 (53%)	12 (40%)	2 (7%)
Total	23 (38%)	30 (50%)	7 (12%)

80 In the beginning

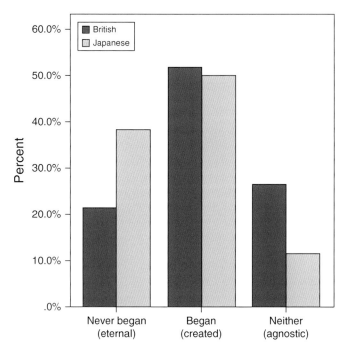

FIGURE 5.4.3 Origin of matter: Percentages of British and Japanese adults selecting "Never began", "Began" and "Neither" options in response to the first cosmological question.

(60% Japanese vs. 40% British) and, by implication, rejected their culture's dominant view that matter has existed eternally. I should immediately clarify that one's agreement with the beginning-of-matter hypothesis does not necessarily imply a preference for a theistic account of the origin of matter, as will become evident when we consider the same participants' responses to the follow-up cosmological question. Nevertheless, the high frequency of the beginning-of-matter views among younger Japanese adults, which is higher than that among their British counterparts, contradicts the claims that Japanese people hold radically different cosmological views than do people in the West by believing that matter has existed eternally and having no concept of "onceness" of time that signifies a beginning event (Watanabe, 1974).

To interpret correctly the finding that a greater number of Japanese than British younger adults selected the beginning-of-matter option, we need to consider their responses to the follow-up cosmological question, namely, their judgements about God's role, if any, in the origin of primary matter. Given the high educational achievement among both groups of younger adults (all university students), it is likely that younger adults from both countries were more aware of the diversity of philosophical and scientific theories and thus better prepared to form their own judgement which, especially in the case of the Japanese participants, was frequently at odds with their culture's traditional view. There is abundant evidence in the participants' comments to suggest that this indeed was the case. Whilst many of those thoughtful views were categorised as corresponding with agnosticism, this was often simply because the statements were not clear instances of either of the two cosmological alternatives but were very much "work in progress" (e.g., "I am changing my view as I go along", said a British student).

In a final comparison looking at the data from the two age groups within each nationality, a different pattern within each country emerged. Whilst the two groups of British adults did not differ significantly in their cosmological preferences, X^2 (1, $N = 60$) = 3.50, $p = .174$, in that the majority of them preferred the beginning-of-matter hypothesis (64% older, 41% younger), older and younger Japanese participants made different choices when answering the same question, X^2 (1, $N = 60$) = 6.01, $p = .050$, Cramer's V = .32. Post-test residual analysis confirmed that the greatest difference between older and younger Japanese adults occurred in relation to the eternal-matter hypothesis (53% older vs. 23% younger). Bearing in mind that almost the same difference was found between older British (18%) and older Japanese adults (53%), it seems clear that it is the older Japanese adults' views about the origin of primary matter that make the greatest contribution to the overall cross-cultural difference between the two national groups. In other words, older but not younger Japanese adults match the stereotype found in the broader literature. When data from children are taken into account, it becomes even more compelling to conclude that the majority of Japanese participants in the current study, children as well as adults, prefer the hypothesis that primary matter has not existed eternally but began at some point in time. Besides, we should recall that 40% of older Japanese participants also selected the beginning-of-matter option as their preferred hypothesis and thereby departed from their culture's prevailing view (Table 5.4.2).

Adults' judgements about God's role in the origin of matter

In contrast to the first cosmological question, where the two nationalities were found to differ significantly in some comparisons, the same participants' responses on the follow-up cosmological question yielded no significant differences. Put differently, when answering the second cosmological question (God's role in the existence of matter), British and Japanese adults were quite similar. The first major similarity to note is that British and Japanese, older as well as younger participants, selected their preferred view about God's role in the origin of matter from among all three possible judgements (Figure 5.4.4). Second, the two nationalities were highly similar in the frequency with which they selected the God-designer option (31% British, 30% Japanese) but diverged on the other two options (God-creator and No role), albeit not significantly so.

The only, albeit marginally, significant difference was that between younger British and younger Japanese adults in their judgements of God's role in the origin of matter, X^2 (2, $N = 62$) = 5.85, $p = .054$, where twice as many Japanese (53%)

82 In the beginning

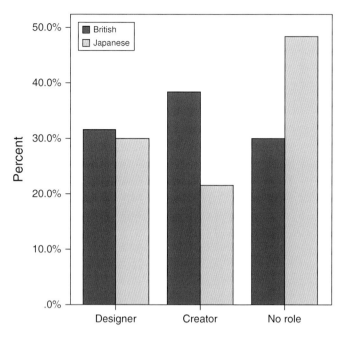

FIGURE 5.4.4 God's role in the origin of matter: Percentages of British and Japanese adults selecting "Designer", "Creator" and "No role" options in response to the follow-up cosmological question.

TABLE 5.4.3 God's role in the origin of matter: Frequencies and percentages of adults' responses according to age group and nationality

	Designer	*Creator*	*No role*
British			
Younger	14 (44%)	10 (31%)	8 (25%)
Older	5 (18%)	13 (46%)	10 (36%)
Total	19 (31%)	23 (38%)	18 (31%)
Japanese			
Younger	10 (33%)	4 (13%)	16 (53%)
Older	8 (53%)	9 (30%)	13 (43%)
Total	18 (30%)	13 (22%)	29 (48%)

as British (25%) younger adults rejected any role for God in the origin of matter. Although this corresponds with the higher total percentage of Japanese (48%) than British (31%) adults who rejected any role for God in the origin of matter, it would be incorrect to conclude from such a trend that Japanese adults have a stronger preference for atheism than British adults. For the total frequency of the Japanese responses identifying God as either creator or designer (52%) is still higher than the responses which deny any role for God (48%) (Table 5.4.3). Seeing that even the responses which reject any role for God in either the origin or structure of matter do not necessarily rule out God's existence, but often restrict it to the moral domain, suggests that at least a half of the Japanese adults in the current sample adhere to hypotheses that are broadly compatible with theism.

In short, it is the pattern of *variation* within each nationality rather than any uniformity that is plainly inconsistent with the claims that Japanese and Western ways of thinking about the world are radically different. The fact that adults from both countries responded in terms of all three possible options when considering the question of how matter began suggests that none of the conceptual possibilities regarding the origin of matter were "foreign" to the members of either national group. Similarly, participants within each nationality varied in their views of God's role in the origin of matter, with 31% British and 22% Japanese adults responding in terms that are not typical of their respective cultures (i.e., designer vs. creator respectively), whilst there were individuals within both nationalities who held the view that God and matter have always coexisted.

Evidence from adults in the tests of cosmological reasoning is thus even more interesting, particularly in conjunction with their comments, as it reveals considerable *individual differences* within each nationality as well as the important *cross-cultural similarities*. The finding that two nationalities, children as well as adults, differed more on the first than the follow-up cosmological question might be explained in terms of the greater and more direct educational and cultural influences on the former than the latter. That is, from an early age people in any culture are exposed, more or less systematically, to myths and scholarly theories about the origin of the world and come to their own view, not just on the basis of their own experience of the physical world but, also, against the background of such input. By contrast, the follow-up cosmological question is more "culture-free" than the first cosmological question in that it is less susceptible to educational and cultural influences. Hence, all participants in the current study are likely to have evinced greater independence of thought when stating their views about God's role in the origin of matter than when making judgements about the origin of matter.

The basic similarity between children and adults in their cosmological reasoning implies that children's cosmological understanding is distinct from their knowledge of the sciences on which cosmological theories rely (e.g., Siegal et al., 2011; Vosniadou, 1994) and may not undergo any radical conceptual organisation that seems to occur in the development of scientific understanding. Indeed, the ease with which many children were answering the two cosmological questions suggests that they had already pondered the answers to both questions as part of their causal development and were ready, and in many instances keen, to reveal them.

Whilst previous research has either claimed or implied that only children explain the origin of the natural world in terms of God whereas adults give mechanistic explanations for its existence (e.g., Evans, 2001; S. Gelman & Kremer, 1991; Kelemen, 1999a,b; Piaget, 1925), the evidence described in the

84 In the beginning

current chapter indicates that children and adults from two cultures with very different cosmological traditions and histories of science both prefer explanations of the natural world and its origin in terms of God. In light of such findings, Wellman and S. Gelman's contention that any theistic hypotheses that children construct when accounting for the primary origins of natural kinds should be treated as "self-constructed errors" is plainly unwarranted (1998, p. 553). Instead, seeing that children's responses to the two cosmological questions are essentially the same as those given by lay adults, and both generations' responses were obtained in the context of their everyday knowledge of the world, children's conjectures about the world as a whole ought to be accepted as fundamentally coherent. Even Hawking conceded that "So long as the universe had a beginning, we could suppose it had a creator", although the physicist gives an equal weight to the possibility that the universe may be completely self-contained, having no boundary or edge, and hence no need for a creator (1988, p. 140–1).

The overall finding of a greater similarity than difference between British and Japanese participants in their cosmological understanding is in agreement with the findings of a survey that compared Japanese and American attitudes to nature (Kellert, 1991). The author of the survey concluded that the American and Japanese public were "similarly pragmatic toward nature" and that Japanese, contrary to their widely known appreciation for nature, in practice valued control and mastery over nature (Kellert, 1991, p. 297). The last point, needless to stress, implies an underlying interest in causal laws and understanding of their application. More broadly, the similarities mentioned hitherto between Japanese and their Western counterparts imply that had Nakamura been in a position to gain insight into how ordinary Japanese people view the world, he may not have needlessly lamented their lack of the Kantian ability to wonder "at both 'the moral law within and the starry heavens above'" when seeking to comprehend the surrounding world (1964, p. 565).

Note

1 I am grateful to Ann Dowker and Claire Davies for their assistance.

6

THE NATURAL-THEOLOGICAL CONCEPT OF GOD

A unique causal agent

"'To whom will you compare me? Or who is my equal?' says the Holy One. Lift your eyes and look to the heavens: Who created all these?"
  (Isaiah, 40:25–26) (The Holy Bible: New international version, 1980)

Throughout this volume I have argued that children's concepts of God should be studied in the context of their understanding of the natural world rather than as something that they acquire through education and culture. According to the natural-theological hypothesis, a spontaneously acquired concept of God is primarily that of a causal agent whereas culturally transmitted religious concepts convey the characteristics of God that are not solely and primarily causal. As such, cultural concepts of God are likely to be acquired by different mechanisms from those that children rely on when spontaneously constructing concepts and theories about the physical world. Evidence described in the previous two chapters indeed shows that children's references to God in the context of their ontological and cosmological reasoning are not fundamentally different from those of adults when both age groups are tested under the same conditions and strongly imply that, for children and adults alike, the concept of God as a causal agent is a simple and coherent concept, qualitatively different from the concept of human agency.

Two other accounts of children's concepts of God that currently dominate developmental literature – anthropomorphism and preparedness – differ from the natural-theological hypothesis in one important respect. They both assume that children do not spontaneously construct a *theological* concept of God (i.e., as neither spatial nor temporal) but depend on their culture and education for its acquisition. As I argue below, however, neither hypothesis envisages a plausible mechanism by which the concept of a transcendent God could emerge from the concepts of empirical agents. Following a brief review of developmental evidence for each hypothesis, I describe data consistent with the natural-theological

86 The natural-theological concept of God

hypothesis and argue that the theological concept of God (i.e., transcendent) children can only acquire spontaneously and do so most evidently in the context of seeking causal explanations for spatial phenomena. Not only would it be difficult to convey such an intuition to young children verbally but, as statements from both children and adults indicate, cultural and educational input does not necessarily have a facilitating role in its development and may even be unhelpful.

The anthropomorphism hypothesis: Theory and evidence

Piaget was among the first developmental psychologists to claim that young children's concept of God is that of a man. In his view, anthropomorphism is typically revealed in children's belief that natural events are caused by "human agency (or divine, but we shall see that this amounts practically to the same thing)" (1977, p. 288). Whilst admitting "the someone" whom natural objects obey "the child may have never explicitly defined in its thought", Piaget nevertheless proclaimed that "it goes without saying that it is man, since man is the *raison d'etre* of everything" (1977, p. 405).

Support for Piaget's claim that children represent God as another human being has come both from the earlier (e.g., Elkind, 1970; Goldman, 1964; Nye & Carlson, 1984) and the more recent developmental research (e.g., Giménez-Dasi, Guerrero & Harris, 2005; Kiessling & Perner, 2014; Lane, Wellman & Evans, 2010, 2012; Makris & Pnevmatikos, 2007). Whilst the earlier researchers investigated children's ideas of God by asking them to draw God or answer questions about God according to children's denominational identity, the more recent studies looked at children's concept of God as an aspect of their theory-of-mind (ToM), a mechanism which enables them to understand that all agents, including God, have minds. According to some thinkers, however, a fully developed ToM does not ensure against anthropomorphism because people intuitively know that minds are embodied and this intuitive knowledge can sometimes "run amok" so that adults, like children, take a "short step" and imagine minds existing out of bodies (Pinker, 2006, p. 8).

A major limitation of the ToM hypothesis is that it does not specify the conditions under which people come to imagine *for the first time* the existence of a mind that differs from any other agents' minds by not having a body. As well as this, the ToM methods used for studying children's concepts of God employ as stimuli objects that are commonly handled by people, such as boxes, pencils, houses, puppets and the like, whilst, at the same time, do not include any stimuli or conditions not associated with humans and which thus might permit children to demonstrate a representation of God as an agent that is distinct from the agents existing in space and time (e.g., Barrett, Richert & Driesenga, 2001; Kiessling & Perner, 2014; Knight, Sousa, Barrett & Atran, 2004; Makris & Pnevmatikos, 2007; Wigger, Paxson & Ryan, 2013). It is thus predictable that children are likely to construe such objects as eliciting behavioural responses that are characteristic of humans, even when God is mentioned as one of the agents, thereby

The natural-theological concept of God **87**

confirming the very assumption that young children are unable to differentiate clearly between the two kinds of agent. Other recent examples of using empirical stimuli for gauging children's ideas of God without, at the same time, including any appropriate controls, come from the studies featuring unusual characters and describing them to children as having "extraordinary" minds; for instance "Mr Smart", whose knowledge does not depend on perception, or "Heroman", who possesses X-ray vision (Lane et al., 2010). Yet both Mr Smart and Heroman are bound to elicit representations of empirical entities and events simply because most children will have met other misters and some may have heard of X-rays in connection with people. Even the agent named "God" was introduced to children in a picture, albeit blurry and prefixed by a disclaimer ("not really a picture of God but let's say it is"; Lane et al., 2010, p. 1489). Equally likely to bias children to anthropomorphism are the questions which ask them about God's location ("Where is God?"; Kiessling & Perner, 2014, p. 1605) and God's appearance ("Do you know what God looks like?"; Guerrero, Enesco & Harris, 2010, p. 129). To answer such questions in a non-anthropomorphic way, children would need a well-developed and specialist vocabulary as well as the social skills needed for challenging such questions coming from adults. Evidence for anthropomorphism was also obtained in studies that did not separate children's religious education, on one hand, and their intuitive understanding of God, on the other, such as when asking them "Was God a little baby a long time ago?" (Giménez-Dasí et al., 2005, p. 288). Final mention is of the supporting evidence for anthropomorphism from those studies which claim that children learn about God's existence from others (e.g., Corriveau, Chen & Harris, 2014; Guerrero et al., 2010; Harris & Koenig, 2006; Lane & Harris, 2014). According to this view, children accept the "testimony" of adults that such a being exists rather than doubt its veracity because they can never perceive any of God's attributes directly (i.e., omniscience, omnipotence, omnipresence) and hence understandably rely on others' knowledge when acquiring such concepts. Yet the questions about God that were put to 4- to 9-year-olds would prove challenging even for many adults: "Is there really God in the world?", "Are you very sure or not very sure that God exists?" and "How do you know that God does/does not exist?" (Guerrero et al., 2010, p. 129). Even so, the researchers found that children's confidence regarding God's existence remained constant across age, whilst their confidence regarding the existence of culturally "endorsed beings" (i.e., from folklore/mythology) decreased with age.

The point of my cursory review of the studies above is to highlight the relevance of the methods used in their potential to bias children towards making crudely (i.e., physically) anthropomorphic references to God. In addition, such studies do not suggest a mechanism by which children acquire the idea of God as a mental agent in the first place or how their knowledge of other human minds makes its acquisition possible. Rather, the proponents of the anthropomorphism hypothesis appear to assume that children already have a concept of God, albeit anthropomorphic, and then contend that children "must overcome or modify

88 The natural-theological concept of God

their intuitive conceptions of agents and increasingly think in counterintuitive, nonanthropomorphic terms" (Lane et al., 2010, p. 1485).

According to a small number of studies investigating anthropomorphism in adults, childhood anthropomorphism is never fully overcome but persists in everyday representations of God. Barrett and Keil (1996), for example, reported that even when adults have acquired a theologically correct understanding of God as neither spatial nor temporal, they still evince a bias to anthropomorphism in everyday reasoning about God. Barrett and Keil's method involved presenting adults with short stories containing information about both God and people, which the participants subsequently recalled and the accuracy of the recalled information was assessed. Barrett and Keil found that many adults recalled information that suggested an anthropomorphic God-concept. Although the authors reject the possibility that the information in the stories may have biased participants to recall God's anthropomorphic characteristics, the stories contain repeated references to "God" as an agent within the world (e.g., "God stopped helping an angel work on a crossword puzzle to help the woman", "God enjoyed the smell", "Uncomp the supercomputer" as a reference to God and the like). Put simply, God and human agents were both depicted as characters that figure in the same situations and perform similar actions, whilst there was no information in the stories to indicate God's ontological otherness (i.e., transcendence) and thereby allow participants to discriminate between the actions that could and could not be plausibly attributed to a transcendent God. One exception to this is the "super-agents" condition (Barrett & Keil, 1996, Study 2), which stipulates several attributes associated with transcendence (e.g., the agent is described as having unlimited attention, no sensory limitations, capable of acting causally at a distance and being from another dimension of existence). Predictably, in my view, this condition elicited significantly less anthropomorphism, with some participants making no errors on the God item. I mention Barrett and Keil's study mainly because it has been cited in the broader literature as having established conclusively the universality and persistence of anthropomorphism in human cognition yet illustrates well the problems besetting most research attempts to verify anthropomorphism in children and adults alike. Indeed, in another study with adults Barrett and Van Orman (1996) concluded that anthropomorphism is not spontaneous but people learn it from Sunday School lessons or children's books.[1]

The preparedness hypothesis: An all-purpose agency concept

According to the preparedness hypothesis, children do not depend on experience with humans in order to acquire a concept of God because their general agent concept already covers many properties of agents, including those of humans and God. Moreover, this general concept of agency equips children to understand a number of God's characteristics in a non-anthropomorphic way ("superknowing, superperceiving, superpowerful") because they start with a "default assumption" that all intentional agents are endowed with super-human properties as the norm (Barrett & Richert, 2003).[2] Whilst children come to learn through experience that none of the agents encompassed by the default concept of agency is actually endowed with "super" abilities, they never encounter God and thus have no opportunities to check God's actual attributes against the default concept of "super" agency and hence retain it. A key aspect of the preparedness hypothesis to stress here is that it also stipulates the characteristics of God that are *not* part of the default concept of "super" agency but are acquired later, notably God's being non-spatial and non-temporal (i.e., transcendent). According to Barrett and Richert, these two characteristics constitute God's "counterintuitive" properties and as such "enjoy no preparedness" but are "conceptually burdensome" for children; such attributes of God children can only acquire through learning from their culture (2003, p. 310).

Yet Barrett and colleagues have accumulated substantial evidence that children treat God's characteristics as different from human and other agents' characteristics. For example, when asked about God's perceptual abilities and beliefs ("If God wanted to show you some crackers, what would God show you inside of?"; Barrett et al., 2001, p. 55), children consistently implied in their responses that God did not have human vision. Such evidence suggests that children may have an intuitive understanding of God's ontological otherness (i.e., exemption from spatial and temporal laws), however, the method used was not sufficient to elicit such understanding in young children. Had they been asked to give justifications for their judgements, children might have been able to articulate their intuitive understanding of God's otherness more clearly. In the absence of such evidence, Barrett and colleagues concluded that children are unlikely to "truly understand God as a different sort of agent and not just a human with a few strange properties (e.g., infallible beliefs, ability to make mountains) that have been overlearned" (Barrett et al., 2001, p. 61; Knight et al., 2004, p. 125).

To sum up, whilst the preparedness hypothesis allows that children may correctly conceptualise a number of God's attributes from the start, it leaves out the most essential characteristics of God's uniqueness, i.e., transcendence of spatial and temporal constraints. I should also stress that leaving transcendence out of the preparedness idea is not an omission but is fully consistent with the aims of the preparedness hypothesis; that is, to provide an account of how children come to acquire a much broader category of agent concepts ("counterintuitive"), which may include "gods, ghosts, ancestor spirits, devils, witches, and angels" as well as God, whilst excluding "powerful humans, rock stars and athletes" (Barrett, 2007, p. 772).

Notwithstanding the difference between the anthropomorphism and preparedness hypotheses regarding the extent to which children's God-concepts overlap with human agency, the two hypotheses are quite similar in their claim that cultural input is necessary for acquiring the theologically correct concept of God, i.e., transcendent. As Barrett and Richert put it: "In the event that children

90 The natural-theological concept of God

are not taught particular divine attributes", "then more salient intentional agent concepts such as the human concept are drawn upon to complete inferential gaps" (2003, p. 310), which ensures the persistence of childhood anthropomorphism as a way of representing God even among adults.

Anthropomorphism in philosophy and theology

In contrast to anthropological and psychological accounts of anthropomorphism, philosophers and theologians have long considered anthropomorphic concepts of God to be necessary on the grounds that humans have no other means but language for expressing such concepts (Farrer, 1967; Ferré, 1984; Kant, 1983; Soskice, 1985). Kant, for example, argued that in thinking about the cause of the world (cosmological reasoning), a certain "subtle" anthropomorphism is justified (1983, p. 568). He also held that any of God's predicates are drawn from finite things *by analogy*, especially from our own mental life, rather than being literal descriptions. Farrer, a philosophical theologian, similarly argued that anthropomorphism was necessary because we can only talk in "natural concepts" (i.e., "the only concepts which convey to us the notion of anything real"), even though our natural concepts cannot apply "as they stand" to a transcendent God (1967, p. 121). Bearing in mind, however, that even mental anthropomorphism (i.e., equating God's mental capacities with those of humans) may seem problematic in philosophy, because thinking and other mental processes occur in time whereas God is a timeless being (Hospers, 1984), the only non-anthropomorphic way of referring to God is apophatic (i.e., mysticism, or *via negativa*), which implies that God cannot be at all articulated in concepts but can only be intuited. Some philosophers have embraced this conundrum and argued that anthropomorphism in the theological language is not only inevitable but is actually desirable because the alternative – complete silence about God – is much less desirable (Ferré, 1984). The profound uncertainty regarding the human capacity to desist from construing references to God as imputing some empirical form to God's transcendence is evident from a letter written by a 6th-century theologian to his fellow monks.

> One must not conceive of eyes or ears, or indeed hands, feet and wings as belonging to God, even though one elects to conceive of such things not as they exist in palpable gross bodies but as existing in fine-drawn immateriality and in correspondence with God's nature; it is utterly silly to entertain such an idea .... For his attributes are wholly ineffable and it would be impossible for those who exist in palpable and gross bodies to be able to understand any essential fact unless we take our own limbs by way of illustrations and thus with difficulty go on to fine-drawn ideas about God.
>
> *(Wickham, 1983, p. 185)*

Philosophical accounts have traditionally emphasised the role of three processes as critically involved in conceptualising God: (1) inferences from observed effects,

The natural-theological concept of God **91**

(2) analogy and (3) negation, whereby all three may occur simultaneously when explaining the existence and origin of finite things (Soskice, 1985; Swinburne, 1991). Thus, for example, starting from the existence of natural and artificial objects and representing them as the effects of divine and human causal action, respectively, we assign human predicates to God *analogically* because of the perceived similarities between the effects of God's and humans' actions, whilst at the same time remaining aware of profound dissimilarities between God and humans (i.e., we negate their identity). As philosophers have maintained, it is the analogies between God and humans that are often liable to being construed as indicating anthropomorphism, mainly because analogies do not separate the two aspects of being a "person": (1) physical, space-occupying object with mass and (2) mental processes of the individual. Seeing, however, that we have a concept of personal characteristics as independent of an organism (i.e., we can conceive of intelligence or imagination as such), their separate occurrence cannot be a contradiction when applied to an immaterial entity (e.g., Harré, 1986; Hospers, 1984; Swinburne, 1997). Developmental research has well documented young children's ability to construct and understand analogy in a variety of tasks (e.g., Goswami, 2001; Inagaki & Hatano, 1987) and their dualist intuition of mental as distinct from physical entities (e.g., Estes et al., 1989; Watson et al., 1998), both of which competencies seem relevant when seeking to determine in what sense children conceptualise God as a person.

The natural-theological hypothesis: Rationale for the current studies

According to the natural-theological hypothesis, children, like the early scientists and their philosophical forerunners, find sufficient information in their everyday experience of the physical world to infer God as a unique causal agent (i.e., intentional agent like no other), without needing any specific cultural input for such an inference other than a linguistic label. In other words, the natural-theological hypothesis assumes that children's ordinary, or typically available, cognitive processes are sufficient to enable them to transcend conceptually the empirical constraints of space and time and imagine or postulate not only novel empirical entities and causal mechanisms (see Chapter 2) but also those that transcend the empirical domain and are thus absolutely and permanently unobservable (Petrovich, 2008). Put differently, the mechanism enabling this empirical-transcendent transition seems to be triggered reliably under the conditions of observing the natural world and constructing causal explanations of empirical phenomena. In Chapters 4 and 5 we saw that, when explaining the origins of natural objects and of matter, children are able to construe this beginning in the primary sense and postulate a non-human causal agent that can account for the existence of such entities by virtue of being ontologically different from the agent(s) responsible for the existence of artificial objects. The key question in this process is whether children's representations of the two kinds of causal agent are

92 The natural-theological concept of God

sufficiently conceptually distinct and can be identified as such verbally. Given that children and adults have recourse to the same basic vocabulary for referring to mentalistic properties of both humans and God, an ability to differentiate the two kinds of causal agency by using such terms consistently and appropriately in each instance would constitute evidence that children have a rudimentary empirical-transcendent distinction. The empirical question is how we might verify such an understanding by relying on the currently available methods of research in developmental psychology.

I suggested earlier that research on children's understanding of mental phenomena as ontologically distinct from physical phenomena provides some useful pointers. For example, Estes and colleagues (1989) presented children with a set of mental entities, including ideas and dreams, in conjunction with physical objects to see whether children can differentiate them consistently. It is pertinent to note that the entities such as *ideas* and *dreams*, whilst unambiguously mental rather than physical, are nonetheless empirical occurrences (i.e., characteristics of embodied beings) and, as such, do not exactly correspond with the empirical-transcendent distinction. In any attempt to ascertain whether children can differentiate humans from God, that is, human mental states from those of God, we need a contrast involving both empirical and transcendent entities as stimuli (i.e., words mapping the contrast between mental entities subject to spatial and temporal constraints and those not being limited by the same constraints). One way of verifying a coherent and plausible concept of God (i.e., non-anthropomorphic) in either children or adults would be by modifying somewhat the taxonomy of existing entities used by Estes and colleagues and asking further questions that might allow children to demonstrate conceptual distinctions similar to those verified by Estes and colleagues but specific to the theological domain. The advantage of such a method is that it requires minimal verbal response from children (e.g., yes vs. no, this one vs. that one, etc.) yet can, in principle, establish a range of attributes that apply to humans but not to God. For instance, one of the criteria used by Estes and colleagues stipulates that real (i.e., physical) objects "afford behavioral-sensory evidence" (1989, p. 46) whereas human mental states cannot be detected by the senses. In my investigations of children's concepts of God, I tried to determine whether preschoolers know that human mental states, although intangible, are nonetheless empirical events (i.e., occur in the brain), whereas God's mental states are *not* located in the space that humans occupy and are therefore radically different from human mental states. Such evidence from children would suggest that they may have some understanding of God's ontological transcendence.

Estes and colleagues' second criterion, with some modifications, also seems relevant to determining whether children's concept of God is physically anthropomorphic. This criterion affirms that real physical objects "have a public existence" (1989, p. 46), whereas human mental states cannot be publicly witnessed. Yet there are ways in which human mental states can be rendered public (e.g., by eliciting people's responses to questions and other stimuli), whereas God's mental states cannot be rendered public by any such means. Again, if children understand such a distinction, this would additionally imply that they have some knowledge that God's action is not subject to the laws of space and time.

Estes and colleagues' third criterion for the mental–physical distinction pertains to the knowledge that a real physical object has a "temporally consistent existence" whereas mental entities do not have "the same sort of consistency" but are transient (1989, p. 46). When addressing the concept of God, it is important to recognise that both forms of existence stipulated by Estes and colleagues (i.e., physical, mental) occur in time and are thus constrained by empirical laws albeit to differing degrees; in contrast, God's mental characteristics are not at all constrained by either space or time. In other words, mental entities such as people's images and dreams are only *less directly* constrained by space and time than are physical objects, but the constraints nonetheless exist.

Finally, Estes and colleagues have also adduced evidence corroborating children's understanding that causation "by thought alone" or "just thinking" can affect people's behaviour whereas physical force is necessary to manipulate physical objects (1989, p. 55). The same distinction is highly relevant to the question of anthropomorphism in God-concepts because it can be used as a measure of children's understanding that a non-anthropomorphic God acts by thought alone whereas people act by using both body and mind. When assessing children's ability to differentiate between God and people as causal agents, my rationale was that by asking them to make *same/different* judgements on a series of attributes of God, on the one hand, and of human beings, on the other, we can come a long way towards ascertaining whether children of preschool age have a rudimentary empirical-transcendent ontological distinction. Whilst developmental psychologists have used similar procedures when studying children's performance in other conceptual tasks, notably when investigating their understanding of the animate–inanimate distinction (e.g., R. Gelman et al., 1983), the same procedures, with some appropriate adjustments, can also be used for studying children's natural-theological understanding.

The other unused methodological resource in this area of research that I mentioned earlier is children's capacity for analogical reasoning. Given the role of analogy in the history of both science and theology, it seems odd that no study of children's analogical reasoning has addressed its application to their concepts of God. Some indications that such an approach could be fruitful comes from the studies investigating children's tendency to "personify" different biological (e.g., grasshopper, rabbit, tulip) and non-biological (e.g., stone) entities when attributing physical and mental properties to the selected targets (Inagaki & Hatano, 1987, 1991). The researchers identified two constraints that influenced children's predictions about the reactions of different objects as analogous to humans: (1) perceived similarities between humans and the target object and (2) factual knowledge about the target. Inagaki and Hatano concluded that five- to six-year-old children use the person analogy in a constrained way rather than indiscriminately when applying it to non-human animate objects but, when they lack the relevant knowledge in terms of which to check their analogy-based

94 The natural-theological concept of God

inferences and predictions, children's analogies can be misleading. Inagaki and Hatano's procedure, too, could be modified for use in testing children's analogical inferences involving God as a "target object". For example, constraint (1) above would predict that if children conceptualise God in abstract terms, their analogical inferences about such a target would only apply to God's mental or psychological properties as similar to people but not any physical properties. If, on the other hand, children's concept of God is that of a physical being rather than an unembodied mind, they should perceive God as identical to a human being, consistent with the anthropomorphism hypothesis. When it comes to constraint (2) above, which stipulates that factual knowledge about the target influences analogical inferences, it is clear that children and adults are equally "novices" in their factual knowledge about God so that the two groups' predictions about God's attributes would be equally and directly relevant to the question of anthropomorphism. Although I have not replicated Inagaki and Hatano's method exactly and systematically, children in my studies offered numerous unsolicited analogical comparisons that are consistent with the predictions based on Inagaki and Hatano's findings in the biological domain as well as with other major studies of children's analogical reasoning (e.g., Goswami, 2001; Holyoak & Thagard, 1995).

In the remainder of this chapter I will describe evidence from the same children and adults who took part in the earlier parts of the project, reported in Chapters 4 and 5, and who made references to God in the context of their reasoning about the world. Because the amount of data obtained from participants concerning their concepts of God exceeds the aims of the current chapter, my focus will be on the data that have a direct bearing on the question of whether children's concept of God as a causal agent is abstract or physically anthropomorphic.

Studies 1 and 2: Concepts of God in British children and adults

Information about participants who took part in Studies 1 (30 children, 30 adults) and 2 (45 children, 24 adults) was provided in Chapter 4. Data pertaining to their concepts of God were reported previously (Petrovich, 1997), so I will only summarise the main findings in the current chapter while describing the cross-cultural findings (in Studies 3 and 4) in more detail.

Participants' representations of God in the first two studies were elicited following their identifications of different objects' origins and answering the primary origin question about one natural entity not shown in a picture (Petrovich, 1997): In Study 1, the entity was the sky and in Study 2 it was either animal or plant "life". Both children and adults responded by selecting one of the three possibilities regarding how the sky or life as such came into being ("By People", "By God" or "By Unknown Power"). Children were encouraged to say what *they* thought rather than what they may have learnt from others or at school. Although these data do not pertain to children's representations of God, they provide a context within which those representations were elicited.

In Study 1, the majority of children selected the option "By God" (53%), followed "By Unknown Power" (20%) and then "By People" (7%), whilst the remaining 20% gave responses not encompassed by the three options above. In Study 2, children in the two stimulus groups (animals, plants) made markedly different attributions regarding the origin of life in that 53% of children in the Plants Group denied that plants have life while the remaining children selected "By Unknown Power" (20%), "By God" (13%) and "By People" (13%) as the source of origin. In contrast, none of the children in the Animals Group explicitly denied that animals have life. The majority of children in this group attributed animal life to God (43%), followed by attributions to "Unknown Power" (33%) and then "People" (7%). The remaining 17% of responses mentioned some other possibility outside of the three options, including two children who did not answer the question. In contrast to children, adults showed a more consistent pattern when attributing the first origin of either the sky or life as such, selecting most frequently "By Unknown Power" (72%) followed by the option "By God" (28%), whilst no adults selected "By People" and none declined to respond. The main similarity between children and adults was in the significantly lower frequency (zero in the case of adults) of attributing a natural entity's primary origin to human agency than to the other two included options. Whilst children's overall preference was for attributing the primary origin of a natural entity to God, adults' preference was for attributing the same entities to an unknown power.

In the God-concept test, which followed the procedure described above, participants were asked about their own representations of God, stressing again that they should say what *they* imagined God to be like. The instruction was followed by three options from which to choose: (1) "Real man", (2) "Something like a person without a body" and (3) "Something like air or gas". They were then asked to provide justifications for their judgements, i.e., answer the question "Why do you think so?". The main research question was whether children would show a systematic preference for the anthropomorphic or the non-anthropomorphic response options.

Many of the children now said that their representation of God was that of a real man. This was surprising given that they are the same children who had previously consistently rejected human agency ("By People") as the source of different natural objects as well as when speculating about the primary origin of a single natural entity. In other words, of the 26 children in Study 1 who responded in accordance with one of the three origin options for a natural item, half (53%) of whom selected "By God" and only 7% "By People", 46% of the same children now selected "Real man" as their image of God while 31% selected "Something like a person without a body" and 23% selected "Something like air or gas" as their preferred representation of God. In Study 2, 41% of children selected "Real man" and another 41% selected "Something like air or gas" as their preferred representations of God whilst 18% opted for "Something like a person without a body". It is important to note that children in both studies made predominantly non-anthropomorphic choices (54% in Study 1,

96 The natural-theological concept of God

59% in Study 2); nevertheless, the occurrence of any anthropomorphic responses is incongruous in that it contradicts the same children's pattern of responding in the earlier parts of the study. It is relevant to point out that adults too sometimes reported own representations of God as corresponding with "Real man" (11%), although the majority reported a non-anthropomorphic representation of God (89%), often using their own wording to convey the abstractness of those representations.

The key evidence in terms of which to interpret the high frequency of "Real man" responses among children in both studies came from their justifications, where the majority of children cited input from religious education, formal or informal, as the source of information about God being a man. For instance, children frequently mentioned seeing God on TV, in books or being told that God had died on the cross.

To sum up, the most relevant implication of children's data from the first two studies is that it would be quite misleading to conclude that children of preschool age have a strong tendency to anthropomorphism without taking account of their justifications for such responses. When this information is taken into account, it becomes evident that children acquire anthropomorphic representations from their culture and religious education rather than constructing them spontaneously when processing everyday causal information about the natural world. The second major implication of the findings from the first two studies is that when studying children's concepts of highly abstract entities, such as the concept of God, direct comparisons with adults can be instructive in the interpretation of children's data. Indeed, the adults who likewise reported their representations of God as corresponding with "Real man" also attributed such concepts to their childhood religious education.

To pursue further the hypothesis that children construct the concept of God as a unique causal agent in the course of their everyday understanding of the physical world rather than receive it from their culture, and that such a concept is unlikely to represent a physically anthropomorphic entity, children from Britain and Japan were compared on the same questions. In order to minimise direct and immediate associations with cultural and educational influences I also tried to include some measure(s) of children's understanding of God that avoided culture-specific terms relevant in such a test.

Study 3: Concepts of God as a causal agent: Evidence from British and Japanese children

Information about the children in the current study was provided in Chapter 4 (Study 3). Following the Origin and Animacy Tasks, all children received first the "Own God-concept" question (also used in Studies 1 and 2), followed by a justification request. In addition, participants in the current study received two further tests, which took the format of a short story: "Fokunom story" ("Fokunomu story" for Japanese participants) and "God story" ("Kamisama story" for Japanese

The natural-theological concept of God **97**

participants) (see Appendix). The Fokunom story portrays an abstract agent whose several characteristics correspond with a theological concept of God as transcendent (i.e., invisible, all-knowing, acts at a distance). By contrast, the God story describes an agent who is limited by several perceptual and sensory constraints that are characteristic of human agents. Upon hearing each story, children received two questions. In the Fokunom story, the questions were: (1) what would the word "Fokunom" mean to the people who had not heard it before and (2) why the participant thought so (justification request). In the God story, participants were asked to say (1) whether the story about God was true or not true, followed by (2) why they thought so (justification request). In addition, they were also asked (1) whether the person mentioned in the story (John/Yamamoto-san) did see God's face and then (2) provide a justification for their judgement. Because many children seemed to understand the question about the truth of the story as being about the truth of God's existence, frequently responding "God is true but the story is not" or saying that the story is true because God is true, only the responses pertaining to the question whether the story protagonist saw God's face were included in data analysis. The three tests above (Own God-concept, Fokunom story and God story) were presented in that order to avoid any potential priming effects of the God story on the Fokunom story and, also, of the two stories on the participants' own representations of God.

Children's responses and justifications on the three God-concept tests were scored independently by four assessors, including myself, according to whether a response was abstract or concrete.[3] On each of the three God-concept tests and on each of the three justification responses the maximum possible score was 2, where 2 signifies abstract or inferential, 1 concrete or literal and zero indicates no response. For example, "Own God-concept" was scored as abstract (i.e., 2) if the child had rejected the option "Real man" (but selected either "Something like a person without a body" or "Something like air or gas"), and their justification response was abstract (i.e., 2) if it was an inference or child's own judgement rather than conveying what others have told them, or mentioning seeing God on TV and the like. In the "Fokunom story", an abstract response was that which identified Fokunom as God (or a spirit)[4] rather than some material entity (e.g., animal, human) whereas an abstract justification was one that stated Fokunom's non-empirical attributes, either those mentioned in the story or in the participants' own words and not any attributes characteristic of material entities. Finally, in the "God story" test, children's responses to the question about seeing God's face were scored as abstract if they had stated that John (or Yamamoto-san) did not see God's face, followed by a justification affirming that God does not have a face or that God's face can only be seen in one's mind, whereas concrete responses were those that suggested a concept of some physical or empirical entity. Accordingly, an overall God-concept score of 6 indicates an abstract concept of God and an overall justification score of 6 indicates that such a concept is held for abstract or inferential reasons rather being a result of assimilated cultural expressions.[5]

98 The natural-theological concept of God

Statistical analysis of children's mean scores on the two measures of abstractness of their theological understanding (i.e., God-concept and Justifications) showed that children's scores differed according to nationality, vocabulary score (VA) and calendar age. More specifically, nationality had a significant effect on both abstractness of God-concepts ($p < .001$) and abstractness of justifications ($p < .001$), whilst children's vocabulary score had a significant effect on abstractness of justifications ($p < .001$) but not on abstractness of God-concepts. Conversely, children's age had an effect on abstractness of God-concepts ($p = .029$) but not on abstractness of justifications. Whilst children's sex did not significantly influence their performance on either measure, a significant interaction between nationality and sex ($p = .006$) occurred in one instance because of a better performance of British girls than British boys, on the one hand, and better performance of Japanese boys than Japanese girls, on the other, although there is no clear explanation for its occurrence in the current sample.

The effect of nationality on the two measures of theological understanding is evident from the scores in Table 6.3.1, with Japanese children's concept of God being more abstract at each age than that of British children, and those in Table 6.3.2, showing that British children's justifications were more abstract than those of Japanese children at each age. The two nationalities were, however, similar in that both achieved significantly higher scores on abstractness of God-concept than on abstractness of justifications.

These patterns of similarities and differences between the two nationalities on the two measures of theological understanding are depicted in Figures 6.3.1 and 6.3.2.

British children's superiority on the justifications responses is consistent with their higher scores on justifications in the Origin Task (Chapter 4) and is best

TABLE 6.3.1 Children's mean scores (standard deviations in parentheses) on abstractness of the overall God-concept (out of six)

Age	British $N = 90$	Japanese $N = 102$
4	4.24 (0.88)	4.61 (1.05)
5	3.73 (0.67)	4.45 (1.09)
6	4.34 (0.75)	4.73 (1.05)
Total	4.09 (0.80)	4.61 (1.06)

TABLE 6.3.2 Children's mean scores (standard deviations in parentheses) on abstractness of justifications (out of six)

Age	British $N = 90$	Japanese $N = 102$
4	2.76 (1.56)	1.36 (1.21)
5	3.21 (1.19)	2.10 (1.26)
6	3.72 (0.81)	2.00 (1.25)
Total	3.27 (1.24)	1.80 (1.30)

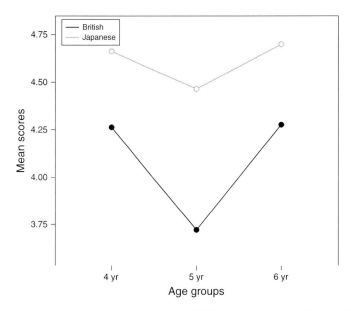

FIGURE 6.3.1 British and Japanese children's mean scores (out of six) on abstractness of the God-concept.

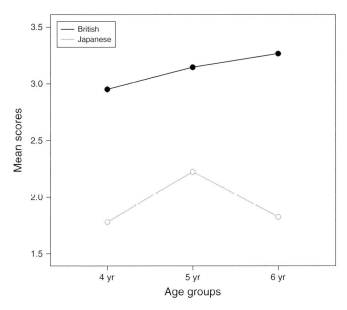

FIGURE 6.3.2 British and Japanese children's mean scores (out of six) on abstractness of justifications.

100 The natural-theological concept of God

explained in terms of their significantly higher vocabulary scores than those of Japanese children of the same age. On the other hand, Japanese children's superiority on abstractness of the God-concept relative to British children may be owed to the nature of their formal religious education (when provided), which is less explicitly anthropomorphic than that of British children. That is, British children more frequently mentioned their religious education as the source of information that God is a man, whereas Japanese children did so much less frequently and usually by appealing to the wider cultural experience of anthropomorphic content such as seeing statues of various divinities in public spaces or watching films about divine beings, including Jesus. In short, children's data are consistent with the proposal that both nationalities construct a concept of God as a causal agent in the context of processing information about the surrounding world and both are influenced by their respective cultures, most directly via its linguistic input (or lack thereof) when articulating their representations of such an agent.

Study 4: Concepts of God as a causal agent: Evidence from British and Japanese children and adults

Children and adults who performed in the Origin and Animacy Tasks of Study 4 (Chapter 4) and whose cosmological judgements were described in Chapter 5, took part in the same three God-concept tests as did children from the two nationalities in Study 3 described above. Because children and adults completed different vocabulary tests, their VA scores were included as a covariate but were analysed separately for each group. Comparisons between the two generations from both nationalities (without their vocabulary scores taken into account) revealed significant differences on both components of their theological understanding, i.e., abstractness of the God-concept ($p < .001$) and abstractness of justifications ($p < .001$). In other words, adults scored higher than did children of any age and British participants from all age groups (except age 6) had a tendency to score higher than their Japanese counterparts on both variables (Table 6.4.1, Figures 6.4.1 and 6.4.2).

TABLE 6.4.1 Mean scores (standard deviations in parentheses) on abstractness of the overall God-concept and abstractness of justifications (out of six)

Age	God-concept		Justifications	
	British	Japanese	British	Japanese
4	3.66 (1.34)	3.61 (1.20)	2.76 (1.43)	1.87 (1.84)
5	3.77 (0.91)	3.64 (1.40)	3.04 (1.34)	2.73 (1.64)
6	3.89 (0.96)	4.33 (1.53)	3.75 (1.01)	2.33 (2.52)
Total	3.77 (1.07)	3.86 (1.38)	3.18 (1.26)	2.31 (2.00)
Adults Young	5.41 (0.87)	4.77 (1.01)	5.19 (0.59)	4.77 (0.90)
Adults Old	5.33 (0.71)	5.13 (1.07)	5.13 (0.90)	4.90 (1.40)
Total	5.37 (0.79)	4.95 (1.04)	5.16 (0.74)	4.83 (1.15)

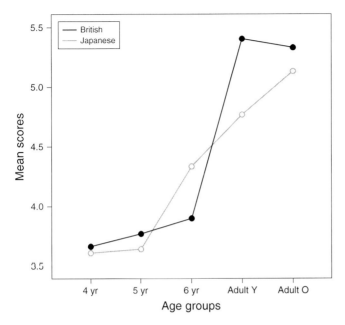

FIGURE 6.4.1 British and Japanese children's and adults' mean scores (out of six) on abstractness of the God-concept.

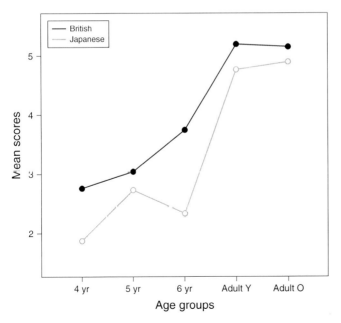

FIGURE 6.4.2 British and Japanese children's and adults' mean scores (out of six) on abstractness of justifications.

102 The natural-theological concept of God

Analysis of children's data, with VA score included as a covariate, revealed that VA score had a significant effect on both components of their theological understanding, that is, abstractness of God-concept ($p < .001$) and abstractness of justifications ($p < .001$), whereas nationality significantly influenced abstractness of justifications, $F(1, 121) = 5.41$, $p = .022$, but not abstractness of God-concepts. Seeing, however, that nationality and language interact closely and, in the case of young children, largely overlap, it may not be possible to separate the effects of each in the current analysis.

Children in the current study, like those in Study 3, scored higher on abstractness of God-concept in each of the three tests than on abstractness of justifications (Table 6.4.2). Independent sample t-tests confirmed that British and Japanese children in the current study did not differ statistically in terms of how abstract their God-concepts are, $t(129) = .454$, $p = .651$, whereas they did differ significantly on abstractness of justifications, $t(76.091) = 2.998$, $p = .004$.

In contrast to children, British and Japanese adults differed significantly both on abstractness of God-concept, $t(120) = 2.30$, $p = .023$, and on abstractness of justifications, $t(101.29) = 2.03$, $p = .045$. As their mean scores indicate (Table 6.4.3), British adults scored consistently higher than did Japanese adults on both tests, although separate comparisons on each of the three concepts of God revealed that

TABLE 6.4.2 Children's mean scores (standard deviations in parentheses) on abstractness of the three God-concepts and the corresponding justifications (out of two).

	British N = 83	Japanese N = 48
God-concept 1	1.33 (0.54)	1.29 (0.68)
God-concept 2	1.22 (0.59)	1.25 (0.64)
God-concept 3	1.23 (0.48)	1.15 (0.54)
Justification 1	1.04 (0.61)	0.75 (0.73)
Justification 2	0.94 (0.61)	0.63 (0.70)
Justification 3	1.19 (0.59)	0.92 (0.82)
God-concept (out of 6)	3.78 (1.08)	3.69 (1.29)
Justification (out of 6)	3.18 (1.31)	2.29 (1.80)

TABLE 6.4.3 Adults' mean scores (standard deviations in parentheses) on abstractness of the three God-concepts and the corresponding justifications (out of two).

	British N = 62	Japanese N = 60
God-concept 1	1.60 (0.66)	1.30 (0.83)
God-concept 2	1.98 (0.13)	1.90 (0.35)
God-concept 3	1.79 (0.41)	1.75 (0.44)
Justification 1	1.50 (0.50)	1.37 (0.55)
Justification 2	1.92 (0.28)	1.83 (0.42)
Justification 3	1.76 (0.47)	1.62 (0.61)
God-concept (out of 6)	5.34 (0.81)	4.95 (1.05)
Justification (out of 6)	5.18 (0.76)	4.82 (1.16)

the two nationalities only differed significantly on the first ("Own God-concept") test, t (112.90) = 2.18, p = .032, but not on the two story tests. It seems that with adults, as with children, "Own God-concept" is only partly one's own inference, whilst it also reflects the ubiquitous cultural input of an anthropomorphic kind. In contrast to children, however, adults' vocabulary scores had no significant effect on any of their test scores.

Several conclusions emerge from the studies reported in this chapter. Whilst it seems clear from the findings that children of preschool age do not "picture man" when they mention God, they nevertheless refer to God in human terms when asked to say what they imagine God to be like. Such a pattern of responding suggests that preschoolers appear to construe the question about their own idea of God as a question asking them to say what they *know* about God. Their only way of answering such a question positively is by appealing to what they have learned through education and the broader cultural input. None of this implies that they do not differentiate between God's and human characteristics when using the same verbal reference terms.

The earlier mentioned studies in this chapter which concluded that children of preschool age do not differentiate between God and people as agents (e.g., Bamford & Lagattuta, 2010; Evans, 2001; S. Gelman & Kremer, 1991; Kelemen, 1999b) did not demonstrate that children conceptualise God's intentions as indistinguishable from human intentions or that they conflate the power of God with that of human beings, yet such evidence would be critical for corroborating anthropomorphism. Whilst we may never be able to unravel the intension of the God-concept for either children or adults, the consistency with which they differentiate God from other causal agents is a measurable aspect of one's core theological knowledge. To evince such knowledge children do not need to be particularly verbally proficient. As long as the task is designed in such a manner that children can anchor their simple verbal (or non-verbal) responses to the questions about specific and purposely arrayed stimuli, or about specific human and divine attributes, and do so reliably in repeated trials, researchers can establish with some confidence that a child probably has a particular concept, in this case that of God as a unique causal agent.

Consistently selecting God and rejecting the human option meets Harré and Madden's (1975) criteria for intelligibility of unverifiable concepts; in other words, the meaning of "God" may not need to be specified further provided that its use is consistent, adequate and serves explanatory purpose. Remarkably, however, young children were often able to specify their ideas about God in some further way. Evidence that they do not confound God's and humans' mental states and actions came most strongly when I asked the children to compare God's and people's actions and any tools used by each type of agent in the making of things as a way of elucidating their references to God's seemingly mundane actions (e.g., making things). For instance, if a child said that God makes things by thinking, then the child made it clear that God thinks without a brain, or if God has a brain, then God's brain is different from the human brain.

104 The natural-theological concept of God

One 6-year-old, when I asked him to clarify his apparent denial that God thinks, simply pronounced "He just knows it" (see also Woolley & Phelps, 2001, p. 156). In other words, God's "radical" difference from humans is in being able to have direct knowledge of the world whereas humans need to rely on effortful mental processes to obtain such knowledge by overcoming the usual spatial and temporal constraints.

Evidence obtained from the Japanese participants in all the components of the current project is manifestly at odds with the literature portrayals of Japanese people as having a vastly different understanding of the world and God than their Western counterparts. In fact, I found that adults from the two countries responded in markedly similar ways on the three God-concept tests as well as when providing justifications for their responses. Some of the most striking examples include adult participants' responses to the Fokunom story when guessing the likely meaning of that word for those encountering it for the first time: "Fokunomu in the story is the same as God or Hotoke-sama" (Japanese); "God, especially the Christian God" (British); "Each one will think that Fokunomu is the God that they know" (Japanese); "God, but this God is not like an Islamic or Christian concept of God … Fokunomu is like a Japanese concept of God" (Japanese). *Pace* Matsumoto's (1996) claim that "the kami idea held by most Japanese is essentially different from the idea of God found in the Judeo-Christian and Muslim traditions" (p. 16), and that Japanese people "have never conceived" of the Shinto kami "as absolute or transcendent in relation to human beings or the world" (p. 16), evidence from the Japanese participants quoted above speaks otherwise. In fact, their responses are in keeping with Hardon's 1965 thesis that the oldest known world religions (including Japanese Shinto, p. 37) are fundamentally monotheistic, demonstrating belief in the unique and transcendent divinity, whereas animism, fetishism and other pagan traditions represent a form of "religious decadence" (p. 26). Hardon goes on to cite ancient Japanese sources which reveal a concept of one "god" to whose powers "man and all other things owe their existence" (p. 215).

In brief, the natural-theological hypothesis advanced in the current book centres on the concept of God as a causal agent, an inference that young children begin to make in the context of multiple comparisons and contrasts (i.e., relational judgements) involving everyday empirical entities while guided by a search for a complete causal explanation. Data reported in the current chapter are consistent with this hypothesis and with its corollary that cultural input is not needed for children to conceptualise God as a unique causal agent. Rather, such input can often be distinctly unhelpful, merely reinforcing the entrenched belief that people from different religious cultures must have different concepts of God.

Notes

1 In a partial replication of Barrett and Keil's procedure that used several of their stories (original condition) as well as altering the same stories by removing any anthropomorphic references to God (modified condition), significantly different results were obtained in the two conditions (Dvorakova, 2011). As expected, adults evinced anthropomorphism in the original but not in the modified condition.

2 Whether children indeed start with a default concept of agency that is "super" potentiated is a separate issue that cannot be discussed here. Research of perceptual and cognitive development in infancy reviewed earlier in this volume suggests that infants have good discriminatory skills in a variety of tasks involving objects. The assumption that they lack the same skills when dealing with agents awaits empirical verification.

3 I am grateful to Kalliopi Chliounaki, Miguel Farrias and Fiona Spence.

4 Some children, but many more adults (Study 4) said that they could not differentiate between "God" and "spirit". Japanese participants also said that they couldn't differentiate clearly between Kami-sama (God), Hotoke-sama or even an angel as all such beings are immaterial rather than having any form.

5 I am grateful to Dr David Popplewell for his input regarding how to arrive at a composite abstractness measure for both variables integral to theological understanding (i.e., God concept and Justifications).

7
THEOLOGY AS A CORE COGNITIVE DOMAIN

In view of the evidence that by the time they are 4- or 5-years-old children can articulate their basic theological idea of God as a unique causal agent, distinct from any empirical agents, and which they acquire as part of their everyday knowledge of the world, I suggested that such understanding might constitute one of the core aspects of their cognitive development.[1]

Whilst developmental psychologists have cogently argued that the issue of what constitutes a core cognitive domain is an empirical question which should be settled by research (e.g., Wellman & S. Gelman, 1998), theology or religion has never been considered as a possible candidate; in fact, a number of scholars have ruled it out as such on the grounds that theology or religion lacks the main characteristics of core domains (e.g., Atran, 1995; Atran & Henrich, 2010; Barrett, 2011; Boyer, 1996, 2003; Boyer & Walker, 2000; Pinker, 2006; Rosengren & Hickling, 2000; Wellman & S. Gelman, 1998) and that transcendence is not a universal concept but a "Western folk category" (Guthrie, 1980, p. 185). The current chapter questions those assumptions and argues that children's intuitive theological understanding meets all the criteria stipulated by developmental psychologists as defining of core domains. In brief, these criteria specify that a core domain differs from non-core domains primarily by involving (a) distinct, domain-specific ontological entities and (b) the causal principles that are uniquely associated with those entities (Carey, 1995; Chi, 1992; R. Gelman, 2000; Wellman & S. Gelman, 1998). Ontological entities in the theological domain differ from those in any other cognitive domain by being neither spatial nor temporal but transcendent and immaterial, whilst the causal mechanisms associated with such entities are assumed to be unlike any mechanisms operational in the world of space and time. The theological domain meets two further criteria stipulated for core domains: (c) unobservability of its entities and causal mechanisms and (d) coherence of a domain's concepts bound by the above criteria (Wellman & S. Gelman, 1998).

Taken together, the criteria above imply that there is no other domain of knowledge apart from theology which involves the existence of transcendent entities and causal action uniquely associated with such entities. Accordingly, it should be possible to predict that if children have an intuitive theological theory, they ought to be able to (a) distinguish theological from non-theological entities consistently and reliably and (b) appeal to causal principles that are uniquely characteristic of such entities. Evidence described in the preceding three chapters suggests that children of preschool age and from two very different cultures meet the criteria above. In other words, they understand that God is ontologically different from any known empirical agents and entities and that God's causal action is radically different from the actions characteristic of empirical agents. Put simply, God's ontological otherness constitutes "the essence of religion in its most rudimentary form" (James, 1961, p. 56).

The concept of transcendence in religion and science

Dictionary and textbook definitions stipulate that transcendent God is completely outside the world of space and time and beyond all possible experience, hence unknowable (Walsh, 1985). Philosophers have argued, however, that whilst God's nature is unknowable, human beings can know intuitively that the transcendent God is utterly distinct from any empirical entities or agents, thus also labelled "the wholly other" (Otto, 1979), "the unconditioned" or "the supersensible" (Kant, 1983). Crucially, by virtue of being neither spatial nor temporal, God can be conceptualised as capable of acting in ways that are impossible for agents within space and time, such as creating the world out of nothingness (Swinburne, 1991). Consequently, although the human mind is endowed with many similar psychological processes as those attributed to God, the human mind is completely different from God's mind in that it is subject to spatial and temporal laws which limit its power greatly as well as qualitatively.

Otto's (1979) account of transcendence as a category in human cognition is of interest to psychology because it stipulates the conditions under which a concept that is not associated with any specific stimuli may emerge, not least because it cannot be taught either verbally or ostensively. According to Otto, the idea of "the wholly other" (also "the holy", "the numinous") is an a priori category that makes religious experience possible under the right conditions, that is, in the presence of "surprising" natural events or "astonishing objects" acting as its environmental "triggers" Otto (1979, p. 27). Although he never mentions children, Otto's account of the origin of this concept is remarkably in tune with contemporary developmental theories. Stated in developmental terms, the idea of the holy ("the wholly other") corresponds with an innate core or a framework concept that underpins and shapes all other religious understanding. Otto's philosophical account can thus be operationalised into a question for developmental psychology about how and under what conditions children come to acquire a concept that has no distinct empirical referents or specific cues yet which they

108 Theology as a core cognitive domain

form spontaneously and early through everyday exposure to the "surprising" stimuli within the natural world.

Not only philosophers and theologians but scientists, too, have made a contribution to elucidating the meaning of transcendence based on their insights deriving from work on the nature of space and matter. According to Fagg (2003), a physicist, transcendence (also labelled "the cosmic inaccessible background" or CIB) is a concept of an unreachable "beyond", which is neither spatial nor temporal yet is commonly referred to by spatial metaphors. Schaefer (2008) also a scientist (chemist), contends that if one pursues the nature of matter to its roots, to the level of atoms and molecules, then one finds oneself in a realm of non-material forms where the notion of matter no longer applies and "actuality turns into potentiality" (p. 341). This realisation forces Schaefer to countenance the possibility that, fundamentally, reality consists of non-material and non-empirical forms, "whose exact nature we will probably never fully comprehend, like the nature of God, but which can be thought to be like the potentiality waves [(Villars, 1987)] of quantum theory" (p. 341). Harré's (1986) construct *referential realism* (RR), which stands for entities inhabiting a realm that is beyond all possible experience (Realm 3) yet can be thought of as having real existence, also resembles theological transcendence. Whether such a concept is scientific depends, according to Harré, on the possibility of translating hypothetical acts of referring into material practices of searching an instance of the kind in question, regardless of whether the search is successful.

We can see, then, why scientists can be intrigued by the similarities between theoretical physics and theology when it comes to conceptualising the most fundamental ontological entities within their respective domains. The *similarity* consists in representing both kinds of postulated entities as existing beyond the bounds of all possible experience (i.e., unobservable and unknowable). The *difference* – and a crucial one at that – is that the postulated entities in physics are assumed to reside in the empirical domain and can thus be searched for by any of the methods available to physicists; in contrast, the postulated entities in theology are assumed to reside in the non-empirical (transcendent) domain and, of course, there are no methods available to any specialist for accessing this domain other than as a domain of human cognition, i.e., through psychological research. Given the pervasiveness of such metaphysical concepts in science as well as theology, one would expect a great deal more psychological research on their role in human cognition. Instead, Piaget's early work Piaget's (e.g., 1924, 1925) is the only source where the concept of transcendence is mentioned in the theological sense and as related to children's understanding of spatial and temporal discontinuities. Unfortunately, Piaget ruled out young children's ability to represent conceptually such discontinuities in abstract terms because of their supposedly pervasive cognitive egocentrism. Post-Piagetian research, however, offers evidence that representation of space in infancy is quite abstract as it can be applied to diverse entities that infants encounter through multiple sensory modalities and which can include objects, actions and sounds in the sequences of their occurrence (Spelke, 1994; Spelke & Kinzler, 2007). Yet, and recalling my earlier point, because the concept of transcendence can be elicited by *any* aspect of the physical world, including any inferred relations among empirical entities, such a concept is even more abstract than the concepts abstracted from the particular empirical categories. By studying children's concepts of transcendent entities, we may thus be able to ascertain whether the abstract–concrete distinctions in the empirical domain, such as those implicit in children's understanding of height, value or ideas (Carey, 1991, 1992), are indeed more difficult for them to master than the empirical-transcendent distinction, as I suggested earlier.

Transcendence: A psychological definition

Transcending conceptual boundaries can be thought of in three ways: (a) going beyond the perceivable features of particular objects, (b) postulating permanently unobservable ontological entities and causal agents within the empirical domain (e.g., black holes, philosophical essences or Harré's Realm 3 denizens) and (c) postulating entities and causal agents beyond the empirical realm itself. There is abundant evidence in developmental research that children of preschool age can conceptualise transcendence in the first sense above by going beyond an object's actual boundaries when looking for causal mechanisms. Children's ability to postulate unobservable and perhaps non-existent empirical causal agents (e.g., essences, magnetic forces) might justify crediting them with a concept of transcendence in sense (b). In this book I have argued that children also seem able to conceptualise transcendence in sense (c).

The concept of transcendence (i.e., God) outlined above is an intuitive concept that demarcates theology as a domain from all other cognitive domains and thereby renders it highly salient. No such clear demarcation exists among the empirical domains of knowledge (e.g., biology, physics or psychology) because ontological entities in those domains involve three-dimensional space occupiers, including living organisms. It could also be argued that theological entities (i.e., God, transcendence) are more abstract than the abstract entities belonging in mathematics and logic because, although highly abstract, mathematical and logical entities (relations) can in many instances be fully and exactly mapped onto different sets or categories of empirical entities to which they relate. No similar correspondence can be envisaged between the core theological concept (God) and any particular empirical occurrence. It is thus interesting that domains such as mathematics, ethics and music, all of which have occasionally been linked with transcendence, have also been mentioned by psychologists as possible candidates for core cognitive domains on account of their distinct, domain-specific ontological entities, even though neither mathematics and logic nor ethics and music meet the criterion of having distinct causal principles associated with the ontological entities of those domains. Theology, on the other hand, implies a causal principle that is uniquely associated with its core ontological entity (i.e., God), hence making it akin to scientific postulates used for referring to entities

110 Theology as a core cognitive domain

as yet unverified or even unverifiable (e.g., "black hole", "field of potential"; Soskice, 1985). It is thus arguable that theology is more similar to core scientific domains than any of the above-mentioned domains (i.e., ethics, mathematics, music) as a potential candidate for inclusion among the core cognitive domains, simply because theology meets *all* of the defining criteria of core domains stipulated by developmental researchers, including the causal criterion.[2]

Psychological research has generally refrained from addressing the question of children's capacity to transcend the empirical domain and postulate causal agents outside of the spatial and temporal realm. Even children's "religious" and other "supernatural" tendencies are discussed in the literature as corresponding with imaginary beings belonging in the world (e.g., Santa Claus, Easter Bunny or Tooth Fairy) rather than in accordance with the theological and philosophical meaning of transcendence. Yet children's acquisition of the core theological concept (God) as part of their everyday understanding of the world merits explanation for a number of reasons. First, as I noted before, the highly abstract nature of this concept, which lacks any direct empirical referents, consists in an inference made under certain empirical conditions that are both similar to and different from the conditions that give rise to other abstract concepts. Second, the core theological concept is theoretical in that it has an explanatory function which, although shared by scientific concepts, is uniquely different from scientific concepts. Third and finally, seeing that the core theological concept is not associated with any *specific* empirical conditions, it may have a more similar developmental path among children from different physical and cultural environments than the concepts that have specific empirical referents. On account of its uniqueness and its relative independence of any particular stimuli, the concept of transcendence or God may thus constitute one of the simplest abstract concepts for children to acquire early and spontaneously as part of their everyday causal and ontological understanding. My own theory about how a concept of this kind might get started in cognitive development as a natural concept is laid out in Chapter 8.

The concept of transcendence: Simplicity and developmental continuity

The argument for the simplicity of the concept of transcendence is based on the premise that its non-observability is both absolute and consistent, quite unlike the non-observability of the empirical entities. In other words, transcendence is inherently unobservable due to its immaterial nature whilst the unobservability of empirical entities is a consequence either of the lack of knowledge about their location or of suitable methods needed for their successful observation (e.g., insides of biological mechanisms, particle physics). Such constraints render any inferences about the unobservable empirical entities more complex to process mentally and even counterintuitive because, initially at least, children obtain information about existing entities through perception and come to understand through experience that physical objects can be temporarily unobservable

Theology as a core cognitive domain **111**

(e.g., as in object permanence). By contrast, the absolute unobservability of transcendent entities means that an intuition of their existence and nature cannot depend on our prior experience or any detailed knowledge about the different aspects of the world but is consistently unavailable to perception. In Otto's (1979) view, the idea of such entities (i.e., transcendence, "the wholly other") is a priori, whose role in cognition is to make religious or theological experience possible. A developmental corollary of Otto's philosophical account is that even young children should be able to conceive of invisible *non-empirical* entities more easily than of those that require information processing skills needed for inferring their occurrence in space and time.

Given the constraints mentioned above, developmental trajectory of the concept of transcendence or God is, in my view, neither that of change (i.e., emergence of new concepts that are not definable in terms of the concepts already held; Carey, 1991) nor enrichment (i.e., forming new beliefs over the concepts already available; Spelke, 1994), but rather continuation or preservation of the initial concept. The rationale for envisioning such a course is in the lack of clarity regarding the nature of information that might lead to its subsequent transformation, seeing that not even all empirical concepts undergo significant structural change during development (Keil, 1981a, Keil, 1981b). Enrichment and conceptual change as developmental mechanisms make most sense when we are dealing with scientific concepts, where the phenomena observed can change under the influence of many factors in the environment. Because scientists are more likely than lay people to encounter situations in which the inadequacies of the earlier conceptions of the same phenomena become clear, whether through experiments, systematic observations or reflection on the previous and current knowledge (Spelke, 1991), scientists' concepts can undergo more dramatic change than that experienced by lay individuals when contradicted by experience. But there are no conceivable opportunities for either experiments or systematic and direct observations of transcendence or God that could lead to any more advanced versions of this concept. Children and adults alike can only reflect on the same "underspecified" physical world and generate inferences about its unobservable causal properties, including those that transcend its boundaries. I mentioned earlier in the volume that the validity of such inferences can be judged in terms of how coherent and compatible with other knowledge they are, rather than by any pragmatic criteria used in science.[3] Confidence regarding the plausibility of children's causal inferences about transcendence should come primarily from the evidence about the validity and coherence of their knowledge of the world, not least because scientific and metaphysical causal inferences are often complementary and should, whenever this seems pertinent, be examined jointly. Given the history of Western science, and its roots in theological thought, it seems perplexing that developmental research of scientific understanding has been advancing for several decades without attempting to bring this issue to the fore.

For the reasons mentioned above, the main developmental task in the case of transcendence or God may thus be no more than ensuring its continuity,

112 Theology as a core cognitive domain

i.e., preserving this concept as unique and distinct in human cognition. This is often harder than it seems; although the concept of transcendence is extremely simple, unique and unchanging, all of which should ensure its salient position in our conceptual repertory, it is these very attributes that, paradoxically, can bring on its premature demise. For this unique concept is destined from its inception to compete with incomparably more numerous, diverse, changing and complex empirical constructs, which continuously demand attention and have the potential to activate other information-processing mechanisms and acquired knowledge, thereby more often than not succeeding in relegating the original concept of transcendence to the earliest stores of memory development.

To summarise thus far, although the core concepts in science, on the one hand, and in theology, on the other, have the same starting point (i.e., the world) and proceed through similar steps (e.g., observation, hypotheses, inferences, formal verification criteria), they are fundamentally different for one developmental reason. Whilst early (children's) and later (adults') concepts of empirical entities may indeed be "incommensurable" because of the qualitatively different information that is available to the developing and mature cognitive systems (Carey, 1988), it is not clear what developmental changes or informational input could lead to the incommensurability of the early and the later core theological concept (i.e., God or transcendence). Encouragingly, the issue of whether the core theological concept undergoes change across life span is not beyond empirical verification. In other words, we should be able to ascertain its developmental status either by direct comparisons between children and adults (e.g., Coley, 2000), or in the context of the related concepts and the intuitive theories in which this concept is embedded, as Carey (1991) proposed in the case of scientific concepts.

My analysis of the conceptual status of transcendence in human cognition may not strike a chord with those philosophers and theologians who have argued against natural theology as a valid starting point in theistic reasoning (Chapter 1). But I have tried to argue, and buttress the argument by empirical evidence, that natural theology is primarily a psychological topic, which is concerned with the concept of God as a causal agent and its origin in cognitive development, rather than a doctrine about God's nature that preoccupies theologians and for which they understandably appeal to divine revelation.

Precursors of transcendence in early development?

The very nature of the concept of transcendence makes it undoubtedly difficult to investigate such a concept directly with very young children. Instead, developmental psychologists must rely on methods that do not require a fully developed vocabulary and, also, on cumulative evidence from other conceptual domains involving abstract distinctions that either imply the concept of transcendence or can be viewed as its precursors. For example, children's intuitive

Theology as a core cognitive domain **113**

grasp of the principles of solidity and continuity that define physical objects may allow them to apprehend the very opposites of those principles, i.e., non-solidity and discontinuity, as also being attributes of existence. Similarly, children's ability to differentiate between objects, on the one hand, and the ideas of those objects, on the other, implies an understanding that abstract entities do not have a spatial location characteristic of physical objects and, according to some recent research, may even include children's ideas about the soul as an aspect of pre-life existence (Emmons & Kelemen, 2014). Below I discuss three instances of conceptual distinctions that are available to young children and which figure in theological reasoning, too. Their theological relevance is in making possible the recognition of miracles as exceptional events that are caused by agents or forces which transcend the domain of spatial and temporal laws rather than merely unusual occurrences due to violations of physical laws.

Causality-by-contact vs. causality-at-a-distance

In his account of causal development, Piaget argued that younger children generally explain physical events in terms of causality-at-a-distance because they lack knowledge and understanding of causal mechanisms.[4] Post-Piagetian research has overturned his claim that children are inherently biased to reason in terms of causality-at-a-distance when responding to empirical sequences by showing that 3- to 5-year-olds commonly assume causality-by-contact as a default when tested in laboratory settings but can accept occurrences at-a-distance as long as such occurrences do not violate the temporal priority rule (Bullock & R. Gelman, 1979). A more recent study with 4-year-olds likewise found that children prefer to use causality-by-contact when making inferences about objects' insides, even though children of this age understand that some causal events can take place at-a-distance (Sobel & Buchanan, 2009). It is pertinent to note that causality-at-a-distance which occurs in the physical world implies a more complex pattern of causal contingencies than does causality-at-a-distance that is initiated beyond the boundaries of the physical world. To begin with, there are many more variables to process selectively and coordinate in the course of empirical causal reasoning than there are when making inferences about non-empirical causal events. In the latter case, all that children (and adults) need to do is envisage the possibility of there being a causal agent capable of producing effects from a distance (i.e., without direct contact), such as the actions commonly ascribed to God; they do not need to have any knowledge of the objects' intrinsic properties or of the mechanisms by which the postulated causal agent acts remotely. Accordingly, when testing children's grasp of causality-at-a-distance within the physical world, on the one hand, and causality-at-a-distance that is assumed to originate beyond the physical world, on the other, the sufficient criterion of accuracy should be children's ability to treat them as distinct forms of causality and do so consistently in repeated

114 Theology as a core cognitive domain

trials and/or different tasks. Ability to differentiate the two causal contingencies is an indication of children's potential to differentiate between *miracle*, as an instance of theological causality-at-a-distance, and *magic,* an event that resembles causality-at-a-distance but is not because it involves natural forces that can be manipulated by those who know how to control them. Because miracles are theological events that cannot be explained in terms of the known physical laws but only in terms of God's causal action (Ward, 2002), they *transcend* rather than violate the usual empirical constraints and hence constitute exceptions to natural laws (Helm, 1991; Polkinghorne, 2002), even if their exceptionality is only in the timing of the events (Humphreys, 2003).

Improbable vs. impossible events

Whilst both the impossible and improbable events contradict the usual patterns of empirical occurrences, only those occurrences that children judge to be *impossible* imply an understanding of fundamental physical laws such as continuity and solidity (Spelke, 1991). By contrast, *improbable* events are those that violate empirical regularities but not physical laws. Shtulman and Carey (2007) investigated this distinction in children aged 4, 6 and 8 years, as well as adults, and found that even the youngest children performed like adults in their judgements of what is impossible; in contrast to adults, however, children failed to affirm that improbable events are actually possible (e.g., that owning a lion as a pet can happen in real life). Shtulman and Carey interpreted the difference between children and adults as reflecting a genuine conceptual difference rather than attributing it to children's insufficient experience. Yet owning a lion as a pet is a very rare occurrence in an environment from which the children were recruited and thus highly unlikely for those children to have come across anyone owning a large and dangerous animal as a pet. Put simply, in the children's world of experience, such events do seem impossible, especially in view of the predictable consequences of keeping a lion in proximity to humans and without the benefit of knowledge that animals can be trained, which was not pre-tested. A related study (Weisberg & Sobel, 2012) subsequently concluded that the probable vs. possible distinction in young children is indeed experience-dependent as it could be elicited more easily in some contexts (story task) than in others (ratings task). The possible–impossible distinction is clearly relevant to children's natural-theological understanding of the world and its laws. Unless they are able to appreciate what events constitute impossible occurrences in the world, children cannot be expected to differentiate miracles as theological events, i.e., those that occur as a result of an exceptional cause, from any other unusual events, such as magic or tricks. It is therefore much more significant for the development of natural-theological understanding that children in Shtulman and Carey's study were able to identify the impossible events in a principled manner, just as adults did, than that they misjudged the probability of the never experienced yet possible events.

Wishing vs. prayer

Children's understanding of prayer as a theological construct is another instance of causality-at-a-distance that implies the empirical-transcendent distinction and what makes prayer akin to miracle rather than wishing and magic. Yet no psychological study has addressed prayer from this viewpoint. Woolley and her colleagues investigated children's ability to differentiate prayer from wishing as an aspect of their developing theory-of-mind (ToM) by questioning 4- to 8-year-olds from Christian backgrounds about the meaning of prayer, its efficacy and "the role of knowledge about God" (2000, p. 120). The researchers concluded that wishing and prayer were on a continuum throughout the life span, with children believing more in wishing and adults in prayer (Woolley, 1997, 2000).

Whilst both wishing and prayer imply mental rather than physical causality, the methods used in the studies above do not reveal whether children understand that prayer and wishing are fundamentally different kinds of action because of the contrasting ontological status of the causal agents involved in each. To establish whether children have a theological concept of prayer, it would be necessary to ascertain whether they can differentiate between the empirical entities and their actions (i.e., in wishing), on the one hand, and those that transcend the empirical boundaries (i.e., in prayer), on the other. Some of Woolley's findings suggest that they can; for example, by 5 years of age, children understand that prayer involves "knowing about God" (2000, p. 123) and that it implies an "interaction between God and thoughts" (p. 125).[5] In view of the paucity of research in this area, Woolley is right to stress the need for further work on "exactly how children conceive of the process of praying" (2000, p. 125). However, situating such work within the ToM framework is unlikely to advance our understanding of whether children conceive of prayer in the theological sense, i.e., differentiate between the empirical and transcendent components of the process of praying. As I argued in the preceding chapter, ToM is a mechanism by which children come to understand the minds of agents that they encounter through experience, notably human, which does not suggest how such experience may give rise to a concept of an unembodied agent with mental properties.

My brief discussion of the three conceptual distinctions above serves to highlight the need for an at least implicit empirical-transcendent contrast as underpinning children's theological understanding. Because, however, developmental researchers have continued to use the terms "magical", "miraculous" and "supernatural" as synonyms for a range of non-scientific entities in children's explanations of physical events, including ghosts, mermaids, fairies, magicians, monsters, angels, gods, witches and wizards, as well as God (e.g., Barrett, 2001; Browne & Woolley, 2004; Canfield & Ganea, 2014; Chandler & Lalonde, 1994; Rosengren & Hickling, 2000; Subbotsky, 1994), it remains unclear whether children in those studies indeed assign to all such agents the same ontological status as hitherto claimed.

116 Theology as a core cognitive domain

Intimations of transcendence in developmental theories

Whilst no psychological research has so far addressed transcendence as a theological concept, at least two contemporary accounts of cognitive development might, in my view, be construed as potentially capable of accommodating such a concept (Carey, 2002; Spelke & Hespos, 2002). Carey's (2002) argument that causality cannot be derived from spatial–temporal descriptions but is a contribution that comes from the mind is one example. The other is Spelke and Hespos' (2002) argument that children have a substantial input in the development of abstract concepts rather than derive such concepts directly from perception.

Although Carey's goal is to explain the origin of empirical or scientific concepts, her point that "the concept of an agent and intentional causality" is at the core of innate causal knowledge (2002, p. 47), and that the "attribution of goals and intentions goes beyond spatio-temporal analysis", even though the input for causal reasoning consists of perceptual properties (p. 50), I see as broad enough to accommodate the concepts of non-empirical agents too, chiefly in view of the level of abstractness that Carey attributes to core causal concepts. Carey's wording thus appears to provide a suitable alternative description of the role of causal reasoning in natural-theological understanding where children, in response to the perceptual input afforded by the spatial–temporal environment, infer an intentional causal agent as distinct from any other agents. Put simply, in natural-theology the transcendent causal agent that the mind "outputs" is an evidence-based inference rather than a figment of the capricious imagination or rote rehearsal of a culturally transmitted concept.

Spelke and Hespos (2002) similarly contend that abstract concepts do not originate in the sensory input but are a product of the mind responding to diverse sensory input. For if there was no such contribution by the mind, cognitive development would take a very long time and much painstaking work in a child's life given the multiplicity and distinctiveness of domain-specific knowledge (e.g., physics, biology, psychology). Spelke and Hespos thus appeal to substantial and incontrovertible evidence that children learn early and quickly about large classes of objects and their intersections, all of which rules out sole reliance on perceptual mechanisms as the source of abstract concepts. They further argue that the acquisition of language enables children to "transcend" the specific domains and "talk about anything we can conceive" (Spelke and Hespos 2002, p. 243). Although Spelke and Hespos do not give any examples of the horizons of conceptual transcendence available to children, their account is compatible with my point that given the complexity which children encounter in different domains of empirical knowledge yet learn to master early and spontaneously, postulating one, altogether different ontological and causal domain must be conceptually simpler than negotiating multiple representations of objects and events in the spatial domain. Put somewhat crudely, it is simpler to conceive of "all this here" (i.e., within space and time) vs. what is "not here", or suchlike, than to group together "the perceived surface layout into entities that are cohesive, continuous, and movable on contact" (Spelke, 1994, p. 439). None of this, of course, is at present possible to verify through research with pre-verbal children because the methods and techniques currently available to developmental researchers set limits to such research.[6]

Both accounts above were given in response to Mandler's proposal that "perceptual analysis" (1988, 2000), or "perceptual meaning analysis" (Mandler 2012), is an innate mechanism by which infants encode sensory information into conceptual categories from birth, whereby "one perception is actively compared to another" (1988, p. 126). Yet even Mandler's proposal might accommodate my hypothesis regarding the origin of the concept of transcendence in everyday experience of the physical world provided that a causal criterion is admitted as critical in the perceptual comparisons that Mandler identifies as necessary. For instance, Mandler (1990) accepts that perceptual analysis – a mechanism which enables simultaneous comparisons and contrasts of two objects – requires some kind of "vocabulary" (p. 240) or "images" (p. 241) in order to yield concepts. She is disinclined to enlist causality for such a role even though a causal criterion would be the best candidate given its status of a "developmental primitive" (Corrigan & Denton, 1996), or an innate experience-enabling mechanism (e.g., Carey, 2002; R. Gelman, 1990; Leslie, 1995; Spelke, 2000). Instead, in her revised proposal Mandler contends that causality follows rather than precedes spatial meaning, i.e., that conceptual primitives are actually "spatial in nature" whereas causality emerges subsequently and becomes added to spatial concepts (2012, p. 222). This begs the question of how infants come to organise spatial arrays without some intuition of priority to guide such organisation, not least because Mandler acknowledges that "concepts of moving things are among the first to be formed" (2012, p. 428). In other words, Mandler considers the concepts such as "move behind", "disappear", "move in" and the like to be spatial, rather than events occurring in space as a result of some cause. It seems that Mandler's reluctance to accept causality as key in the construction of spatial concepts stems from her equating the notion of cause with "force" (Piagetian sense) and not with "change" (Aristotelian sense), leading her to assert that "we have no evidence that young infants ascribe force to their causal perceptions" (Mandler's 2012, p. 432). The point is that they don't need to; instead, when change occurs within a spatial array, children appear to respond by seeking to identify its cause.

Transcendence and language development

Whilst it is generally accepted that language plays an important role in the development of abstract concepts, there is a consensus among developmental researchers that even before acquiring a language, infants grasp a number of relational or abstract concepts (e.g., Mandler, 2004; Nelson, 2011; Spelke & Hespos, 2002; Waxman, 2003). According to Nelson, for example, in order to learn the names of things "infants must have available, or be able to form, concepts of the things

118 Theology as a core cognitive domain

named allowing identification and reference to members of the conceptual category" (2011, p. 97). Although Nelson's primary concern is with the concepts of objects (i.e., empirical entities), notably their function or "relation in activity" as the basis for concept formation (2011, p. 97), the same developmental sequence (i.e., words becoming mapped onto already formed concepts) may be valid for abstract concepts too. Nelson's point that no psychological research has attempted to elucidate the acquisition of abstract concepts because of its preoccupation with "objects and object names" is pertinent (2011, p. 99). Some of the reasons for this bias are, in her view, trivial (e.g., easy to study in the laboratory or possible to learn through ostensive methods) but a more troublesome reason is the presumption among researchers that children have a tendency to learn mostly object names. Nelson's own evidence challenges this assumption by showing that some of the earliest children's words include "characteristics of the natural world (wind, rain, snow)" rather than mundane objects (2011, p. 99). Needless to say, such evidence is highly relevant to the topic of this volume as it implies that children from early on pay attention to the wider natural world as they seek to understand it.

Spelke and Hespos have similarly argued that children appear to approach the task of language learning equipped with many conceptual distinctions already in place. In their view, "many of our foundational concepts are clearest during the infancy period" (2002, p. 244), that is, before the onset of language, which is why as adults we may lack the words needed to convey some of our rudimentary concepts (see also Keil, 1981a, b). A major drawback of an early (i.e., pre-verbal) onset of foundational abstract concepts is that, with age, people become less sensitive to those conceptual distinctions that are not marked by their language, a point consistent with Bauer and Wewerka's (1995) findings with infants aged 13 to 20 months. The researchers tested children's memory for simple event sequences and then assessed them at different levels of delay, ranging from one to twelve months. Bauer and Wewerka found that, regardless of age and delay interval, children showed memory for the events both verbally and non-verbally; however, those children who had a more developed language at the time of experiencing the events remembered more. In other words, being able to encode verbally the events at the time of experiencing them reliably predicted the extent to which children verbally indicated memory for those events after the delay. It is interesting, however, that children's memory for an event did not depend upon their ability to code it verbally nor was language necessary at the time of encoding for children to express their memory verbally at a later time. "It would seem that children are capable of 'translating' their early preverbal memories into verbal form" at a later time (Bauer & Wewerka, 1995, p. 491). Still, the availability of language to allow verbal encoding conferred significant advantages (e.g., verbal infants were able to acquire additional information by understanding better the experimenter's narrative accompanying the events).

Before commenting on the implications of Bauer and Wewerka's findings for the development of natural-theological understanding, it is worth noting that their method consisted of manipulating physical objects that could be named. This is clearly not possible in the case of highly abstract concepts that lack association with any specific stimuli, notably God or transcendence. Nevertheless, a significant implication of Bauer and Wewerka's study for the concept of transcendence is that children's ability to "translate" early memories of ontological distinctions into verbal expressions at a later time may allow them to label an implicit concept thereof later, upon acquiring the appropriate label. We saw in Chapter 4 that the concept *natural,* as an all-inclusive abstract category, also lacks a verbal label in some languages (e.g., Japanese). Yet Japanese children and adults have a clear working concept of "natural in general" and use it in the same way as British children and adults do when tested by the same procedures.

The possibility that transcendence or God is a pre-verbal intuitive concept which, because it lacks a verbal label at the time of its onset, may not retain a secure place in one's conceptual inventory is highly pertinent to my attempt to explain its origin in everyday understanding of the world and its subsequent fate. In other words, although pre-verbal children may be able to intuit the concept(s) mapping the empirical-transcendent distinction, notably along the dimension of causality, they are unlikely to retain this intuition in explicit memory by the time they reach adulthood unless they are systematically and sufficiently often exposed to the words corresponding with those conceptual mappings. This condition, I suspect, is not always met even in the case of children raised in religious environments. Seeing that inferences about God in the context of one's experience of the natural world are not easy to code verbally or communicate, lack of opportunities for their rehearsal and thus long-term retention present greater challenges than do scientific concepts.[7]

Notes

1 Non-core domains (e.g., chess, history, phonetics) include concepts and skills that do not elicit theory construction and are acquired by learning from others rather than spontaneously (e.g., Chi, 1992; R. Gelman, 2000).
2 Whilst some philosophers have argued that metaphysical causal accounts do not provide causes but only reasons (e.g., Hospers, 1984), and Kant held that God is not the cause but the ground of all possibility (Wood, 1992), the postulate of God as a causal agent plays a key role in completing a causal enquiry originating in the empirical domain (e.g., Swinburne, 1991).
3 Philosophical arguments for God's existence from religious experience are a version of pragmatic tests, however, the notion of "religious experience" in such arguments is considerably broader than the concept of God as a causal agent considered in this volume (see Franks Davis, 1989; Proudfoot, 1985).
4 For example, Piaget (1924) claimed that children under 7 or 8 years of age consider miracles to be a common occurrence because they do not differentiate between physical determinism and moral necessity and hence accept that man's caprice can rule natural events. Elsewhere he argued that action-at-a-distance is non-rational as it originates in the child's egocentrism, the source of both efficacy and phenomenalism as forms of primitive causality (Piaget & Kraft, 1925).
5 Bamford and Lagattuta's (2010) finding that 4-year-olds do not view prayer as having an instrumental value in dealing with negative emotions does not demonstrate

that children of this age have no understanding of prayer as a fundamentally different form of communication. Rather, children's consistent affirmations that "God can know what you are thinking" (2010, p. 89) imply that 4-year-olds have an intuition of God's ontological otherness, consistent with a theological concept of prayer.

6 A further obstacle facing researchers of infant cognition that Spelke highlights is in their peers setting "an impossible standard", i.e., that one should only accept cognitive interpretations after all other possible perceptual and sensory interpretations have been tried and found insufficient (2000, p. 39).

7 As Kikas (1998) demonstrated, scientific concepts, too, are subject to forgetting unless they can be rehearsed.

8

INNATENESS OF RELIGION WITHIN THE LIMITS OF SCIENCE ALONE

Thus far I have argued that the evidence discussed in this volume is consistent with the natural-theological hypothesis, i.e., the concept of God as a unique causal agent is an intuitive concept that children acquire early and spontaneously through their experience of the physical world, where they construct many of their other concepts in the presence of certain innate constraints. In the current chapter I attempt to develop an account of how those constraints might operate to give rise to the core theological concept (i.e., God). When suggesting that the core theological concept is innately specified, I rely on the wider developmental evidence, some of which was reviewed earlier in this volume, as well as on the criteria used for determining conceptual innateness, namely: (a) early and spontaneous onset in development, (b) little or no change across age and (c) cross-cultural similarities within a conceptual domain (e.g., Carey, 1991; Carey & Spelke, 1994; Pinker, 2006). In other words, the nativist position implies that children and adults from different cultures have the same core intuitions and organise core knowledge in the same way even though many differences may emerge in later development as a result of education and learning. Contemporary accounts of the origin and development of human knowledge thus converge on agreement that nature and nurture provide two equally important sources (Elman et al., 1996) and that innate knowledge structures encourage and facilitate, rather than stifle, learning and further development (R. Gelman & Brenneman, 1994).

The question regarding the exact contribution of innate structures to different developmental domains has generated a variety of views within human sciences (see Mameli & Bateson, 2006). Elman and colleagues, for example, are highly sceptical that any aspects of knowledge can be strictly innate (i.e., independent of nurture) because innateness implies specific neuronal circuits, where each neurone has a pre-specified role. As they put it, innately specified knowledge would "most likely … have to be in the form of fine-grained patterns of

122 Innateness of religion

synaptic connectivity at the cortical level, i.e., cortical micro-circuitry" (1996, p. 25). Their argument against representational or conceptual innateness relies on substantial evidence from vertebrate animals which shows that any group of neurones can learn anything given sufficient experience (the plasticity argument). For example, when investigators alter the nature of cortical input, the cortex is capable of taking on neuro-anatomical and physical properties that are appropriate for the information it receives. Alterations in the cortical input can be made by transplanting plugs of foetal cortex from one area to another, by inflicting damage to the sensory surface or by redirecting inputs from their typical area (e.g., visual) to a different area (e.g., auditory). Such evidence undoubtedly implies that, initially at least, neurones are not designated for specific tasks but appear to be equipotential.

Whilst no human behaviour can be strictly "genetic" (i.e., exclusively a product of the information contained within the genes), certain aspects thereof seem to be more biologically constrained than those behaviours that are largely culturally determined. To emphasise the different levels of genetic influence on behaviour, Elman and colleagues draw on Johnson and Morton's (1991) distinction between *innate* and *primal* behavioural outcomes. According to this distinction, "innate" pertains to interactions occurring within the organism itself, that is, "between the genes and their molecular and cellular environments without recourse to information from outside the organism" (1996, p. 22). In contrast, "primal" behaviours are those that are shaped by the interactions between the organism (genetic information) and external environment, and which are common to all members of the species. Importantly, the outcomes of both types of interaction involving the genes are "inevitable", that is, are specific to a given species within its natural environment so that there is little variability among its individual members. Elman and colleagues acknowledge, moreover, that the boundary between innate and primal behaviours is not always clear and can shift as a result of research; for instance, what used to be classified as innate in earlier research was later shown to result from pre-natal learning. Because of the fluid boundaries between the two terms, "innate" has continued to be used by developmental scientists for all aspects of behaviour that are influenced both by the genes and the environment (e.g., Baillargeon, 2008). It is this "interactionist" connotation of innateness that provides a framework for my account of the origin of the core theological concept and the distinction between the physical (empirical) and metaphysical (transcendent) domains of thought and knowledge.

Metaphysical concepts and the brain

The two conceptual domains at the centre of natural-theological understanding – physical and metaphysical – might also be differentiated in terms of the cortical representation of each. Whilst innateness in terms of cortical micro-circuitry may well be the only way in which physical (i.e., empirical) concepts are represented cortically, the highly abstract metaphysical concepts such as transcendence (God) need not be cortically implemented in the same way as physical concepts. The possibility of a differential cortical representation of empirical and non-empirical concepts derives from the nature of input characteristic of each. Whilst empirical concepts are typically associated with some specific sensory input, representations of non-empirical entities do not imply any specific physical input but consist of abstracted properties and inferred relations that lack exact correspondence to anything given in experience.

My proposal above is consistent with Karmiloff-Smith's point that connectionist models of conceptual origins can appear adequate in the case of humans mainly because such accounts do not consider developmental evidence regarding higher cognitive functions such as, for instance, children's theories (in Elman et al., 1996). When, however, human capacity for theoretical knowledge is taken into account, it becomes clear that such a capacity is not determined solely by sensory input, as is the knowledge acquired by the lower organisms who receive sensory input directly controlled by the investigators. Rather, our theoretical knowledge implies some internal input as well, notably causality (e.g., Carey, 2002; R. Gelman, 1991). Such input may be of a kind that cannot be mapped onto anything specific within the environment, in agreement with Kant's theory of a priori categories of understanding and their role in knowledge acquisition. Consequently, none of the evidence against the innateness of physical concepts is necessarily fatal to the possibility of innateness of some metaphysical concepts, including the core theological concept of transcendence or God. Elman and colleagues indeed acknowledge that evidence from rats "does not mean that there is no case for innate constraints on higher cognitive processes" and they do not entirely rule out the possibility that neurones are born "knowing" what kinds of representations they are destined to take on (1996, p. 27). Wellman and S. Gelman similarly grant that it is conceivable that "certain representations may be innately specified" (1998, p. 527).

Karmiloff-Smith's argument (in Elman et al., 1996) that connectionist models do not account for children's theoretical thought permits a conjecture that, in the case of the core theological concept (i.e., God), we may conceive of the brain as functioning under the conditions of a permanently non-specific input in the sense that no stimuli in the environment could be said to be more specifically associated with the content of such a concept, i.e., be its better referent. Instead, the brain seems to construct a basic theological concept of a transcendent causal agent (i.e., God) from the perceived objects and events as well as the relations abstracted or inferred within the world. The reliability with which such a concept is invoked or triggered under certain empirical conditions (e.g., when explaining the origins of natural and artificial objects) points to its developmental inevitability as it fulfils all three behavioural criteria of innateness mentioned earlier, namely, early and spontaneous onset, child–adult developmental continuities in its deployment and cross-cultural similarities.

124 Innateness of religion

Although very little developmental research has tested the hypothesis of conceptual nativism directly, Shultz and Mareschal (1997) quote one study (Nolfi et al., 1990) where some network genotypes were actually shown to be capable of simulating representational innateness. Whilst the details of this study are not directly relevant to theological concepts, it is pertinent to point out that until we know more about the exact mechanisms of cortical representation, some form of conceptual nativism remains a "plausible hypothesis" (Elman et al., 1996, p. 371). One of the tasks for future research could thus be to look for ways of simulating non-empirical concepts other than just moral, which Elman (2005) considers to be exotic even though the core theological concept (i.e., transcendence) would present a far greater challenge in this respect. One of the proposals for testing innateness in developmental research advocates the use of teaching experiments as a way of determining if children's early concepts are innate (Baillargeon, 2002). This, however, is only feasible in the case of physical concepts because it is far from clear what new information we could systematically vary in order to see how it might affect infants' concepts of highly abstract entities, such as that of the transcendent God.

To sum up thus far: The chief argument against conceptual innateness rests on the evidence that is consistent with brain plasticity (i.e., the fact that the neurones can learn to respond to anything). This argument certainly seems valid in the case of scientific concepts, i.e., representations of empirically occurring entities. But the plasticity argument does not account for all concepts' origins. It does not tell us, for instance, what the neurones are responding to when representing metaphysical entities and abstract relations such as those that involve transcendence, Harré's Realm 3 beings, Fagg's CIB and the like. It should also be said that some neuroscience findings are compatible with both the nativist and brain plasticity hypotheses (e.g., Dehaene-Lambertz, Dehaene & Hertz-Pannier, 2002). According to their study with 3-month-old infants, the precursors of adult cortical language areas are already active by this age, that is, well before the onset of speech production. Yet, whilst the adult brain responds differently when listening to the native as opposed to a foreign language, no such difference was observed in the infant temporal lobe.

Innate constraints and the core theological concept: A hypothesis

Whilst the state of an initial equipotentiality of neurones is manifestly incompatible with there being any innately specified physical concepts, the very same condition of the developing brain may provide a basis for understanding innateness (or behavioural inevitability) of the core theological concept. The argument is this: Because the core theological concept lacks any *specific* sensory input (i.e., is empirically "amodal"), the only innately specified "content" of such a concept could be some mechanism(s) capable of detecting and responding to relational input in the form of rudimentary contrasts and comparisons (i.e., trans-domain, see Chapter 3). On this hypothesis, any aspect of the world that interacts with the cognitive-perceptual mechanisms, notably causal, is in principle capable of eliciting the core theological concept. Put differently, the core theological concept could be an emergent property of the permanently equipotential (undesignated) neurones, for which the world as a whole (i.e., any aspect thereof) may provide an input for those neurones to pick up. Hence it is possible that only in the condition of equipotentiality are the neurones capable of detecting multiple relations between and among stimuli in the environment, which, in turn, leads to inferences of transcendent entities as distinct from empirical entities whenever certain cognitive pressures obtain (e.g., when seeking causal explanations). Thus, for example, perceiving artefacts not only as individual objects but as members of the whole class of artificial objects, which are similar on account of their origin (i.e., human-made), sets up a comparative framework for encoding and processing all natural items as similar in the same causal-origin sense (i.e., not human-made), thereby giving rise to a single or unifying principle by which all natural items come to be seen as belonging in one ontological category. The key point here is that, unlike objects and their characteristics, the causal relations inferred to exist between the objects and their source(s) of origin permit grouping of all and any natural objects in a single category, which I discussed in more detail in Chapter 4.

The possibility that only the undesignated neurones can pick up the metaphysically relevant information implies that those neurones are, *de facto*, designated for such a task. In other words, the initially uncommitted neurones may actually be committed from the start to play a more general role (e.g., infer relations, envisage possibilities, intuit novel entities). The alternative would be to assume – an option tentatively considered by Elman and colleagues (1996) – that abstract concepts in general are representationally pre-specified and hence remain constant throughout development. The plausibility of this alternative when applied to the core theological concept, i. e., transcendent God, lies in the fact that there is no conceivable specific experience or evidence to account for either the origin or subsequent change of its core content.

Quartz's (1993) analysis of parallel-distributed processing (PDP) models as consistent with conceptual nativism (in a robust sense) matches this alternative. According to Quartz, PDP models have built into their architecture a "highly restricted hypothesis space that contains the target function or at least an acceptable approximation to it" Quartz (1993, p. 233) Such fixed architecture ensures that training by examples is simply learning the "truth conditions for a concept that the network already has available to it" (1993, p. 233). Quartz also points out that because PDP networks are limited to an *a priori* defined or fixed hypothesis space, they are efficient in simple situations, when examples fit the hypothesis, but poor in complex domains. I suggest that this is indeed how the core theological concept should be understood, as a simple representation of an unobservable entity with unique causal powers. Put differently, an innate

126 Innateness of religion

concept of God is a very basic concept of a transcendent causal agent and as such is not suited to the task of handling complex explanatory demands of the physical world where the specialised sciences can come up with more specific and detailed solutions. Rather, the core theological concept corresponds to a tightly constrained hypothesis, with a small number of defining criteria that lead to the formation of broad, well defined and mutually exclusive ontological categories, often of a dichotomous kind. According to the hypothesis advanced in this volume children construct the concept of transcendence through the opportunities for contrasts and comparisons that are available empirically (i.e., among physical objects) and to which they have abundant access. R. Gelman's constructivist model, according to which any innate skeletal structures that "outline the kind of data needed for their further development", seems to make a similar point albeit with reference to concepts belonging in the empirical domain (1991, p. 314).

Whether the two accounts of representational origins above – innateness and brain plasticity – can in practice be operationally differentiated is at present unclear and may not matter when the core theological concept is concerned. For the existence of undesignated neurones, on the one hand, and representational innateness, on the other, both equally entail its developmental inevitability. To account for the developmental inevitability of such concepts it may be sufficient to postulate certain innate mechanisms capable of identifying some of the basic ways in which objects behave or interact (Baillargeon, 1995), or some "mechanisms for singling out entities" within a domain (Carey & Spelke, 1994, p. 170), as well as being capable of establishing elementary causal connections or inferences. In other words, the basic cognitive-perceptual processes characteristic of all humans (even under the conditions of considerable mental and physical handicap) may be the only genetic component required for instigating interactions with the world, any aspect of which can afford the information needed for engendering a core theological concept. My point is that all of those ways of being innate – neuronal plasticity, representational nativism and general cognitive mechanisms – equally allow for an early and universal occurrence of the core theological concept in human development, consistent with the natural-theological hypothesis.

The proposal above also seems broadly compatible with "neural constructivism" as an account of conceptual innateness, which posits some "general, intrinsic processes along with environmentally derived neural activity carrying domain-specific information" (Quartz & Sejnowski, 1997, p. 539). For Quartz and Sejnowski acknowledge that "No learner can be completely assumption-free since pure tabula rasa learning is impossible – there must be some built-in assumptions" (1997, p. 555). There are, however, two caveats implicit in their account that should be mentioned when discussing the core theological concept. The first is Quartz and Sejnowski's definition of neural constructivism as a learning account, which implies that it should be possible to specify the exact nature of input that gives rise to the theological domain.

I noted earlier, however, that the opposite is true in the case of the core theological concept, i.e., there is no way of telling which aspects of the world are those that trigger the concept of God (transcendence) more reliably or predictably than any other. The second caveat is that Quartz and Sejnowski's "built-in assumptions" are not assumptions, strictly speaking, but tools or mechanisms used in the learning process and which include generic initial cortical circuitry, conduction velocities, subcortical organisation, learning rates and hierarchical development. Nevertheless, because Quartz and Sejnowski state clearly that the built-in biases are "consistent with a largely equipotential cortex" (1997, p. 555), such a state of the cortex does allow for a broad compatibility between their "neural constructivism" hypothesis and the natural-theological hypothesis considered here, which assumes that the core theological concept is innately specified (see below).[1]

As for the question whether children's and adults' consistent and reliable responses in terms of God as a causal agent can be construed as evidence for "behavioural constructivism", the answer depends on the extent to which behavioural constructivism presupposes neural constructivism, i.e., is "the outcome of cortical specialisation" (Johnson, Bates, Elman, Karmiloff-Smith & Plunkett, 1997, p. 569). The neural constructivist assumption has been challenged for its supposition of a tight correspondence between cognitive modularity and neural modularity on the grounds that cognitive functions could be neurally implemented in a highly distributed fashion even though they comprise a module at the cognitive level (e.g., Scholl, 1997).

In summary, the origin of two broad conceptual domains – physical and metaphysical – can be differentiated according to the nature of input presupposed by each (i.e., specific and non-specific, respectively). Physical concepts may indeed require fewer or no innate representational constraints because there exists in the world *specific* sensory input for such concepts from the moment of birth and some of this input can be picked up by the organism before birth. Accordingly, even the principles of solidity and continuity of objects, which Spelke (e.g., 1994) defines as the core or innate principles of physical knowledge, are likely to benefit from some form of environmental input right from birth. In contrast, no similarly *specific* environmental input can be envisaged as necessary and sufficient in the case of the core theological concept, i.e., God or transcendence. According to the natural-theological hypothesis, abstract concepts of this kind seem to be supported only by a very generalised and intricate matrix of inferred relations between or among objects and events within the environment when guided by a search for causal explanation. It is important to stress that this hypothesis is quite different from the premise of strict nativism according to which some concepts may need no environmental input of any kind. Rather the reverse: On my hypothesis, the whole world can be said to provide the input needed for the core or basic theological inference, although only a portion thereof may in reality be necessary to give rise to such inferences.[2] Crucially, therefore, an "innate" concept of a transcendent deity proposed here *requires* experience for

128 Innateness of religion

its deployment.[3] It follows that my account of the natural-theological concept of God as deriving from everyday perception and understanding of the world and being a foundational concept of the theological domain is equally compatible with empiricist accounts of development. For as Newcombe points out, the two types of account – nativist and empiricist – differ less than at first appears. In both instances environmental input is necessary, whether merely to trigger certain "specific content-laden modules" or to enable infants to interact with the world, which "will (almost) inevitably develop the sorts of structures that are needed for adaptive function" (2002, p. 400). Elman and colleagues' point is similar, namely, to identify a behaviour as innate does not mean that "there is a single genetic locus or set of genes which have the specific function of producing the behavior in question" (1996, p. 357) but rather that "given normal developmental experiences, it is a highly probable outcome" (1996, p. 319).

The nativist hypothesis has retained its place in scientific psychology because of its potential to account for very early knowledge acquisition as well as any developmental continuities from childhood to adulthood. Nevertheless, in spite of the many significant achievements and methodological innovations, neuroscience is still not in a position to verify the nativist hypothesis for two main reasons. First, the complexity of interactions between the genetic component and the environment throughout development practically rules out any precise pinpointing of the contribution made by each source. Second, the lack of information regarding what specific input might conceivably constitute stimuli for the core theological concept strengthens the case for postulating innate representational constraints as critical in the emergence of this concept in early development. Consequently, cognitive or behavioural evidence remains a crucial source of data relevant to the issue of conceptual innateness in the domain of physical and metaphysical cognition alike. Cognitive and developmental psychology are therefore two key areas of experimental psychology to undertake the task of explaining the origin of each. As Estes and Bartsch write in their response to Quartz and Sejnowski's (1997) target article, "in the endeavour to understand how the mind emerges from the brain, developmental psychology has a certain priority" and add that developmental research "should not just guide theories of neural development: it should tightly constrain them" (1997, p. 562).

Notes

1 Although Quartz (1999) suggests that the neural constructivist perspective corresponds with the Piagetian perspective in that it views representations as constructions made during interaction between developmental mechanisms and the environment, the similarity with Piaget is only apparent. According to Piaget, the new-born's mind is profoundly egocentric, i.e., laden with "distorting" assumptions and biases, which takes several years of development to correct before any constructive interactions between the child and the environment can take place (Petrovich, 1988). Until then, the early interactions give rise to misconceptions rather than coherent concepts.

2 It would be difficult to conceive of an organism's viable existence if no input from the world was reaching it. For all input to cease, one would have to be biologically dead because even those born congenitally blind, deaf or limbless would still be able to obtain sufficient input from the environment through their remaining bodily functions.

3 This is consistent with Kant's (1983) epistemology, which maintains that without the empirical input, *a priori* categories of human understanding could not by themselves lead to knowledge as they are merely tools for transforming the mass of unstructured ongoing experience into ideas rather than being ideas in themselves.

9

CONCLUSIONS, EXCLUSIONS AND SOME IMPLICATIONS

In this book I have tried to argue that children's motive to understand the world as a whole – its structure as well as origin – underpins their ability to differentiate reliably between natural and artificial objects as distinct ontological categories. The natural–artificial ontological dichotomy thus represents a rudimentary yet correct theory of the world, which children construct by relying on a causal criterion that is extrinsic rather than intrinsic to objects (i.e., is relational) and as such can account for the objects' primary or ultimate, as opposed to ante-cedent-derived, origin. Contrary to the claims that "no theory can ever hope to continuously make principled distinctions among all the possible entities it applies to" (Keil, 1989, p. 277), the natural–artificial ontological dichotomy, as a rudimentary theory of the world as a whole, does allow children and adults alike to do just that. I further argued that, by virtue of its coherence, such a theory gives credence to children's speculative reasoning and their conjectures about the characteristics of God as a causal agent rather than those depicted by diverse cultures and traditions.

Whilst it can be relatively easy to establish that children differentiate consist-ently between natural and artificial objects from the viewpoint of the objects' primary or ultimate origin, it is harder to explain how and when they acquire a concept of primary origin as its criterion, except that they do not rely solely or mainly on the strategies previously suggested in the literature and which may include the objects' size, distance and capacity for self-sustained or self-initiated activities (S. Gelman & Kremer, 1991). Although such strategies do figure in children's justifications of natural objects' origins, they cannot be criti-cal because children also know that humans do not make many small sized natural items such as pebbles, insects and specks of dust, many of which also happen to be near children and which they can handle. Nor is it likely that chil-dren rely on adult testimony when acquiring beliefs about unobservable entities

Conclusions, exclusions and some implications **131**

(e.g., Canfield & Ganea, 2014; Harris & Koenig, 2006; Harris, Pasquini, Duke, Asscher & Pons, 2006). Rather, evidence from several sources indicates that parents have little or no influence on their children's beliefs. For example, when interacting with their 20- and 36-month-old children parents "rarely mentioned non-obvious features such as insides, innate potential, origins, or essences" and never discussed origins with 20-month-old children (S. Gelman, Coley & Gottfried, 1994, p. 355). Similarly, parental beliefs had no direct influence on children's beliefs about the origins of species until adolescence (Evans, 2001) and no effect on 4- to 6-year-old children's religious beliefs (Vaden & Woolley, 2011, p. 1130). Piaget's records, too, imply that any information about objects' origins that preschool children may receive from others is typically in response to children's questions (see Piaget, 1977).

A possible criticism of my proposal that children acquire the natural–artificial ontological dichotomy as part of their own effort to understand the surrounding world in causal terms is that children rely on their learning experience rather than deduction from a causal principle when telling the origin of natural and artificial objects. Hence, the criticism goes, because children do not see people make natural objects, they can say that such objects are not human-made. The answer to this criticism must be that children do not see most of the artefacts being made either, yet extant developmental literature is in agreement that children have no difficulties identifying artefacts as objects made by people. In other words, the criticism begs the question how children come to know that people make artefacts given that they do not witness the making of most artificial objects in their environment or receive systematic teaching about their origin. According to my proposal, children can correctly deduce the origin of any object from the available information afforded by the object and the already held causal principles, notably the scope and power of human action. Consequently, what children learn and discover about artefacts, and in light of their general causal knowledge, allows them to infer that *some* objects in the world people do not make.

Not only do young children understand that natural events are those which take place without human intervention (e.g., S. Gelman & Kremer, 1991; Keil, 1986; Petrovich, 1988), but they go further and ask how, or by what cause, such entities first came to be. Like adults, children answer such questions by speculating about the primary cause(s), thereby stretching their enquiry beyond the level of identifying causal antecedents from which a specific entity derives and beginning to consider how matter itself emerged.

Following a review and discussion of evidence about causal development in different domains of knowledge (Chapter 2), I also suggested that identifying objects according to primary origin should be easier at any age than identifying the correct antecedent causal mechanisms on the grounds that judgements about primary origin do not require detailed knowledge of the objects' intrinsic structural and causal characteristics but only an inference of a plausible object-extrinsic source. This prediction was borne out most clearly in the current studies when the extrinsic criterion was stated in terms of human causal action,

132 Conclusions, exclusions and some implications

which children used to identify items as natural or artificial, but not as clearly when they had to specify the non-human source of natural origins (e.g., evolution, God). Children's equally good performance when identifying familiar and unfamiliar items also implies that familiarity with the criterion, rather than with particular objects, is what facilitates children's reliable use of human causal agency as a criterion when categorising objects as natural or artificial.

In light of considerable developmental evidence that even very young children have a good grasp of the physical laws as valid for specific domains of the world, and that preschool children are able to construct theories which honour the coherence and validity of those laws, in Chapter 3 I proposed that children's everyday knowledge of scientific domains (i.e., physics, biology and psychology) is directly relevant to their natural-theological understanding. For children's scientific knowledge implies that they conceptualise, largely correctly, the boundaries within which different empirical laws hold, which, in turn, facilitates their understanding of further contrasts, notably visible–invisible or material–immaterial, both within and outside of those domains. Importantly, such contrasts are also captured by the empirical-transcendent distinction as a component of children's intuitive knowledge and without which it would be impossible for them to represent God in non-anthropomorphic terms. Consequently, to accept the validity of either children's or adults' conjectures about God as the primary or ultimate cause of natural entities, evidence is needed that their concept of God is plausible, that is, represents an agent that is ontologically distinct from other entities by virtue of not being constrained by either space or time. Abundant evidence from different areas of developmental research mentioned in this book, which documents young children's ability to reason in terms of invisible or unobservable characteristics, is consistent with this rationale. Put differently, children's non-anthropomorphic representations of God encompass the characteristics that are not just hidden from view but are ontologically distinct from human characteristics. Findings described in Chapter 6 corroborate such a concept in children and adults alike, notwithstanding their considerable verbal limitations that are bound to frustrate one's ability to convey those understandings fully.

Evidence reported in Chapters 4, 5 and 6 taken together suggests that children and adults from two cultures with very different histories of science commonly postulate God as the cause of the world and matter as such although many, especially adult participants, engage in considering alternative possibilities.[1] My main conclusion from the evidence described in Chapter 5 is that cosmological judgements, in all age groups, invariably involve God's agency, regardless of whether those judgements terminate in the acceptance or rejection of God's role in the origin of matter. Natural-theological understanding from childhood to adulthood thus seems to be remarkably consistent with the reasoning recurrent in the history of scientific thought and which can be traced to the earliest records of human yearning to understand the cosmos. Based on the current findings, together with the wider developmental research and theory reviewed earlier, in Chapter 7 I argued that theological understanding constitutes a core domain in human

Conclusions, exclusions and some implications **133**

cognition on the grounds that it meets all the developmental criteria for identifying core domains, in addition to emerging early and universally. In Chapter 8 I ventured the view that a concept as tightly constrained by its eliciting conditions (i.e., God as a causal agent) is likely to be innate in the same way that several other domain concepts are considered to be innate.

A notable omission from the current volume is the work on religion carried out in anthropology, cultural or evolutionary, neurotheology and genetics. The main reason for leaving out those approaches is that none address the origin of religious thought in individual development, especially not the concept of God as a causal agent. Thus, although most of the omitted accounts emphasise "naturalness" of religion, this is not in the natural-theological sense espoused in the current volume but in the sense of religion being a natural by-product of cognitive processes that evolved for survival purposes in the physical world which, however, have a tendency to "misfire" in response to certain environmental influences and give rise to counterintuitive notions. According to those approaches, religion is a by-product of the ability to reason about other human minds (Bering, 2006; Pinker, 2006), of the perceptual mechanisms which evolved for detecting agents (Guthrie, 1980) or of any common-sense and intuitive cognitive capacities that become counterintuitive as a result of exposure to cultural content (Boyer, 1994b, 1996). From the viewpoint of developmental psychology, however, accounts of religion as counterintuitive are problematic for two main reasons. First, to the extent that the God-concept is a by-product of "intuitive" (i.e., empirical) concepts, notably those in biology, physics and psychology, such a concept can only be anthropomorphic. Second, and related to the above point, the proponents of the counterintuitiveness view of religion assume that people of any age conceptualise human and divine entities as being on a continuum rather than as ontologically distinct, yet do not cite any psychological evidence to corroborate such a continuum in human cognition.

A more relevant, albeit overlooked, contribution to the study of religion is Boyer's explicit distinction between anthropological, on the one hand, and psychological interests, on the other. Specifically, Boyer makes it clear that, as an anthropologist, his interests are in the recurrence and transmission of "counterintuitive" religious concepts rather than in those notions that occur universally and constitute "the minimal point" in any religion (1994a, p. 392). Boyer further admits that he finds nothing of interest in "the very vague notion of 'supernatural' entities and agency" (1994b, p. 9) and, most important, recognises that "modern anthropology does not have much to say about the 'origins' of religious ideas because it does not know how to describe the acquisition and representation of ideas in general" (1994b, p. viii). Boyer's demarcation of the anthropological approach to religion is of value in that it highlights its key differences from the psychological approach, especially developmental, where research and theory *are* driven by an interest in those aspects of early cognition that may indeed be universal, however "minimal" their role in adult cognition might seem to be. It is thus curious that Boyer's anthropological ideas have

134 Conclusions, exclusions and some implications

inspired a great deal of developmental research on counterintuitiveness of children's religious understanding, without any attempt to determine first what aspects of their religious understanding might be *intuitive*.

One other omission from the current book that ought to be mentioned concerns God's moral agency. Although this book does not address the moral aspects of God as a component of natural-theological understanding, this is solely because of my aim to focus on those issues that figure in both science and the historical natural theology, namely, explanations of the natural world in causal terms and any inferences about God as its cause. Such an aim does not assume that the originators of modern science viewed God's moral attributes as irrelevant to their understanding of the world but only that they did not see them as amenable to being investigated by the methods then available for studying nature. Subsequent developments within science and its methodological advances have immeasurably broadened its scope so that study of the mind is now a scientific domain in its own right. Put simply, whilst it is understandable that the idea of science in the 17th and 18th centuries was limited to the physical world, with any psychological questions investigated by philosophy, modern psychology can now investigate mental life in all its diversity by using scientific methods. Needless to say, such a study ought to encompass *all* aspects of human reasoning about God, including God's moral attributes.

In these closing paragraphs I can mention briefly some of the implications arising from the findings reported in this volume. Religious education is the most obvious yet never discussed topic in developmental research; not only school-based religious education, which is not offered as a subject to children in many parts of the world, but religious education in the broader sense that may involve children and adults alike. The strongest case for its relevance was made by the research participants, most eloquently by British adults, who frequently and squarely put the blame on their own educational history for depriving them of opportunities to discuss the issues addressed in the current study ("not a common conversation topic") and thereby acquire the language needed for articulating and refining their ideas about those issues.

When Bruner stated that "any idea could be taught in some 'intellectually honest' form to children of any age" (in Brown, Metz & Campione, 1996, p. 156), he had in mind scientific education, yet the same rationale should hold in the case of religious education. As Brown and colleagues have argued in relation to science, learning is best done in a community of learners who engage in discussion, questioning and criticism. "Over time, the community of learners adopts a common voice and common knowledge base, a shared system of meaning, beliefs, and activity" (1996, p. 162), simply because meaning, as such, is constantly negotiated and refined. Religious language is a particularly good example where meaning-negotiation may prove productive. Although it has long been accepted in theological scholarship that religious experience is ineffable (James, 1902), its ineffability may, to a large degree, be a consequence of not having developed a language for articulating its content and thereby rendering it more effable. This is not to say that scientific and theological entities are equally ineffable and that both acquire meaning via language in the same way. In contrast to science, lack of opportunities to be influenced by language can sometimes be advantageous in philosophy and theology. For this reason, perhaps, it has been suggested that young children are more likely to produce profound philosophical judgements than older children as they have been less exposed to education that often stifles such thought (Matthews, 1980). To know, however, when language can no longer convey meaning, evidence-based insight into its potential scope ought to be our best guide.

Notes

1 The similarities between children and adults in the studies reported in this volume, notably regarding those aspects of the world that do not require detailed factual knowledge but involve reflection and speculation, are consistent with other research reporting continuities between children and adults at the behavioural (e.g., "cognitive biases") as well as the brain level, based on observing each group's performance in Piagetian tasks (Leroux et al., 2009).

REFERENCES

Ahn, W., Kalish, C., Gelman, S. A., Medin, D. L., Luhmann, C., Atran, S., Coley, J., & Shafto, P. (2001). Why essences are essential in the psychology of concepts. *Cognition*, *82*, 59–69.

Alters, B. J. & Nelson, C. E. (2002). Teaching evolution in higher education. *Evolution*, *56* (10), 1891–1901.

Amsel, E., Klaczynski, P. A., Johnston, A., Bench, S., Close, J., Sadler, E., & Walker, R. (2008). A dual-process account of the development of scientific reasoning: The nature and development of metacognitive intercession skills. *Cognitive Development*, *23*, 452–471.

Annett, M. (1959). The classification instances of four common class concepts by children and adults. *British Journal of Educational Psychology*, *29*, 223–236.

Arieti, A. & Wilson, P. A. (2003). *The scientific and the divine: Conflict and reconciliation from ancient Greece to the present*. New York, NY: Rowman & Littlefield Publishers Ltd.

Arterberry, M. E. & Bornstein, M. H. (2001). Three-month-old infants' categorization of animals and vehicles based on static and dynamic attributes. *Journal of Experimental Child Psychology*, *80*, 333–346.

Atran, S. (1995). Causal constraints on categories and categorical constraints on biological reasoning across cultures. In D. Sperber, D. Premack, & A. J. Premack (Eds.), *Causal cognition: A multidisciplinary debate* (pp. 205–233). Oxford, UK: Clarendon Press.

Atran, S. & Henrich, J. (2010). The evolution of religion: How cognitive by-products, adaptive learning heuristics, ritual displays, and group competition generate deep commitments to prosocial religions. *Biological Theory*, *5* (1), 18–30.

Au, T. K. (1994). Developing an intuitive understanding of substance kind. *Cognitive Psychology*, *27* (1), 71–111.

Avargués-Weber, A., Dyer, A. G., Combe, M., & Giurfa, M. (2012). Simultaneous mastering of two abstract concepts by the miniature brain of bees. *PNAS*, *109* (19), 7481–7486.

Backscheider, A. G., Shatz, M., & Gelman, S. A. (1993). Preschoolers' ability to distinguish living kinds as a function of regrowth. *Child Development*, *64*, 1242–1257.

Baillargeon, R. (1994). Physical reasoning in young infants: Seeking explanations for impossible events. *British Journal of Developmental Psychology*, *12*, 9–33.

138 References

Baillargeon, R. (1995). A model of physical reasoning in infancy. In C. Rovee-Collier & L. P. Lipsitt (Eds.), *Advances in infant research* (Vol. 9, pp. 305–371). Norwood, NJ: Ablex.

Baillargeon, R. (2002). The acquisition of physical knowledge: A summary in eight lessons. In U. Goswami (Ed.), *Blackwell handbook of childhood cognitive development* (pp. 47–83). Oxford, UK: Blackwell Publishers Ltd.

Baillargeon, R. (2008). Innate ideas revisited: For a principle of persistence in infants' physical reasoning. *Perspectives on Psychological Science, 3* (1), 2–13.

Bamford, C. & Lagattuta, K. H. (2010). A new look at children's understanding of mind and emotion: The case of prayer. *Developmental Psychology, 46* (1), 78–92.

Barbour, I. (1998). *Religion and science: Historical and contemporary issues.* London, UK: SCM Press Ltd.

Barrett, J. L. (2001). How ordinary cognition informs petitionary prayer. *Journal of Cognition and Culture, 1* (3), 259–269. DOI:10.1163/156853701753254404

Barrett, J. L. (2007). Cognitive science of religion: What is it and why is it? *Religion Compass, 1* (6), 768–786.

Barrett, J. L. (2011). Cognitive science of religion: Looking back, looking forward. *Journal for the Scientific Study of Religion, 50* (2), 229–239.

Barrett, J. L. & Keil, F. C. (1996). Conceptualising a nonnatural entity: Anthropomorphism in God concepts. *Cognitive Psychology, 31,* 219–247.

Barrett, J. L. & Richert, R. A. (2003). Anthropomorphism or preparedness? Exploring children's God concepts. *Review of Religious Research, 44* (3), 300–312.

Barrett, J. L., Richert, R. A., & Driesenga, A. (2001). God's beliefs versus mother's: The development of nonhuman agent concepts. *Child Development, 72* (1), 50–65.

Barrett, J. L. & Van Orman, B. (1996). The effects of image-use in worship on God concepts. *Journal of Psychology and Christianity, 15* (1), 38–45.

Bauer, P. J. & Wewerka, S. S. (1995). One- to two-year-olds' recall of events: The more expressed, the more impressed. *Journal of Experimental Child Psychology, 59,* 475–496.

Beecroft, R. (2014). *Effects of religious belief on teaching and learning of evolution in A-level biology.* Unpublished research project, University of Oxford.

Behl-Chadha, G. (1996). Basic-level and superordinate-like categorical representations in early infancy. *Cognition, 60,* 105–141.

Bering, J. M. (2006). The cognitive psychology of belief in the supernatural. *American Scientist, 94,* 142–149.

Berry, R. J. (1986). What to believe about miracles. *Nature, 322,* 321–322.

Bertenthal, B. I. (1996). Origins and early development of perception, action, and representation. *Annual Review of Psychology, 47,* 431–459.

Bishop, B. A. & Anderson, C. W. (1990). Student conceptions of natural selection and its role in evolution. *Journal of Research in Science Teaching, 27,* 415-428.

Blakemore, C. (2009, February 22). Science is just one gene away from defeating religion. *The Observer.* Online at http://www.guardian.co.uk/commentisfree/2009/feb/22/genetics-religion

Booth, A. (2008). The cause of infant categorization? *Cognition, 106,* 984–993.

Booth, A., Waxman, S., & Huang, Y. (2005). Conceptual information permeates word learning in infancy. *Developmental Psychology, 41,* 491–505.

Boyer, P. (1994a). Cognitive constraints on cultural representations: Natural ontologies and religious ideas. In L. A. Hirschfeld & S. A. Gelman (Eds.), *Mapping the mind: Domain specificity in cognition and culture* (pp. 391–411). Cambridge, UK: Cambridge University Press.

Boyer, P. (1994b). *The naturalness of religious ideas: A cognitive theory of religion.* Berkeley, CA: University of California Press.

Boyer, P. (1996). What makes anthropomorphism natural: Intuitive ontology and cultural representations. *Journal of the Royal Anthropological Institute (N. S.), 2,* 83–97.

Boyer, P. (2003). Religious thought and behaviour as by-products of brain function. *Trends in Cognitive Sciences, 7* (3), 119–124.

Boyer, P. & Ramble, C. (2001). Cognitive templates for religious concepts: Cross-cultural evidence for recall of counter-intuitive representations. *Cognitive Science, 25,* 535–564.

Boyer, P. & Walker, S. (2000). Intuitive ontology and cultural input in the acquisition of religious concepts. In K. S. Rosengren, C. N. Johnson, & P. L. Harris (Eds.), *Imagining the impossible: Magical, scientific, and religious thinking in children* (pp. 130–156). Cambridge, UK: Cambridge University Press.

Broadbent, D. (1972). *Behaviour.* London, UK: Methuen & Co.

Brooke, J. (1991). *Science and religion: Some historical perspectives.* Cambridge, UK: Cambridge University Press.

Brown, A. L., Metz, K. E., & Campione, J. C. (1996). Social interaction and individual understanding in a community of learners: The influence of Piaget and Vygotsky. In A. Tryphon & J. Vonéche (Eds.), *Piaget-Vygotsky: The social genesis of thought* (pp. 145–170). Hove, UK: Psychology Press.

Browne, C. A. & Woolley, J. D. (2004). Preschoolers' magical explanations for violations of physical, social, and mental laws. *Journal of Cognition and Development, 5* (2), 239–260.

Brush, S. (1992). How cosmology became a science. *Scientific American, 267,* 62–70.

Bryant, P. E. (1974). *Perception and understanding in young children.* London, UK: Methuen & Co.

Bryce, T. G. K. & Blown, E. J. (2013). Children's concepts of the shape and size of the earth, sun and moon. *International Journal of Science Education, 35* (3), 388–446.

Bullock, M. (1984). Preschool children's understanding of causal connections. *British Journal of Developmental Psychology, 2,* 139–148.

Bullock, M. (1985). Animism in childhood thinking: A new look at an old question. *Developmental Psychology, 21,* 217–225.

Bullock, M. & Gelman, R. (1979). Children's assumptions about cause and effect: Temporal ordering. *Child Development, 50,* 89–96.

Bullock, M., Gelman, R., & Baillargeon, R. (1982). The development of causal reasoning. In W. J. Friedman (Ed.), *The developmental psychology of time* (pp. 209–245). New York: Academic Press, Inc.

Caldwell-Harris, C. L. (2012). Understanding atheism / non-belief as an expected individual differences variable. *Religion, Brain & Behavior, 2* (1), 4–47.

Callanan, M. A. & Oakes, L. M. (1992). Preschoolers' questions and parents' explanations: Causal thinking in everyday activity. *Cognitive Development, 7,* 213–233.

Canfield, C. F. & Ganea, P. A. (2014). "You could call it magic". What parents and siblings tell pre-schoolers about unobservable entities. *Journal of Cognition and Development, 15* (2), 269–286.

Carey, S. (1985). *Conceptual change in childhood.* Cambridge, MA: The MIT Press.

Carey, S. (1988). Conceptual differences between children and adults. *Mind & Language, 3* (3), 167–181.

Carey, S. (1991). Knowledge acquisition: Enrichment or conceptual change? In S. Carey & R. Gelman (Eds.), *The epigenesis of mind: Essays on biology and cognition* (pp. 257–291). Hillsdale, NJ: Psychology Press.

Carey, S. (1992). The origin and evolution of everyday concepts. In R. Giere (Ed.), *Minnesota Studies in the Philosophy of Science: Cognitive models of science* (Vol. 15, pp. 89–128) Minneapolis, MN: University of Minnesota Press.

140 References

Carey, S. (1995). On the origin of causal understanding. In D. Sperber, D. Premack, & A. J. Premack (Eds.), *Causal cognition: A multidisciplinary debate* (pp. 268–308). Oxford, UK: Clarendon Press.

Carey, S. (2002). The origin of concepts: Continuing the conversation. In N. L. Stein, P. J. Bauer, & M. Rabinowitz (Eds.), *Representation, memory, and development: Essays in honor of Jean Mandler* (pp. 43–52). London, UK: Lawrence Erlbaum Associates.

Carey, S. & Spelke, E. (1994). Domain-specific knowledge and conceptual change. In L. A. Hirschfeld & S. A. Gelman (Eds.), *Mapping the mind: Domain specificity in cognition and culture* (pp. 169–200). Cambridge, UK: Cambridge University Press.

Carr, B. (2006). Cosmology and religion. In P. Clayton & Z. Simpson (Eds.), *The Oxford handbook of religion and science* (pp. 139–155). Oxford, UK: Oxford University Press.

Chandler, M. J. & Lalonde, C. E. (1994). Surprising, magical and miraculous turns of events: Children's reactions to violations of their early theories of mind and matter. *British Journal of Developmental Psychology, 12*, 83–95.

Chi, M. (1992). Conceptual change within and across ontological categories: Examples from learning and discovery in science. In R. Giere (Ed.), *Minnesota studies in the philosophy of science: Cognitive models of science* (Vol. 15, pp. 129–186).. Minneapolis, MN: University of Minnesota Press.

Chinn, C. A. & Brewer, W. F. (2000). Knowledge change in response to data in science, religion, and magic. In K. S. Rosengren, C. N. Johnson, & P. L. Harris (Eds.), *Imagining the impossible: Magical, scientific, and religious thinking in children* (pp. 334–371). Cambridge, UK: Cambridge University Press.

Cimpian, C. A. & Erickson, L. C. (2012). Remembering kinds: New evidence that categories are privileged in children's thinking. *Cognitive Psychology, 64*, 161–185.

Cimpian, A. & Petro, G. (2014). Building theory-based concepts: Four-year-olds preferentially seek explanations for features of kinds. *Cognition, 131*, 300–310.

Cohen, L. B. (1988). An information-processing approach to infant cognitive development. In L. Weiskrantz (Ed.), *Thought without language* (pp. 211–228). Oxford, UK: Clarendon Press.

Coles, P. (2005). The state of the universe. *Nature, 433*, 248–256.

Coley, J. D. (2000). On the importance of doing comparative research: The case of folk biology. *Child Development, 71* (1), 82–90.

Collins, F. S. (2007). *The language of God*. London, UK: Pocket Books.

Coltheart, M. (2006). What has functional neuroimaging told us about the mind (so far)? *Cortex, 42*, 323–331.

Concise Oxford English Dictionary, 9th edition. (1995). Oxford, UK: Clarendon Press.

Corrigan, R. & Denton, P. (1996). Causal understanding as a developmental primitive. *Developmental Review, 16*, 162–202.

Corriveau, K. H., Chen, E. E., & Harris, P. L. (2014). Judgments about fact and fiction by children from religious and nonreligious backgrounds. *Cognitive Science, 1 – 30.* DOI:10.1111/cogs.12138

Currie-Jedermann, J. L. (1984). The role of function in conceptual development. *Canadian Journal of Behavioral Science, 16* (2), 83–98.

Cyranoski, D. (2010). Japanese view of the natural world. *Nature, 466*, 1046.

Dawkins, R. (2006). *The God delusion*. London, UK: Bantam Press.

Dehaene-Lambertz, G., Dehaene, S., & Hertz-Pannier, L. (2002). Functional neuroimaging of speech perception in infants. *Science, 298*, 2013–2015.

Denney, N. W. & Acito, M. A. (1984). Classification training in 2- and 3-year-old children. *Journal of Experimental Child Psychology, 17*, 37–48.

Dolgin, K. G. & Behrend, D. A. (1984). Children's knowledge about animates and inanimates. *Child Development, 55,* 1646–1650.

Doumas, L. A. A., Hummel, J. E. & Sandhofer, C. M. (2008). A theory of the discovery and predication of relational concepts. *Psychological Review, 115* (1), 1–43.

Dvorakova, L. (2011). *Anthropomorphism in God concepts.* Unpublished MSc dissertation, University of Oxford.

Einstein, A. (1940). Science and religion. *Nature, 3706,* 605–607.

Elkind, D. (1970). The origins of religion in the child. *Review of Religious Research, 12,* 25–42.

Ellis, G. & Silk, J. (2014). Defend the integrity of physics. *Nature, 516,* 321–323.

Elman, J. L. (2005). Connectionist models of cognitive development: Where next? *Trends in Cognitive Sciences, 9* (3), 111–117.

Elman, J. L., Bates, E. A., Johnson, M. H., Karmiloff-Smith, A., Parisi, D., & Plunkett, K. (1996). *Rethinking innateness: A connectionist perspective on development.* Cambridge, MA: The MIT Press.

Emmet, D. (1966). *The nature of metaphysical thinking.* London, UK: Macmillan.

Emmons, N. A. & Kelemen, D. (2014). Development of children's pre-life reasoning. *Child Development, 85* (4), 1617–1633.

Erickson, J. E., Keil, F. C., & Lockhart, K. L. (2010). Sensing the coherence of biology in contrast to psychology: Young children's use of causal relations to distinguish two fundamental domains. *Child Development, 81* (1), 390–409.

Estes, D. & Bartsch, K. (1997). Constraining the brain: The role of developmental psychology in developmental cognitive neuroscience. *Behavioral and Brain Sciences, 20* (4), 562–563.

Estes, D., Wellman, H. M., & Woolley, J. D. (1989). Children's understanding of mental phenomena. In H. W. Reese (Ed.), *Advances in child development and behavior* (Vol. 22, pp. 41–87). San Diego, CA: Academic Press.

Evans, E. M. (2000). The emergence of beliefs about origins of species in school-age children. *Merrill-Palmer Quarterly, 46* (2), 221–254.

Evans, E. M. (2001). Cognitive and contextual factors in the emergence of diverse belief systems: Creation versus evolution. *Cognitive Psychology, 42,* 217–266.

Evans, E. M. (2008). Conceptual change and evolutionary biology: A developmental analysis. In S. Vosniadou (Ed.), *International handbook of research on conceptual change* (pp. 263–294). New York, NY: Routledge.

Fagg, L. W. (2003). Are there intimations of divine transcendence in the physical world? *Zygon, 38* (3), 559–572.

Farrer, A. (1967). *Faith and speculation.* London, UK: Adam & Charles Black.

Ferré, F. (1984). In praise of anthropomorphism. *International Journal for Philosophy of Religion, 16,* 203–212.

Fontana Dictionary of Modern Thought. (1979). London, UK: Fontana Books.

Franks Davis, C. (1989). *The evidential force of religious experience.* Oxford, UK: Clarendon Press.

Frazier, B. N., Gelman, S. A., & Wellman, H. M. (2009). Preschoolers' search for explanatory information within adult-child conversation. *Child Development, 80* (6), 1592–1611.

Friedman, W. J. (2001). The development of an intuitive understanding of entropy. *Child Development, 72* (2), 460–473.

Gelman, R. (1990). First principles organize attention to and learning about relevant data: Number and the animate-inanimate distinction as examples. *Cognitive Science, 14,* 79–106.

142 References

Gelman, R. (1991). Epigenetic foundations of knowledge structures: Initial and transcendent constructions. In S. Carey & R. Gelman (Eds.), *The epigenesis of mind: Essays on biology and cognition* (pp. 293–322). Hillsdale, NJ: Psychology Press.

Gelman, R. (2000). Domain specificity and variability in cognitive development. *Child Development, 71* (4), 854–856.

Gelman, R. (2002). On animates and other worldly things. In N. L. Stein, P. J. Bauer, & M. Rabinowitz (Eds.), *Representation, memory, and development: Essays in honor of Jean Mandler* (pp. 75–87). London, UK: Lawrence Erlbaum Associates.

Gelman, R. & Brenneman, K. (1994). First principles can support both universal and culture-specific learning about number and music. In L. A. Hirschfeld & S. A. Gelman (Eds.), *Mapping the mind: Domain specificity in cognition and culture* (pp. 369–390). Cambridge, UK: Cambridge University Press.

Gelman, R., Spelke, E. S., & Meck, E. (1983). What pre-schoolers know about animate and inanimate objects. In D. Rogers & J. A. Sloboda (Eds.), *The acquisition of symbolic skills* (pp. 297–326). New York, NY: Plenum Publishing Corporation.

Gelman, S. A. (1988a). Children's expectations concerning natural kind categories. *Human Development, 31*, 28–34.

Gelman, S. A. (1988b). The development of induction within natural kind and artifact categories. *Cognitive Psychology, 20*, 65–95.

Gelman, S. A., Coley, J. D., & Gottfried, G. M. (1994). Essentialist beliefs in children: The acquisition of concepts and theories. In L. A. Hirschfeld & S. A. Gelman (Eds.), *Mapping the mind: Domain specificity in cognition and culture* (pp. 341–365). Cambridge, UK: Cambridge University Press.

Gelman, S. A. & Koenig, M. A. (2003). Theory-based categorisation in early childhood. In D. H. Rakison & L. M. Oakes (Eds.), *Early category and concept development: Making sense of the blooming, buzzing confusion* (pp. 330–359). London, UK: Oxford University Press.

Gelman, S. A. & Kremer, K. E. (1991). Understanding natural cause: Children's explanations of how objects and their properties originate. *Child Development, 62*, 396–414.

Gelman, S. A. & Noles, N. S. (2011). Domains and naïve theories. *WIREs Cognitive Science, 2*, 490–502.

Gelman, S. A. & Opfer, J. E. (2002). Development of the animate-inanimate distinction. In U. Goswami (Ed.), *Blackwell handbook of childhood cognitive development* (pp. 151–166). Malden, MA: Blackwell Publishers.

Gentner, D., Anggoro, F. K., & Klibanoff, R. S. (2011). Structure mapping and relational language support children's learning of relational categories. *Child Development, 82* (4), 1173–1188.

Gervais, W. M. & Norenzayan, A. (2012). Analytic thinking promotes religious disbelief. *Science, 236*, 493–496.

Gibbs, W. W. (1998). Beyond physics. *Scientific American*, August, 20–22.

Giménez-Dasi, M., Guerrero, S., & Harris, P. L. (2005). Intimations of immortality and omniscience in early childhood. *European Journal of Developmental Psychology, 2* (3), 285–297.

Gobbini, M. A., Gentili, C., Ricciardi, E., Bellucci, C., Salvini, P., Laschi, C., Guazzelli, M., & Pietrini, P. (2011). Distinct neural systems involved in agency and animacy detection. *Journal of Cognitive Neuroscience, 23* (8), 1911–1920.

Goedert, K. M., Ellefson, M. R., & Rehder, B. (2014). Differences in the weighting and choice of evidence for plausible versus implausible causes. *Journal of Experimental Psychology: Learning, Memory, and Cognition, 40* (3), 683–702.

Goldman, R. (1964). *Religious thinking from childhood to adolescence*. London, UK: Routledge.

References 143

Goldstone, R. L. (1994). The role of similarity in categorization: providing a groundwork. *Cognition*, *52*, 125–157.

Goldwater, M. B. & Gentner, D. (2015). On the acquisition of abstract knowledge: Structural alignment and explication in learning causal system categories. *Cognition*, *137*, 137–153.

Golinkoff, R. M., Harding, C. G., Carlson, V., & Sexton, M. E. (1984). The infant's perception of causal events: The distinction between animate and inanimate objects. In L. P. Lipsitt & C. Royce-Collier (Eds.), *Advances in infancy research* (Vol. 3, pp. 145–151). Norwood, NJ: Ablex Publishing Corporation.

Gopnik, A., Sobel, D. M., Schultz, L. E., & Glymour, C. (2001). Causal learning mechanisms in very young children: Two-, three-, and four-year-olds infer causal relations from patterns of variation and covariation. *Developmental Psychology*, *37* (5), 620–629.

Gopnik, A. & Wellman, H. M. (1994). The theory theory. In L. A. Hirschfeld & S. A. Gelman (Eds.), *Mapping the mind: Domain specificity in cognition and culture* (pp. 257–293). New York, NY: Cambridge University Press.

Goswami, U. (1992). *Analogical reasoning in children*. Hove, UK: LEA Publishers.

Goswami, U. (2001). Analogical reasoning in children. In D. Gentner, K. Holyoak, & B. Kokinov (Eds.), *The analogical mind: Perspectives from cognitive science* (pp. 437–470). Cambridge, MA: MIT Press.

Gould, S. J. (1997). Nonoverlapping magisteria. *Natural History*, *106*, 16–22.

Grayling A. C. (2012). *The Oxford Student*, 26th April. Interview with Susheel Gokarakonda, pp. 20–21.

Greif, M. L., Kemler Nelson, D. G., Keil, F. C., & Gutierrez, F. (2006). What do children want to know about animals and artifacts? Domain-specific requests for information. *Psychological Science*, *17* (6), 455–459.

Gross, N. & Simmons, S. (2009). The religiosity of American college and university professors. *Sociology of Religion*, *70* (2), 101–129.

Guerrero, S., Enesco, I., & Harris, P. L. (2010). Oxygen and the soul: Children's conceptions of invisible entities. *Journal of Cognition and Culture*, *10*, 123–151.

Guilford, J. P. (1967). *The nature of human intelligence*. New York, NY: McGraw-Hill Book Co.

Guthrie, S. E. (1980). A cognitive theory of religion. *Current Anthropology*, *21* (2), 181–203.

Haldane, J. S. (1924). Biology and religion. *Nature*, *2865* (114), 468–471.

Halliwell, J. (1991). Quantum cosmology and the creation of the universe. *Scientific American*, December, 76–85.

Hardon, J. A. (1965). *Religions of the world*. London, UK: Robert Hale Ltd.

Harré, R. (1983). *The philosophies of science*. Oxford, UK: Oxford University Press.

Harré, R. (1986). *Varieties of realism*. Oxford, UK: Basil Blackwell.

Harré, R. (1993). *Laws of nature*. London, UK: Duckworth.

Harré, R. & Madden, E. H. (1975). *Causal powers*. Oxford, UK: Blackwell.

Harris, P. L. (1997). The last of the magicians? Children, scientists, and the invocation of hidden causal powers. *Child Development*, *68* (6), 1018–1020.

Harris, P. L. (2000). On not falling down to earth: Children's metaphysical questions. In K. S. Rosengren, C. N. Johnson, & P. L. Harris (Eds.), *Imagining the impossible: Magical, scientific, and religious thinking in children* (pp. 157–178). Cambridge, UK: Cambridge University Press.

Harris, P. L. & Koenig, M. (2006). Trust in testimony: How children learn about science and religion. *Child Development*, *77* (3), 505–524.

Harris, P. L., Pasquini, E. S., Duke, S., Asscher, J. J., & Pons, F. (2006). Germs and angels: The role of testimony in young children's ontology. *Developmental Science*, *9* (1), 76–96.

144 References

Hatano, G. & Inagaki, K. (1994). Young children's naïve theory of biology. *Cognition*, *50*, 171–188.

Hatano, G., Siegler, R. S., Richards, D. D., Inagaki, K., Stavy, R., & Wax, N. (1993). The development of biological knowledge: A multi-national study. *Cognitive Development*, *8*, 47–62.

Hawking, S. (1988). *A brief history of time*. London, UK: Bantam Books.

Hegel, G. W. F. (1959). *Encyclopedia of Philosophy* (transl. G. E. Mueller). New York, NY: Philosophical Library.

Helm, P. (1991). The miraculous. *Science & Christian Belief*, *3* (1), 83–95.

Hickling, A. K. & Gelman, S. A. (1995). How does your garden grow? Early conceptualization of seeds and their place in the plant growth cycle. *Child Development*, *66* (3), 856–876.

Holyoak, K. J. & Cheng, P. W. (2011). Causal learning and inference as a rational process: The new synthesis. *Annual Review of Psychology*, *62*, 135–163.

Holyoak, K. J. & Thagard, P. (1995). *Mental leaps: Analogy in creative thought*. Cambridge, MA: The MIT Press.

Hospers, J. (1984). *An introduction to philosophical analysis*. 2nd ed. London, UK: Routledge & Kegan Paul.

Huang, I. (1930). Children's explanations of strange phenomena. *Psychologische Forschung*, *14*, 63–182.

Huang, I. (1943). Children's conception of physical causality: A critical summary. *Journal of Genetic Psychology*, *63*, 71–121.

Humphreys, C. (2003). *The miracles of Exodus: A scientist's discovery of the extraordinary natural causes of the Biblical stories*. London, UK: Continuum.

Hunter, M. (2009). *Boyle: Between God and science*. New Haven, CT & London, UK: Yale University Press.

Inagaki, K. & Hatano, G. (1987). Young children's spontaneous personification as analogy. *Child Development*, *58*, 1013–1020.

Inagaki, K. & Hatano, G. (1991). Constrained person analogy in young children's biological knowledge. *Cognitive Development*, *6*, 219–231.

Isaacs, S. (1929). Critical notes: The child's conception of the world, by Piaget. *Mind*, *38*, 506–513.

James, E. O. (1961). *Comparative religion*. London, UK: Methuen.

James, W. (1902/1979). *The varieties of religious experience: A study in human nature*. Glasgow, UK: Collins Sons & Co.

Johnson, C. N. (1997). Crazy children, fantastical theories, and the many uses of metaphysics. *Child Development*, *68*, 1024–1026.

Johnson, M. H., Bates, L., Elman, J., Karmiloff-Smith, A., & Plunkett, K. (1997). Constraints on the construction of cognition. *Behavioral and Brain Sciences*, *20* (4), 569–570.

Kalish, C. W. & Gelman, S. A. (1992). On wooden pillows: Multiple classifications and children's category-based inductions. *Child Development*, *63*, 1536–1557.

Kant, I. (1983). *The critique of pure reason* (transl. N. Kemp Smith). London, UK: The Macmillan Press.

Kawasaki, K. (1990). A hidden conflict between Western and traditional concepts of nature in science education in Japan. *Bulletin of the School of Education, Okayama University*, *33*, 203–214.

Keil, F. C. (1979). *Semantic and conceptual development: An ontological perspective*. Cambridge, MA: Harvard University Press.

Keil, F. C. (1981a). Constraints on knowledge and cognitive development. *Psychological Review*, *88* (3), 197–227.

Keil, F. C. (1981b). Children's thinking: What never develops? *Cognition*, *10*, 159–166.

Keil, F. C. (1983). On the emergence of semantic and conceptual distinctions. *Journal of Experimental Psychology: General*, *112* (3), 357–385.

Keil, F. C. (1986). The acquisition of natural kind and artifact terms. In W. Demopoulos & A. Marras (Eds.), *Language learning and concept acquisition* (pp. 133–153). Norwood, NJ: Ablex Publishing Corporation.

Keil, F. C. (1989). *Concepts, kinds, and cognitive development*. Cambridge, MA: The MIT Press.

Keil, F. C. (1991). The emergence of theoretical beliefs as constraints on concepts. In S. Carey & R. Gelman (Eds.), *The epigenesis of mind: Essays on biology and cognition* (pp. 237–256). Hillsdale, NJ: Psychology Press.

Keil, F. C. (1995). The growth of causal understanding of natural kinds. In D. Sperber, D. Premack, & A. J. Premack (Eds.), *Symposia of the Fyssen Foundation: Causal cognition: A multidisciplinary debate* (pp. 234–267). Oxford, UK: Clarendon Press.

Keil, F. C. (2012). Running on empty? How folk science gets by with less. *Current Directions in Psychological Science*, *21* (5), 329–334.

Keil, F. C. & Silberstein, C. S. (1996). Schooling and the acquisition of theoretical knowledge. In D. R. Olson & N. Torrance (Eds.), *The handbook of education and human development: New models of learning, teaching and schooling* (pp. 621–645). Oxford, UK: Blackwell Publishers.

Kelemen, D. (1999a). The scope of teleological thinking in preschool children. *Cognition*, *70*, 241–272.

Kelemen, D. (1999b). Why are rocks pointy? Children's preference for teleological explanations of the natural world. *Developmental Psychology*, *35* (6), 1440–1452.

Kelemen, D., Callanan, M. A., Casler, K., & Pérez-Granados, D. R. (2005). Why things happen: Teleological explanation in parent–child conversations. *Developmental Psychology*, *41* (1), 251–264.

Kelemen, D. & DiYanni, C. (2005). Intuitions about origins: Purpose and intelligent design in children's reasoning about nature. *Journal of Cognition and Development*, *6* (1), 3–31.

Kellert, S. R. (1991). Japanese perceptions of wildlife. *Conservation Biology*, *5* (3), 297–308.

Kiessling, F. & Perner, J. (2014). God-mother-baby: What children think they know. *Child Development*, *85* (4), 1601–1616.

Kikas, E. (1998). The impact of teaching on students' definitions and explanations of astronomical phenomena. *Learning and Instruction*, *8* (5), 439–454.

Knight, N., Sousa, P., Barrett, J. L., & Atran, S. (2004). Children's attributions of beliefs to humans and God: Cross-cultural evidence. *Cognitive Science*, *28*, 117–126.

Kobayashi, S. (1993). *Savages in a civilised society: Young people's drift away from science and technology*. International Symposium for the Public Understanding of Science and Technology and Science and Mathematics Education of Youth. Science Museum, Tokyo, Japan (October 2–5, 1992).

Koslowski, B. & Masnick, A. (2002). The development of causal reasoning. In U. Goswami (Ed.), *Blackwell handbook of childhood cognitive development* (pp. 257–281). Oxford, UK: Blackwell Publishers Ltd.

Kosugi, D., Ishida, H., & Fujita, K. (2003). 10-month old infants' inference of invisible agent: Distinction in causality between object motion and human action. *Japanese Psychological Research*, *45* (1), 15–24.

Kotovsky, L. & Gentner, D. (1996). Comparison and categorization in the development of relational similarity. *Child Development*, *67*, 2797–2822.

Kuhn, D. (1989). Children and adults as intuitive scientists. *Psychological Review*, *96* (4), 674–689.

146 References

Kuhn, D. (2002). What is scientific thinking and how does it develop? In U. Goswami (Ed.), *Blackwell handbook of childhood cognitive development* (pp. 371–393). Oxford, UK: Blackwell Publishers Ltd.

Kuhn, D. (2012). The development of causal reasoning. *WIREs Cognitive Science*, 3, 327–335. DOI:10.1002/wcs.1160

Kurtz, K. J., Boukrina, O., & Gentner, D. (2013). Comparison promotes learning and transfer of relational categories. *Journal of Experimental Psychology: Learning, Memory and Cognition*, 39 (4), 1303–1310.

Kuzmak, S. D. & Gelman, R. (1986). Young children's understanding of random phenomena. *Child Development*, 57, 559–566.

Lane, J. D. & Harris, P. L. (2014). Confronting, representing, and believing counterintuitive concepts: Navigating the natural and the supernatural. *Perspectives on Psychological Science*, 9 (2), 144–160.

Lane, J. D., Wellman, H. M., & Evans, E. M. (2010). Children's understanding of ordinary and extraordinary minds. *Child Development*, 81 (5), 1475–1489.

Lane, J. D., Wellman, H. M., & Evans, E. M. (2012). Sociocultural input facilitates children's developing understanding of extraordinary minds. *Child Development*, 83 (3), 1007–1021.

Larson, E. J. & Witham, L. (1999). Scientists and religion in America. *Scientific American*, September, 78–83.

Leddon, E. M., Waxman, S. R., & Medin, D. L. (2008). Unmasking "alive": Children's appreciation of a concept linking all living things. *Journal of Cognition and Development*, 9 (4), 461–473.

Legare, C. H. & Gelman, S. A. (2008). Bewitchment, biology, or both: The co-existence of natural and supernatural explanatory frameworks across development. *Cognitive Science*, 32, 607–642.

Lennox, J. (2009). *God's undertaker: Has science buried God?* 2nd ed. Oxford, UK: Lion Hudson Plc.

Leroux, G., Spiess, J., Zago, L., Rossi, S., Lubin, A., Turbelin, M., Mazoyer, B., Tzourio-Mazoyer, N., Houdé, O., & Joliot, M. (2009). Adult brains don't fully overcome biases that lead to incorrect performance during cognitive development: An fMRI study in young infants completing a Piaget-like task. *Developmental Science*, 12 (2), 326–338.

Leslie, A. M. (1988). The necessity of illusion: Perception and thought in infancy. In L. Weiskrantz (Ed.), *Thought without language* (pp. 185–210). Oxford, UK: Clarendon Press.

Leslie, A. M. (1995). A theory of agency. In D. Sperber, D. Premack, & A. J. Premack (Eds.), *Causal cognition: A multidisciplinary debate* (pp. 121–149). Oxford, UK: Clarendon Press.

Lindsay, A. D. (1934). *Kant*. London, UK: Ernest Benn.

Lloyd, G. (1995). Ancient Greek concepts of causation in comparativist perspective. In D. Sperber, D. Premack, & A. J. Premack (Eds.), *Causal cognition: A multidisciplinary debate* (pp. 536–556). Oxford, UK: Clarendon Press.

Lombrozo, T. (2006). The structure and function of explanations. *Trends in Cognitive Sciences*, 10 (10), 464–470.

Lombrozo, T. (2007). Simplicity and probability in causal explanation. *Cognitive Psychology*, 55, 232–257.

McCauley, R. N. (2000). The naturalness of religion and the unnaturalness of science. In F. C. Keil & ilson R. A. W (Eds.), *Explanation and cognition* (pp. 61–85). Cambridge, MA: The MIT Press.

McGrath, A. E. (2001). *A scientific theology: Nature, Part 1*. Edinburgh, UK: T & T Clark.

McLeish, T. (2014). *Faith and wisdom in science*. Oxford, UK: Oxford University Press.

Makris, N. & Pnevmatikos, D. (2007). Children's understanding of human and supernatural mind. *Cognitive Development, 22*, 365–375.

Mameli, M. & Bateson, P. (2006). Innateness in the sciences. *Biology & Philosophy, 21*, 155–188.

Mandler, J. M. (1988). How to build a baby: On the development of an accessible representational system. *Cognitive Development, 3*, 113–136.

Mandler, J. M. (1990). A new perspective on cognitive development in infancy. *American Scientist, 78*, 236–243.

Mandler, J. M. (1999). Seeing is not the same as thinking: Commentary on "Making sense of infant categorization". *Developmental Review, 19*, 297–306.

Mandler, J. M. (2000). Perceptual and conceptual processes in infancy. *Journal of Cognition and Development, 1*, 3–36.

Mandler, J. M. (2004). Thought before language. *Trends in Cognitive Sciences, 8* (11), 508–513.

Mandler, J. M. (2012). On the spatial foundations of the conceptual system and its enrichment. *Cognitive Science, 36*, 421–451.

Mandler, J. M. & McDonough, L. (1993). Concept formation in infancy. *Cognitive Development, 8*, 291–318.

Mandler, J. M. & McDonough, L. (1998). On developing a knowledge base in infancy. *Developmental Psychology, 34*, 1274–1278.

Margett, T. E. & Witherington, D. C. (2011). The nature of preschoolers' concepts of living and artificial objects. *Child Development, 82* (6), 2067–2082.

Markman, E., Cox, B., & Machida, S. (1981). The standard object-sorting task as a measure of conceptual organisation. *Developmental Psychology, 17* (1), 115–117.

Massey, C. & Gelman, R. (1988). Preschoolers' ability to decide whether a photographed unfamiliar object can move itself. *Developmental Psychology, 24*, 307–317.

Matan, A. & Carey, S. (2001). Developmental changes within the core of artifact concepts. *Cognition, 78*, 1–26.

Matsumoto, S. (1996). Introduction. In N. Tamaru & D. Reid (Eds.), *Religion in Japanese culture* (pp. 13–26). Tokyo, Japan: Kodanisha International.

Matthews, G. B. (1980). *Philosophy and the young child*. Cambridge, MA: Harvard University Press.

Mayr, E. (1961). Cause and effect in biology. *Science, 134*, 1501–1506.

Medawar, P. (1984). *The limits of science*. New York, NY: Harper & Row.

Medin, D. (1989). Concepts and conceptual structure. *American Psychologist, 44*, 1469–1481.

Meltzoff, A. N. (1990). Towards a developmental cognitive science. In The development of neural bases of higher cognitive functions, *Annals of the New York Academy of Sciences, 608*, 1–37.

Meltzoff, A. N. (2002). Imitation as a mechanism of social cognition: Origins of empathy, theory of mind, and the representation of action. In U. Goswami (Ed.), *Blackwell handbook of childhood cognitive development* (pp. 6–25). Oxford, UK: Blackwell Publishers Ltd.

Miller, G. A. (2010). Mistreating psychology in the decades of the brain. *Perspectives on Psychological Science, 5* (6), 716–743.

Mitchell, B. (1973). *The justification of religious belief*. London, UK: Macmillan.

Mitchell, J. P., Heatherton, T. F., & Macrae, C. N. (2002). Distinct neural systems subserve person and object knowledge. *PNAS, 99* (23), 15238–15243.

148 References

Moore, A. (2010). Should Christians do natural theology? *Scottish Journal of Theology*, *63* (2), 127–145.

Morrison, P. & Gardner, H. (1978). Dragons and dinosaurs: The child's capacity to differentiate fantasy from reality. *Child Development*, *49*, 642–648.

Murphy, G. L. & Medin, D. L. (1985). The role of theories in conceptual coherence. *Psychological Review*, *92* (3), 289–316.

Nadelson, L. S. & Sinatra, G. M. (2009). Educational professionals' knowledge and acceptance of evolution. *Evolutionary Psychology*, *7* (4), 490–516.

Nakamura, H. (1964/1985). *Ways of thinking of Eastern peoples: India-China-Tibet- Japan.* Honolulu, HI: University of Hawaii Press.

Needham, A. W. (2016). *Learning about objects in infancy.* Florence, Italy: Taylor & Francis.

Nelson, K. (2011). "Concept" is a useful concept in developmental research. *Journal of Theoretical and Philosophical Psychology*, *31* (2), 96–101.

Nelson, K. & Ware, A. (2002). The reemergence of function. In N. L. Stein, P. J. Bauer, & M. Rabinowitz (Eds.), *Representation, memory, and development: Essays in honor of Jean Mandler* (pp. 161–184). Mahwah, NJ: LEA Publishers.

Newcombe, N. S. (2002). The nativist-empiricist controversy in the context of recent research on spatial and quantitative development. *Psychological Science*, *13* (5), 395–401.

Nye, W. C. & Carlson, J. S. (1984). The development of the concept of God in children. *The Journal of Genetic Psychology*, *145*, 137–142.

Ochiai, M. (1989). The role of knowledge in the development of life concept. *Human Development*, *32*, 72–78.

Ogawa, M. (1986). Toward a new rationale of science education in a non-western society. *European Journal of Science Education*, *8* (2), 113–119.

Ogawa, M. (1998). A cultural history of science education in Japan: An epic description. In W. W. Cobern (Ed.), *Socio-cultural perspectives on science education* (pp. 139–161). London, UK: Kluwer Academic Publishers.

Ono, S. (1962). *Shinto.* Tokyo, Japan: Charles E. Tuttle Publishing Co.

Otto, R. (1979). *The idea of the holy.* Oxford, UK: Oxford University Press.

Passingham, R. E. & Rowe, J. B. (2015). *A short guide to brain imaging.* Oxford, UK: Oxford University Press.

Pauen, S. (2002). Evidence for knowledge-based category discrimination in infancy. *Child Development*, *73* (4), 1016–1033.

Peacocke, A. R. (1993). *Theology for a scientific age: Being and becoming – natural, divine and human.* London, UK: SCM.

Petrovich, O. (1988). *An examination of Piaget's theory of childhood artificialism.* Unpublished D.Phil. thesis, University of Oxford.

Petrovich, O. (1997). Understanding of non-natural causality in children and adults: A case against artificialism. *Psyche en Geloof*, *8*, 151–165.

Petrovich, O. (1999). Preschool children's understanding of the dichotomy between the natural and the artificial. *Psychological Reports*, *84*, 3–27.

Petrovich, O. (2008). Natural theological understanding in children from different religious cultures: Evidence and theory. Keynote lecture, "Spirituality, human development and well-being" conference, 24–25 July, University of Western Sydney, Australia.

Piaget, J. (1924). Etude Critique: L'Experience Humaine et la Causalité Physique de Leon Brunschvicg. *Journal de Psychologie Normal et Pathologique*, *21*, 586–607.

Piaget, J. (1925). La representation du monde chez l'enfant. *Revue de Theologie et de Philosophie*, *13*, 191–214.

Piaget, J. (1977). *The child's conception of the world.* St. Albans, UK: Palladin.

Piaget, J. & Kraft, H. (1925). De quelques forms primitives de causalité chez l'enfant. Phénoménisme et efficace. *L'Année Psychologique, 26*, 31–71.

Pinker, S. (2006). The evolutionary psychology of religion. In P. McNamara (Ed.), *Where God and science meet: How brain and evolutionary studies alter our understanding of religion* (Vol. 1, pp. 1–9). Westport, CT: Praeger Publishers.

Polkinghorne, J. (1987). *One world: The interaction of science and theology.* London, UK: SPCK.

Polkinghorne, J. (2002). The credibility of the miraculous. *Zygon, 37* (3), 751–757.

Pratt, C. & Bryant, P. E. (1990). Young children understand that looking leads to knowing (so long as they are looking into a single barrel). *Child Development, 61,* 973–982.

Proudfoot, W. (1985). *Religious experience.* Berkeley, CA: University of California Press.

Quartz, S. R. (1993). Nativism, neural networks, and the plausibility of constructivism. *Cognition, 48,* 223–242.

Quartz, S. R. (1999). The constructivist brain. *Trends in Cognitive Sciences, 3* (2), 48–57.

Quartz, S. R. & Sejnowski, T. J. (1997). The neural basis of cognitive development: A constructivist manifesto. *Behavioral and Brain Sciences, 20,* 537–596.

Quinn, P. C. (2002a). Category representation in young infants. *Current Directions in Psychological Science, 11* (2), 66–70.

Quinn, P. C. (2002b). Early categorization: A new synthesis. In U. Goswami (Ed.), *Blackwell handbook of childhood cognitive development* (pp. 84–101). Oxford, UK: Blackwell Publishers Ltd.

Rakison, D. H. & Yermolayeva, Y. (2010). Infant categorisation. *WIREs Cognitive Science, 1,* 894–905.

Rees, M. (1999). *Just six numbers.* London, UK: Weidenfeld & Nicholson.

Rees, M. (2011). *The Romanes Lecture,* 2 November, University of Oxford.

Rhodes, M., Gelman, S. A., & Karuza, J. C. (2014). Preschool ontology: The role of beliefs about category boundaries in early categorization. *Journal of Cognition and Development, 15* (1), 78–93.

Richards, D. D. (1989). The relationship between the attributes of life and life judgements. *Human Development, 32,* 95–103.

Richards, D. D. & Siegler, R. S. (1986). Children's understanding of the attributes of life. *Journal of Experimental Child Psychology, 42,* 1–22.

Roberts, K. & Cuff, M. D. (1989). Categorisation studies of 9- to 15-month-old infants: Evidence for superordinate categorisation? *Infant Behavior and Development, 12,* 265–288.

Rosch, E., Mervis, C. B., Gray, W. D., Johnson, D. M., & Boyes-Braem, P. (1976). Basic objects in natural categories. *Cognitive Psychology, 8,* 382–439.

Rosengren, K. S. & Hickling, A. K. (2000). Metamorphosis and magic: The development of children's thinking about possible events and plausible mechanisms. In K. S. Rosengren, C. N. Johnson, & P. L. Harris (Eds.), *Imagining the impossible: Magical, scientific and religious thinking in children* (pp. 75–98). Cambridge, UK: Cambridge University Press.

Ross, G. (1980). Categorization in 1- to 2-year-olds. *Developmental Psychology, 16,* 391–396.

Saxe, R., Tenenbaum, J. B., & Carey, S. (2005). Secret agents: Inferences about hidden causes by 10- and 12-month-old infants. *Psychological Science, 6* (12), 995–1001.

Schaefer, L. (2008). Nonempirical reality: Transcending the physical and spiritual in the order of the one. *Zygon, 43* (2), 329–352.

Scholl, B. J. (1997). Neural constraints or cognitive modularity? *Behavioral and Brain Sciences, 20* (4), 575–576.

150 References

Schulz, L. E. (2012). The origins of enquiry: Inductive inference and exploration in early childhood. *Trends in Cognitive Sciences, 16* (7), 382–389.

Schulz, L. E., Goodman, N. D., Tenenbaum, J. B., & Jenkins, A. C. (2008). Going beyond the evidence: Abstract laws and preschoolers' responses to anomalous data. *Cognition, 109,* 211–223.

Shtulman, A. (2012). Scientific knowledge suppresses but does not supplant earlier intuitions. *Cognition, 124,* 209–215.

Shtulman, A. & Carey, S. (2007). Improbable or impossible? How children reason about the possibility of extraordinary events. *Child Development, 78* (3), 1015–1032.

Shultz, T. R. (1982). Causal reasoning in the social and non-social realms. *Canadian Journal of Behavioural Science, 14,* 307–322.

Shultz, T. R. & Kestenbaum, N. R. (1985). Causal reasoning in children. *Annals of Child Development, 2,* 195–249.

Shultz, T. R. & Mareschal, D. (1997). Rethinking innateness, learning, and constructivism: Connectionist perspectives on development. *Cognitive Development, 12,* 467–490.

Shultz, T. R. & Shamash, F. (1981). The child's conception of intending act and consequence. *Canadian Journal of Behavioral Science, 13* (4), 368–372.

Siegal, M., Butterworth, G., & Newcombe, P. A. (2004). Culture and children's cosmology. *Developmental Science, 7* (3), 308–324.

Siegal, M., Nobes, G., & Panagiotaki, G. (2011). Children's knowledge of the Earth. *Nature Geoscience, 4,* 130–132.

Simons, D. J. & Keil, F. C. (1995). An abstract to concrete shift in the development of biological thought: The *insides* story. *Cognition, 56,* 129–163.

Sloutsky, V. (2009). Theories about "theories": Where is the explanation? *Trends in Cognitive Sciences, 13* (8), 331–332.

Sobel, D. M. & Buchanan, D. W. (2009). Bridging the gap: Causality-at-a-distance in children's categorization and inferences about internal properties. *Cognitive Development, 24,* 274–283.

Soskice, J. M. (1985). *Metaphor and religious language.* Oxford, UK: Clarendon Press.

Southcott, R. & Downie, J. R. (2012). Evolution and religion: Attitudes of Scottish bioscience students to the teaching of evolutionary biology. *Evo Edu Outreach, 5,* 301–311. DOI:10.1007/s12052-012-0419-9

Spelke, E. S. (1991). Physical knowledge in infancy: Reflections on Piaget's theory. In S. Carey & R. Gelman (Eds.), *The epigenesis of mind: Essays on biology and cognition* (pp. 133–169). Hillsdale, NJ: Psychology Press.

Spelke, E. S. (1994). Initial knowledge: Six suggestions. *Cognition, 50,* 431–445.

Spelke, E. S. (2000). Nativism, empiricism, and the origins of knowledge. In D. Muir & A. Slater (Eds.), *Infant development: The essential readings* (pp. 36–51). Oxford, UK: Blackwell.

Spelke, E. S. & Hespos, S. J. (2002). Conceptual development in infancy: The case of containment. In N. L. Stein, P. J. Bauer, & M. Rabinowitz (Eds.), *Representation, memory, and development: Essays in honor of Jean Mandler* (pp. 223–246). London, UK: Lawrence Erlbaum Associates.

Spelke, E. & Kinzler, K. (2007). Core knowledge. *Developmental Science, 10* (1), 89–96.

Sperber, D., Premack, D., & Premack, A. J. (1995). *Causal cognition: A multidisciplinary debate.* Oxford, UK: Clarendon Press.

Springer, K. & Keil, F. C. (1989). On the development of biologically specific beliefs: The case of inheritance. *Child Development, 60,* 637–648.

Stavy, R. & Wax, N. (1989). Children's conceptions of plants as living things. *Human Development, 32,* 88–94.

Strauss, M. S. (1979). Abstraction of prototypical information by adults and 10-month-old infants. *Journal of Experimental Psychology: Human Learning and Memory, 5*, 618–632.

Subbotsky, E. (1994). Early rationality and magical thinking in pre-schoolers: Space and time. *British Journal of Developmental Psychology, 12*, 97–108.

Subbotsky, E. (1996). *The child as a Cartesian thinker: Children's reasoning about metaphysical aspects of reality.* Hove, UK: Psychology Press.

Sugarman, S. (1982). Developmental change in early representational intelligence: Evidence from spatial classification strategies and related verbal expressions. *Cognitive Psychology, 14*, 410–449.

Sugarman, S. (1983). *Children's early thought: Developments in classification.* Cambridge, UK: Cambridge University Press.

Swinburne, R. (1991). *The existence of God.* Oxford, UK: Clarendon Press.

Swinburne, R. (1997). *The evolution of the soul.* Oxford, UK: Clarendon Press.

Tambiah, S. J. (1990). *Magic, science, religion and the scope of rationality.* Cambridge, UK: Cambridge University Press.

The Holy Bible: New international version. (1980). London, UK: Hodder and Stoughton.

Tracy, J. L., Hart, J., & Martens, J. P. (2011). Death and science: The existential underpinnings of belief in Intelligent Design and discomfort with evolution. *PLoS ONE, 6* (3), 1–13.

Turner, M. (2010). No miracle in the multiverse. Review of Hawking, S. & Mlodinow, L. (2010). The grand design: New answers to the ultimate questions of life. Bantam Press. *Nature, 467*, 657–658.

Vaden, V. C. & Woolley, J. D. (2011). Does God make it real? Children's belief in religious stories from the Judeo-Christian tradition. *Child Development, 82* (4), 1120–1135.

Van den Berg, R., Vogel, M., Josic, K., & Ma, W. J. (2012). Optimal inference of sameness. *PNAS, 109* (8), 3178–3183.

Vosniadou, S. (1994). Universal and culture-specific properties of children's mental models of the earth. In L. A. Hirschfeld & S. A. Gelman (Eds.), *Mapping the mind: Domain-specificity in cognition and culture* (pp. 412–429). Cambridge, UK: Cambridge University Press.

Vosniadou, S. & Brewer, W. F. (1994). Mental models of day / night cycles. *Cognitive Science, 18*, 123–183.

Wallace, W. A. (1974). *Causality and scientific explanation* (Vol. 2). An Arbor, MI: University of Michigan Press.

Walsh, M. J. (1985). *A history of philosophy.* London, UK: Geoffrey Chapman.

Ward, K. (1985). *Rational theology and the creativity of God.* Oxford, UK: Basil Blackwell.

Ward, K. (2002). Believing in miracles. *Zygon, 37* (3), 741–750.

Watanabe, M. (1974). The conception of nature in Japanese culture. *Science, 183*, 279–282.

Watanabe, M. (1976). *The Japanese and Western science.* Philadelphia, PA: University of Pennsylvania Press.

Watson, J. K., Gelman, S. A., & Wellman, H. M. (1998). Young children's understanding of the non-physical nature of thoughts and the physical nature of the brain. *British Journal of Developmental Psychology, 16*, 321–335.

Waxman, S. R. (2003). Links between object categorization and naming: Origins and emergence in human infants. In D. H. Rakison & L. M. Oakes (Eds.), *Early category and concept development: Making sense of the blooming, buzzing confusion* (pp. 213–241). Oxford, UK: Oxford University Press.

Waxman, S. R. & Gelman, S. A. (2009). Early word-learning entails reference, not merely associations. *Trends in Cognitive Sciences, 13* (6), 258–263.

152 References

Weisberg, D. S. & Sobel, D. M. (2012). Young children discriminate improbable from impossible events in fiction. *Cognitive Development, 27,* 90–98.

Wellman, H. M. & Gelman, S. A. (1992). Cognitive development: Foundational theories of core domains. *Annual Review of Psychology, 43,* 337–375.

Wellman, H. M. & Gelman, S. A. (1998). Knowledge acquisition in foundational domains. In W. Damon, D. Kuhn, & R. S. Siegler (Eds.), *Handbook of child psychology* (pp. 523–574). New York, NY: John Wiley & Sons, Inc.

White, L. (1967). The historical roots of our ecologic crisis. *Science, 155,* 1203–1207.

White, P. A. (2006). The causal asymmetry. *Psychological Review, 113* (1), 132–147.

Wickham, L. R. (Ed.) (1983). *Cyril of Alexandria – Select Letters.* Oxford, UK: Clarendon Press.

Wigger, J. B., Paxson, K., & Ryan, L. (2013). What do invisible friends know? Imaginary companions, God, and theory of mind. *The International Journal for the Psychology of Religion, 23,* 2–14.

Wiles, M. (1976). *What is theology?* Oxford, UK: Oxford University Press.

Wood, A. W. (1992). Rational theology, moral faith, and religion (pp. 394–416). In P. Guyer (Ed.), *The Cambridge companion to Kant.* Cambridge, UK: Cambridge University Press.

Woolley, J. D. (1997). Thinking about fantasy: Are children fundamentally different thinkers and believers from adults? *Child Development, 68* (6), 991–1011.

Woolley, J. D. (2000). The development of beliefs about direct mental-physical causality in imagination, magic, and religion. In K. S. Rosengren, C. N. Johnson, & P. L. Harris (Eds.), *Imagining the impossible: Magical, scientific and religious thinking in children* (pp. 99–129). Cambridge, UK: Cambridge University Press.

Woolley, J. D. & Phelps, K. (2001). The development of children's beliefs about prayer. *Journal of Cognition and Culture, 1* (2), 139–166.

Zuckerman, M., Silberman, J., & Hall, J. A. (2013). The relation between intelligence and religiosity: A meta-analysis and some proposed explanations. *Personality and Social Psychology Review, 17* (4), 325–354.

APPENDIX

Fokunom story (British version)

In a faraway country people believe in Fokunom. Fokunom cannot be seen, however, people believe that Fokunom made the first animals and plants. When people become ill, they hope that Fokunom can help them. This is because Fokunom always knows what people anywhere in the world think and feel, even if they do not say anything. Fokunom can help any person, at any time, even though people cannot see Fokunom.

Fokunomu story (Japanese version)

The story content is identical to the Fokunom story (British version) except that for Japanese participants the character's name is in a syllabic form common to many Japanese words.

God story (British version)

A man called John became ill one day and went to look for God to ask for help. But God had gone to visit another ill person in a village nearby and did not know that John needed God's help at that time. Later, God returned and tried to explain to John what had happened. John saw on God's face that God was sorry for not being there to help him.

Kamisama story (Japanese version)

The story content is identical to the God story (British version) except that the person interacting with God is now called Yamamoto-san.

AUTHOR INDEX

Acito, M. A. 37
Ahn, W. 19
Alexander, Dennis 3
Alters, B. J. 59
Amsel, E. 7
Anderson, C. W. 59
Annett, M. 36–37
Arieti, A. 4
Arterberry, M. E 36, 39
Asscher, J. J. 131
Atran, S. 33, 86, 106
Au, T. K. 28

Backscheider, A. G. 29
Baillargeon, R. 19–20, 28, 36, 122, 124, 126
Bamford, C. 103, 119n5
Barbour, I. 5, 24, 69
Barrett, J. L. 86, 88–89, 106, 115
Bartsch, K. 128
Bates, L. 127
Bateson, P. 121
Bauer, P. J. 118–119
Beecroft, R. 64
Behl-Chadha, G. 36
Behrend, D. A. 44
Bering, J. M. 133
Berry, R. J. (Sam) 3, 69
Bertenthal, B. I. 28–29, 36
Bishop, B. A. 59
Blakemore, C. 4–5
Blown, E. J. 71
Booth, A. 36

Bornstein, M. H. 36, 39
Boukrina, O. 35
Boyer, P. 1, 25, 106, 133
Boyes-Braem, P. 35
Boyle, R. 3, 24
Brenneman, K. 121
Brewer, W. F. 5, 18, 71
Broadbent, D. 6
Brooke, J. 2–3, 24
Brown, A. L. 23, 134
Browne, C. A. 115
Brush, S. 69
Bryant, P. E. 29, 36
Bryce, T. G. K. 71
Buchanan, D. W. 113
Bullock, M. 19–20, 44, 113
Butterworth, G. 71

Caldwell-Harris, C. L. 3
Callanan, M. A. 18
Campione, J. C. 23, 134
Canfield, C. F. 115, 131
Carey, S. 20, 25, 28, 30, 33, 35, 44, 46, 106, 109, 111–112, 114, 116, 117, 121, 123, 126
Carlson, V. 29, 86
Carr, B. 69
Casler, K. 18
Chandler, M. J. 115
Chen, E. E. 87
Cheng, P. W. 21
Chi, M. 11, 25, 33, 106
Chinn, C. A. 5, 18

Author Index

Cimpian, C. A. 35–36
Cohen, L. B. 66n6
Coles, P. 26
Coley, J. D. 18, 21, 30, 112, 131
Collins, Francis 3, 24
Coltheart, M. 5
Corrigan, R. 20, 117
Corriveau, K. H. 87
Cox, B. 37
Cuff, M. D. 35
Currie-Jedermann, J. L. 37
Cyranoski, D. 47

Dawkins, R. 4
Dehaene-Lambertz, G. 124
Dehaene, S. 124
Denney, N. W. 37
Denton, P. 20, 117
DiYanni, C. 8, 71–72
Dolgin, K. G. 44
Downie, J. R. 59
Driesenga, A. 86
Duke, S. 131
Dvorakova, L. 104n1
Dyson, Freeman 3

Einstein, A. 5
Elkind, D. 86
Ellefson, M. R. 19
Ellis, G. 70
Elman, J. L. 121–125, 127–128
Emmet, D. 33
Emmons, N. A. 113
Enesco, I. 87
Erickson, J. E. 25, 36, 37
Estes, D. 29, 91, 92–93, 128
Evans, E. M. 8, 54, 71–72, 83, 86, 103, 131

Fagg, L. W. 108
Farrer, A. 90
Ferré, F. 90
Frazier, B. N. 17
Friedman, W. J. 20
Fujita, K. 20

Ganea, P. A. 115, 131
Gardner, H. 37, 39
Gelman, R. 11, 19, 20, 25, 28–29, 33, 37–38, 44, 93, 106, 113, 117, 121, 123, 126
Gelman, S. A. 1, 7–8, 11, 13, 16–18, 21, 23, 25–26, 28–29, 33–35, 37, 39, 83–84, 103, 106, 123, 130–131
Gentner, D. 35–36

Gervais, W. M. 3
Gibbs, W. W. 70
Giménez-Dasi, M. 86
Glymour, C. 13
Goedert, K. M. 19
Goldman, R. 86
Goldstone, R. L. 23
Goldwater, M. B. 36
Golinkoff, R. M. 29, 36
Goodman, N. D. 18
Gopnik, A. 13, 18, 23
Goswami, U. 35, 91, 94
Gottfried, G. M. 18, 21, 131
Gould, S. J. 5
Gray, W. D. 35
Grayling, A. C. 6
Greif, M. L. 18
Gross, N. 3
Guerrero, S. 86 87
Guthrie, S. E. 106, 133
Gutierrez, F. 18

Haldane, J. S. 5
Hall, J. A. 3
Halliwell, J. 69
Harding, C. G. 29
Hardon, J. A. 104
Harré, R. 8, 15, 19–20, 30, 69, 91, 103, 108
Harris, P. L. 1, 86–87, 131
Hart, J. 64
Hatano, G. 29, 46, 91, 93–94
Hawking, S. 4, 26, 68, 84
Hegel, G. W. F. 14
Helm, P. 114
Henrich, J. 106
Hertz-Pannier, L. 124
Hespos, S. J. 27, 116–118
Hickling, A. K. 29, 106, 115
Holyoak, K. J. 20–21, 94
Hospers, J. 8, 13, 68, 90–91
Huang, I. 15–16, 36
Hume, David 6, 69
Humphreys, Colin 3, 24, 114
Hunter, M. 2–3

Inagaki, K. 29, 91, 93–94
Isaacs, S. 15–16
Ishida, H. 20

James, E. O. 107
James, W. 134
Jenkins, A. C. 18
Johnson, D. M. 35
Johnson, M. H. 127

156 Author Index

Kalish, C. 28
Kant, I. 2, 8, 13–14, 68–69, 90, 107, 123
Karmiloff-Smith, A. 123, 127
Karuza, J. C. 23
Kawasaki, K. 47
Keil, F. C. 14, 18, 21, 24–25, 29, 32–35,
    37, 88, 111, 118, 130–131
Kelemen, D. 8, 18, 71–72, 83, 103, 113
Kellert, S. R. 84
Kemler Nelson, D. G. 18
Kestenbaum, N. R. 20
Kiessling, F. 86–87
Kikas, E. 7
Kinzler, K. 36, 109
Knight, N. 86, 89
Kobayashi, S. 47
Koenig, M. A. 23, 29, 39, 87, 131
Koslowski, B. 13, 19, 40
Kosugi, D. 20
Kotovsky, L. 35
Kremer, K. E. 8, 16–17, 83, 103, 130–131
Kuhn, D. 7, 13, 23, 39
Kurtz, K. J. 35
Kuzmak, S. D. 20

Lagattuta, K. H. 103, 119n5
Lalonde, C. E. 115
Lane, J. D. 1, 86–88
Larson, E. J. 3
Leddon, E. M. 37, 46
Legare, C. H. 7
Lennox, John 2–4, 70
Leslie, A. M. 27, 36, 117
Lindsay, A. D. 14, 20
Lloyd, G. 24
Lockhart, K. L. 25
Lombrozo, T. 13–14, 19

McCauley, R. N. 18–19
McDonough, L. 21, 36
McGrath, A. E. 2
McLeish, T. 5–6, 24
Machida, S. 37
Madden, E. H. 20, 103
Makris, N. 86
Mameli, M. 121
Mandler, J. M. 21, 28, 35, 36–37, 117
Mareschal, D. 124
Margett, T. E. 37
Markman, E. 37
Martens, J. P. 64
Masnick, A. 13, 19, 40
Massey, C. 29, 44
Matan, A. 35

Matsumoto, S. 104
Matthews, G. B. 135
Meck, E. 37
Medawar, P. 69
Medin, D. 23, 37, 46
Meltzoff, A. N. 19, 21, 29, 39
Mervis, C. B. 35
Metz, K. E. 23, 134
Miller, G. A. 5–6
Miller, Ken 3
Mitchell, B. 25
Moore, A. 2
Morrison, P. 37, 39
Murphy, G. L. 23

Nadelson, L. S. 59
Nakamura, H. 47–48, 84
Needham, A. 28, 35
Nelson, K. 36, 59, 117–118
Newcombe, N. S. 128
Newcombe, P. A. 71
Nobes, G. 71
Noles, N. S. 1, 26
Norenzayan, A. 3
Nye, W. C. 86

Oakes, L. M. 18
Ochiai, M. 44, 46
Ogawa, M. 33, 47, 65, 73
Ono, S. 48, 73
Opfer, J. E. 37
Otto, R. 107, 111

Panagiotaki, G. 71
Pasquini, E. S. 131
Passingham, R. E. 5
Pauen, S. 36
Paxson, K. 86
Peacocke, A. R. 78
Pérez-Granados, D. R. 18
Perner, J. 86, 87
Petro, G. 35
Petrovich, O. 38, 41, 71, 91, 94, 131
Phelps, K. 104
Piaget, J. 8, 15, 23, 39, 70–71, 83, 86, 108,
    113, 131
Pinker, S. 86, 106, 121, 133
Plunkett, K. 127
Pnevmatikos, D. 86
Polkinghorne, John 3, 24, 114
Pons, F. 131
Pratt, C. 29
Premack, A. J. 13
Premack, D. 13

Author Index

Quartz, S. R. 125–128
Quinn, P. C. 21, 36, 65

Ramble, C. 25
Rees, M. 7, 68, 69
Rehder, B. 19
Rhodes, M. 23, 36
Richards, D. D. 37, 46
Richert, R. A. 86, 89
Roberts, K. 35
Rosch, E. 35
Rosengren, K. S. 106, 115
Ross, G. 21, 35, 36
Rowe, J. B. 5
Ryan, L. 86

Saxe, R. 20
Schaefer, L. 108
Scholl, B. J. 127
Schulz, L. E. 13, 18, 20
Sejnowski, T. J. 126–127, 128
Sexton, M. E. 29
Shamash, F. 21
Shatz, M. 29
Shtulman, A. 7, 114
Shultz, T. R. 19, 20–21, 124
Siegal, M. 71, 83
Siegler, R. S. 37, 46
Silberman, J. 3
Silberstein, C. S. 24–25
Silk, J. 70
Simmons, S. 3
Simons, D. J. 35, 37
Sinatra, G. M. 59
Sloutsky, V. 23
Sobel, D. M. 13, 113–114
Soskice, J. M. 90–91, 110
Sousa, P. 86
Southcott, R. 59
Spelke, E. S. 25, 27–28, 36–37,
    109, 111, 114, 116–118, 121,
    126–127

Sperber, D. 13
Springer, K. 29
Stavy, R. 46
Strauss, M. S. 21
Subbotsky, E. 115
Sugarman, S. 21, 36, 39
Swinburne, R. 10, 13, 68–69, 91, 107

Tambiah, S. J. 3, 24, 70
Tenenbaum, J. B. 18, 20
Thagard, P. 94
Tracy, J. L. 64
Turner, M. 69

Vaden, V. C. 131
Van Orman, B. 88
Vosniadou, S. 71, 83

Walker, S. J. 106
Wallace, W. A. 14
Walsh, M. J. 107
Ward, K. 25, 114
Ware, A. 36
Watanabe, M. 47–48, 73, 80
Watson, J. K. 91
Wax, N. 46
Waxman, S. R. 23, 36–37, 46, 117
Weisberg, D. S. 114
Wellman, H. M. 7, 11, 13, 17, 21, 23, 25,
    29, 33, 84, 86, 106, 123
Wewerka, S. S. 118–119
White, L. 1, 47, 63
Wickham, L. R. 90
Wigger, J. B. 86
Wiles, M. 2
Wilson, P. A. 4
Witham, L. 3
Witherington, D. C. 37
Wood, A. W. (in Guyer, 1992) 14
Woolley, J. D. 29, 104, 115, 131

Zuckerman 3

SUBJECT INDEX

"alive", meaning of 38, 44–47, 53–54, 63
analogy 39, 90–91, 93
Animacy Task 44–46, 49, 53, 55–56, 59, 62, 73, 96, 100
Animals Group (vs. Plants Group) 44–45, 95
animate–inanimate; *see* dichotomies
animism 47–48, 104
antecedent-derived origin 22n2, 24, 46, 130; *see also* derived origin
anthropological, accounts xii, 1, 90, 133
anthropomorphism 11, 85, 93, 94; in children and adults 96, 103, 104n1, 132, 133; hypothesis of 86–88; in philosophy and theology 90–91; *see also* God-concepts
artificialism 70

biology: children's knowledge of 28–29; *see also* animate–inanimate
brain: metaphysical and religious cognition 5, 122–124, 126, 128

categorisation: causal 21; by origin 21, 32–37, 40, 55; 125; *see also* dichotomies
causal: criteria 34, 46, 66n3; explanations 8, 13–15, 26, 68, 86, 91; God as causal agent 2, 11, 48, 65, 85, 94, 100, 103–104, 112, 127, 133; mechanisms 8, 13–14, 16–19, 21, 25, 30, 32, 34, 43, 46–47, 52–53, 55, 72, 109, 131; reasoning 8, 14–15, 17–21, 47, 71, 78, 113, 116

causality: at-a-distance 113–115; by contact 113; empirical 15, 21, 22n1, 30, 113; physical vs. metaphysical 13–14, 28, 71, 111
causes: extrinsic vs. intrinsic 8, 14, 34
classification *see* categorisation
conceptual nativism hypothesis 121, 124, 125, 128
constructivism 11, 126–127
core domains of knowledge: characteristics 25–26, 106–107; *see also* biology; physics; psychology; theology
core theological concept 11, 109–110, 112, 121–128; *see also* God-concept; transcendence
cosmology: adults' conjectures 100, 132; children' conjectures 75, 100, 132; reasoning in 10, 68–71, 73–74, 79, 83, 85; theory 9, 26, 69, 71
creationist responses 72–73
culture: influences on British children 64–65, 95; on Japanese children 47–48, 58, 65, 76, 78; Japanese vs. Western 33, 54, 63, 73, 83, 104

derived origin 8, 14, 34, 48–54, 60, 64; *see also* primary origin
Direct Question Task 16–17 *see also* Open Ended Task
dichotomies 33, 36–38, 44–46; animate-inanimate 33, 37–38, 44, 93; empirical-transcendent 14–15, 91–93, 109, 115, 119, 122, 132; mental-physical 33,

92–93; natural-artificial 10, 14, 33–35, 37–39, 42–44, 56, 64, 130–131
distinction *see* dichotomies
domain-specific: causal principles 25; entities 26, 106, 109; theories 9, 25–26; *see also* scientific

education: influences of 21, 83, 96, 100, 135; religious 87, 96, 134; scientific 7, 24, 58, 134
empirical-transcendent; *see* dichotomies
evolutionary: anthropology 133; psychology 11; responses by adults 61–62, 64; by children 56, 58–59, 64
extrinsic vs. intrinsic *see* causes

Fokunom story 96–97, 104

God concepts: abstractness of 96, 98–102; in adults 100, 102, 132; in children 98, 100, 102, 132; as cultural product 73, 85, 96, 103–104; and moral attributes 2–3, 134; in natural-theological hypothesis 11, 85, 92; in preparedness hypothesis 88–90; *see also* anthropomorphism
God story 96–97

impossible vs. improbable events 114; *see also* plausibility
infants: categorisation abilities 21, 36; causal understanding in 19–20, 38–39; physical object knowledge 27–28
innateness: core theological concept 11, 121–128; domains of knowledge 25, 116; neuronal basis 121–126; *see also* constructivism
intrinsic vs. extrinsic *see* causes

justifications: abstractness of 96–98, 100, 102; in natural-artificial categorisation 38, 41, 43–44, 46, 51, 58–59, 62, 130; and vocabulary 54–55

language: and abstract concepts 116–118; and anthropomorphism 90; effects in Origin and Animacy Tasks 46, 53, 64–65; and religious education 134

memory: concept rehearsal 7–8, 112; and verbal development 118–119
mental–physical *see* dichotomies
metaphysical: concepts 4, 13, 32; and the brain 122–124; in children's

spontaneous questions 15–18, 70–71, 131; research of 27, 108; theories 9, 11, 24–26, 28, 30; *see also* trans-domain theories
miracles 113–114

nativist hypothesis *see* conceptual nativism hypothesis
natural-artificial *see* dichotomies
natural objects: vs. artificial 33–34, 38–39, 40–41, 64, 91, 123; imitations of 40–44, 45–46; inanimate 38, 44, 46, 48, 56, 65; origins of, 8, 14–15, 34, 47–48, 51–52, 54, 56, 58, 61, 64–65, 71–72, 130–131; remote vs. familiar 16–17
natural-theological hypothesis 11, 91–94, 127–128
natural theology: historical xii, 1 3, 5, 8, 112, 134
neural constructivism 126–127

ontological knowledge: children's construction of 9, 21, 32–33, 132; defined 25, 32–33, 35; in theological domain 106–107; *see also* natural–artificial dichotomy
Open Ended Task 16–17
Origin Task 44–46, 48–49, 51–53, 56, 57–62
"Own God-concept" test 96–97, 103

parallel-distributed processing (PDP) models 125
physics: children's knowledge of 27–28
physical-metaphysical 13–14, 71, 111, 115, 122, 127–128; *see also* mental–physical
plausibility: in causal reasoning 19, 20, 30–31
prayer 119n5; *see also* wishing vs. prayer
preparedness hypothesis 88–90
primary origin: conjectures 16, 64–65, 71–73, 77–78, 94–95; criteria 34, 52–53; definition 8; vs. derived 14; reasoning process 54–55, 131
psychology: children's knowledge of 29–30; and religion 4–6; as scientific domain 134; *see also* mental–physical

randomness 20
religion: as culture 5, 25; concepts of 18–19, 25–26, 104, 133; definitions 1–2; and science 3–6
Royal Society Charter 3

160 Subject Index

scientific: concepts 4, 7, 13, 24, 110–112, 116, 119, 124; domains 1, 15, 24–25, 29, 71, 110, 132; theories 7, 9, 24, 27, 30, 80
single natural category *see* natural–artificial dichotomy
studies background 40–41
Study 1 41–44, 94–96
Study 2 44–47, 94–96
Study 3 48–56, 96–100
Study 4 56–65, 100–103
supernatural: meaning of 1, 3, 7, 15, 19–20, 110, 115

theology: anthropomorphism in 90–91; children's theory 9, 26; as core cognitive domain 11, 106–107, 109–112, 132–133; defined 1–2; and science 5–6; *see also* natural theology
theory definition 23
theory-of-mind (ToM) 86, 115
trans-domain theories 9, 26, 124
transcendence: concepts in philosophy and religion 14–15, 88, 106–109; developmental continuity 110–112, 116–119; vs. empirical understanding 91–92, 112–115; psychological definition of 109–110; in science 15, 108

wishing vs. prayer 115

PLATES 1 and 2   Selected examples of objects used in Clear Contrast condition

PLATE 1

PLATE 2

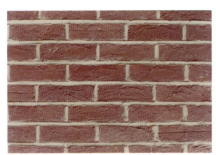 

PLATES 3 and 4 Selected examples of objects used in Matched Contrast condition

PLATE 3

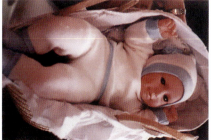

PLATE 4

PLATES 5 and 6 Selected examples of objects used in Unmatched Contrast condition

PLATE 5

PLATE 6

PLATES 7 and 8 Selected examples of objects used as control or dummy pairs

PLATE 7

PLATE 8